PRAISE FOR

The Wilder Life

"McClure exhibits an admirable modern-day pioneer spirit, humorously throwing herself into the history of the *Little House* series with equal amounts of enthusiasm and skepticism. Fans of the *Little House* series will eat up this book like a hot johnnycake, and well they should, because McClure highlights that intangible something about the series that strikes a deep chord in even the most casual reader."

—*Minneapolis Star Tribune*

"*The Wilder Life* . . . has the power to charm even those who shudder at the thought of gingham, calving, or salt pork. As a child reader, my tastes ran more toward Anglophilia and stories without parents, and still I devoured this memoir like Laura 'Half-Pint' Ingalls chowing down on Ma's vanity cakes. . . . *The Wilder Life* features as much humor as it does reminiscence and reportage. The result is at once endearing and very funny. Even a casual Ingalls admirer like myself can understand why one of McClure's friends felt her knees buckle with awe in a Missouri museum when she saw *Pa's actual fiddle* on display. *The Wilder Life* explores not only the uneasy interplay of fact and fiction but also those disorienting moments when the icons of childhood—places, people, and things of nearly divine power—suddenly materialize in our adult lives. McClure's touch is as light as Ma's best biscuits, but the result still sticks to your ribs." —Laura Miller, *Salon*

"Even for people who've never read Laura Ingalls Wilder's work, *The Wilder Life* is an insightful, entertaining look at our relationship with pop culture, how it changes from youth to adulthood, how it intersects with the real world, and how other people relate to the personal things we love." —*The A.V. Club (The Onion)*

"McClure chronicles all of these adventures with wry humor . . . those who have dreamed of wearing prairie dresses and traveling in a covered wagon will find this sojourn into Laura World enlightening."

—*Time Out New York*

continued . . .

"Deeply human, darkly hilarious . . . an entertaining and touching book—and an essential for *Little House* fans."

—NPR "What We're Reading" blog

"Wendy McClure really put her money where her sunbonnet is. . . . You need not have been an obsessive fan of Laura Ingalls Wilder in order to appreciate McClure's memoir *The Wilder Life*—because, really, she's not just talking about this one series, but about the magic childhood books can hold throughout one's life. . . . Breezy and funny and fun."

—Jezebel.com

"Highly engaging, often hilarious book . . . the author's pilgrimage arrives at what feels like well-earned literary nostalgia."

—*The Boston Globe*

"A friendly way for the millions of Laura's fans to reconnect."

—*St. Paul Pioneer Press*

"Reading McClure's account . . . feels like catching up with one dear friend and meeting another." —*The Christian Science Monitor*

"Smart and sweetly hilarious . . . *The Wilder Life* is a trip worth taking."

—*St. Petersburg Times*

"Funny, insightful . . . McClure's journey will elicit laughter and some new reflections on why, exactly, Laura's stories have held readers in enduring enchantment." —*Christianity Today*

"Thoughtful and thorough . . . *The Wilder Life* [has] the feeling of a chat between friends, an exploration of the *Little House* stories with close confidants and fans." —*The Capital Times*

"Readers don't need to be Wilder fans to enjoy this funny and thoughtful guide to a romanticized version of the American expansion west."

—*Publishers Weekly* (starred review)

"Intensely enjoyable . . . McClure perfectly captures that haunting brew of wistfulness and nostalgia." —*BookPage* (top pick)

"Prairie lovers will thrill to follow the journey of one of their own."

—*Booklist*

"I thought no one could love Laura Ingalls Wilder as much as I do, but Wendy McClure does. *The Wilder Life* is a tribute to the *Little House* books that's both reverent and irreverent—in a thoughtful, hilarious way. I couldn't put it down."
—Gretchen Rubin, author of *The Happiness Project*

"A howlingly funny, historically thorough, and irresistibly mad trip down the rabbit hole of the Laura Ingalls/*Little House* obsession that has consumed an entire generation of women. I spent seven years on the prairie and this book made me want to run out and buy a butter churn! Mandatory reading for all 'bonnetheads'—and the people who love them!"
—Alison Arngrim, TV's Nellie Oleson and *New York Times* bestselling author of *Confessions of a Prairie Bitch*

"Wendy McClure's *The Wilder Life* evoked such almost palpable nostalgia that I felt like I was walking into my childhood dollhouse every time I opened the book. It is so warmly written—so funny and real—it made *Little House on the Prairie* come more fully to life than a million episodes of the TV show. As a person who has been obsessed with many things from my armchair, I ate up Wendy's adventures. I absolutely loved this book."
—Julie Klam, author of *You Had Me at Woof*

"*The Wilder Life* perfectly captures the wistful, poignant, goofy nature of *Little House* lust. It also offers some important lessons on late-nineteenth century land rights and butter churning. Now that's my kind of book!"
—Meghan Daum, author of *Life Would Be Perfect If I Lived in That House*

"*The Wilder Life* is a funny and poignant account about figuring out how to reconcile childhood obsessions with our adult selves. I was a huge Laura Ingalls Wilder fan as a girl, and Wendy McClure has reminded me of how deep that love runs. She's done all the footwork and analysis for me so that I don't have to jump on the next plane to South Dakota. Thanks, Wendy!"
—Tracy Chevalier, author of *Remarkable Creatures* and *Girl with a Pearl Earring*

ALSO BY WENDY McCLURE

I'm Not the New Me

The Amazing Mackerel Pudding Plan

The
WILDER LIFE

MY ADVENTURES IN THE LOST WORLD
OF *LITTLE HOUSE ON THE PRAIRIE*

Wendy McClure

RIVERHEAD BOOKS

New York

RIVERHEAD BOOKS
An imprint of Penguin Random House LLC
375 Hudson Street
New York, New York 10014

The names and identities of some individuals in this book have been changed to protect their privacy. Laura Ingalls Wilder changed a few names, too, you know.

The Library of Congress has catalogued the Riverhead hardcover edition as follows:

McClure, Wendy.
    The Wilder life : my adventures in the lost world of Little house on the prairie / Wendy McClure.
        p.   cm.
    Includes bibliographical references.
    ISBN 978-1-59448-780-4
    1. Wilder, Laura Ingalls, 1867–1957—Appreciation.   2. Wilder, Laura Ingalls, 1867–1957. Little house on the prairie.   3. Frontier and pioneer life in literature.   I. Title.
    PS3545.I342Z768   2011   2010044960
    813'.52—dc22

First Riverhead hardcover edition: April 2011
First Riverhead trade paperback edition: April 2012
Riverhead trade paperback ISBN: 978-1-59448-568-8

Printed in the United States of America
10   9   8   7   6   5   4   3

Cover design by Kelly Blair
Book design and illustrations by Meighan Cavanaugh
Front cover art © 1953, 1981 by Garth Williams. Used by permission of HarperCollins Publishers

For Dad, with love.

And for Chris, who read the books.

CONTENTS

The
WILDER LIFE

1.

Our Past Life

I WAS BORN in 1867 in a log cabin in Wisconsin and maybe you were, too. We lived with our family in the Big Woods, and then we all traveled in a covered wagon to Indian Territory, where Pa built us another house, out on high land where the prairie grasses swayed. Right?

We remember the strangest things: the way rabbits and wild hens and snakes raced past the cabin to escape a prairie fire, or else how it felt when the head of a needle slipped through a hole in the thimble and stuck us hard, and we wanted to yell, but we didn't. We moved on to Minnesota, then South Dakota. I swear to God it's true: we were a girl named Laura, who lived and grew up and grew old and passed on, and then she became a part of us somehow. She existed fully formed in our heads, her memories swimming around in our brains with our own.

Or that's how it felt to me at least. That's how it still feels sometimes, if I really think about it. I mean I don't believe in reincarnation, and obviously Laura Ingalls Wilder didn't either, not with her respectable Protestant singing-off-key-in-wooden-churches upbringing. It's just how reading the Little House books was for me as a kid. They gave me the uncanny sense that I'd experienced everything she had, that I had nearly drowned in the same flooded creek, endured the grasshopper plague of 1875, and lived through the Hard Winter. It's a classic childhood delusion, I know, and in my typically dippy way I tended to believe that the fantasy was mine alone, that this magical past-life business was between Laura and me and no one else. Surely *I* was the only one who had this profound mind-meld with her that allowed me to feel her phantom pigtails tugging at my scalp; I had to be the only one who was into the books that much.

This was despite the fact that I was just one of the millions of kids who discovered Wilder's books in the 1970s and '80s, not too long after the entire nine-book series was released in paperback in 1971, and around the same time the TV show *Little House on the Prairie* aired on NBC. Girls in earlier eras would have read the books in hardcover editions, perhaps as gifts from nice relatives who themselves loved the books as children.

(And let's be honest here: if you didn't already know and love the Little House books, they would look and sound an awful lot like something your grandmother would foist upon you as a present, what with their historically edifying qualities and family values—basically, the literary equivalent of long underwear. In fact, I'm surprised that *my* grandmother didn't give them to me, though had she done so, they might have gone unread, along with the etiquette guide and the thick, small-print, illustration-free book about the Amish. Thank you, Grandma. Sorry, Grandma.)

Readers of my generation, though, could buy the Little House books cheap through Scholastic Book Clubs, and a great many more found their way to them after watching the TV show. And we were maybe the first generation of readers to be completely out of recollection range for the era these books recorded—we were born so late in the century that even our grandparents had only secondhand knowledge of covered wagons and dresses with bustles. The books were no longer really about anyone's "good old days" anymore—nobody *I* knew, at least—and as a result the world they described, the woods and prairies and big sloughs and little towns, seemed to me almost as self-contained and mystical as Narnia or Oz.

Except even better, because unlike those wholly fictional realms, the "Laura World," as I'd come to think of it, was a little more permeable. It shared space with the actual past, so things from it could make their way into my world, where I would look for them everywhere. No doubt it helped that countless family restaurants and steak emporiums of my 1970s suburban childhood went for rustic, antique-strewn decorating themes, with knickknack shelves full of tin cups and assorted old-timey crap. It didn't take much more than, say, the sight of a dusty glass oil lamp on the wall above a booth at a suburban Bonanza to make me feel like I was communing with Laura while I ate my cottage fries. Which I preferred to think of as "pan-fried potatoes."

Not like I was a dorky kid or anything.

Since I edit children's books for a living, I get asked a lot about my favorite books as a kid. When I tell people I loved the Little House books, I know it's a perfectly respectable answer, the sort of thing folks expect me to say. Then sometimes they go on and ask me whether I also loved various other Important Children's Books, like *Where the Wild Things Are* and *The Little Prince* and *The House at Pooh Corner*, and I'll do my best for a while, trying to play along, and then at some point I have to hem and haw and shrug because, well, you know what I really liked? I liked books that had pictures of toast in them.

 Well, not *just* toast, but, you know, cups and ladles and baskets and hats, lovingly rendered, all in their places in a room or even just in little vignettes, but at any rate, *things,* in all their thinginess. I had, and loved, a battered 1960s-era "pictionary" with wagons and hot dogs and butter dishes floating in plotless arrangements on the page. I pored over the page spreads in Richard Scarry's Book of Something-or-Other, looking at all the little rooms whose contents were meticulously catalogued and the dressed-up raccoons and pigs and squirrels who sat in them, drinking "coffee" and listening to the "radio" and eating, yes, "toast."

(Though yes, there are those of you who will no doubt point out that, actually, the Little House books have hardly any toast at all, that in fact *The Long Winter* is the only book in the series in which toast appears, and then only once do the Ingallses get to even butter it before the town gets snowed in and provisions run low, and then the toast is eaten plain or dipped in tea for the next five months and two hundred pages, and the flour that they make the bread from in the first place is ground from seed wheat in the coffee mill with the little iron hopper and the tiny wooden drawer, and after Ma bakes the bread she makes a button lamp, because do you remember the button lamp, in the saucer, with the little square of calico that she twists up and greases into a wick? Shall we go on?)

Toast or no toast, I think I've made my point here.

The Little House world is at once as familiar as the breakfast table and as remote as the planets in *Star Wars*. If you had every last log cabin and covered wagon and iron stove needed to conjure this world up, you couldn't, not completely: it's a realm that gets much of its power from single things—the lone doll, trundle bed, china shepherdess, each one realer than real.

⚘

Most of the Little House books I read came from the public library, usually off the paperback racks—the Harper Trophy editions with the yellow borders and spines, their corners worn soft after years of circulation. Sometimes I found the battered old hardcovers on the shelves, multiple copies of each book in thick plastic jackets. I remember studying the list of books in the series; their titles appeared in small caps in the front matter of every book, and I loved the way the list had its own rhythm: *Little House in·the Big Woods. Little House on the Prairie. Farmer Boy. On the Banks of Plum Creek. By the Shores of Silver Lake. The Long Winter.* Of course I memorized them. *Little Town on the Prairie. These Happy Golden Years. The First Four Years.* The words plodded along reliably, like the feet of Indian ponies.

And, oh my God: I wanted to live in one room with my whole family and have a pathetic corncob doll all my own. I wanted to wear a calico sunbonnet—or rather, I wanted to *not* wear a calico sunbonnet, the way Laura did, letting it hang down her back by its ties. I wanted to do *chores* because of those books. Carry water, churn butter, make headcheese. I wanted dead rabbits brought home for supper. I wanted go out into the backyard and just, I don't know, grab stuff off trees, or uproot things from the ground, and bring it all inside in a basket and have my parents say, "My land! What a harvest!"

There were a host of other things from the books that I remember I wanted to do, too, such as:

Make candy by pouring syrup in the snow.

Make bullets by pouring lead.

Sew a seam with tiny and perfectly straight stitches.

Have a man's hands span my corseted waist, which at the time didn't seem creepy at all.

Twist hay into sticks.

Eat salt pork.

Eat fat pork.

Keep a suckling pig as a pet.

Chase a horse and/or ox into a barn stall.

Ride on the back of a pony just by hanging on to its mane.

Feel the chinook wind.

I say I wanted to do all these things, though that may not have been what I truly desired. For instance, the sewing presented itself in the form of my grandma's embroidery lessons, but despite my early Little House–inspired enthusiasm, I didn't have the patience; couldn't take how slow and laborious it was to stitch just one letter on the sampler I was doing. The needle kept becoming unthreaded, and more than once I accidentally sewed the embroidery hoop to my skirt. I was trying to spell out MY NAME IS WENDY MCCLURE. It felt like homework, and after a while I wondered what was the advantage of writing one's name this way, when you could just take a Magic Marker and be done in ten seconds. I got as far as MY NAM before Grandma finished it for me. Though I was relieved, I knew that Ma Ingalls wouldn't have let Laura off the hook so easily. I understood, deep down, that I lived in a different world from Laura's, one where grandmas appreciated just that you tried, and that you didn't *have* to know how to stitch the letters of your name, and that you could just watch *The Love Boat* instead. It's not that I really wanted to make bullets or race around on ponies, it's that I wanted to be in Laura World and do them.

And Laura World, for all its enticing remnants washed in on the tides of time and antique shops, was another world, and to visit it was all but unthinkable. From what I could tell, the places where the Ingalls family lived were either mythical nowheres, like the Big Woods and the Prairie, or else impossible to find: Where, on a map of Minnesota in one's parents' 1970 encyclopedia set, would one even begin to look for the unnamed town in *On the Banks of Plum Creek?* And De Smet, South Dakota, where the family had settled at last, was in one of those big empty states at the top of the map, as remote, it seemed, as the moon. I knew that some kind of actual *there* existed from the books, but somehow I never considered that any of them could be reached from where I was.

For our summer vacations my family took camping road trips, long, epic ones sometimes, to the southwest, where my grandparents lived, or east to New England. We'd seen the Liberty Bell in Philadelphia and Paul Revere's house in Boston; if the places where Laura Ingalls Wilder had lived were really important, if there was anything to see, I supposed my mom or dad would know about it. Though of course in my mind the only old places where you could go were places where history happened, and I didn't think of Laura's life as history. It was more alive than that, and more secret somehow, too.

Although I never asked if we could visit any of the places where she lived, I remember spending one long day in the car as we traveled through central Kansas, keeping up an extended reverie in which I hoped that we'd come across the cabin the Ingallses abandoned at the end of *Little House on the Prairie*. We'd see it in the distance, waiting for someone to come back to it. I wanted that someone to be me: I wanted to find that door and open it and complete the story.

For a while I had a close imaginary friendship with the Laura of *On the Banks of Plum Creek*, who felt closest to my age in those books. I was eight or nine; I had knowingly conjured her up to talk with her in my head. I daydreamed that she'd shown up in the twentieth century and I had to be her guide.

I've discovered from talking to friends that this was a common desire. My friend Amy, for instance, wanted to "show her around" (that was the exact phrase she says she remembers using: *show her around*). Surely a fantasy this specific must mean something. I suppose it allowed us to infuse our own world with Laura-like wonder as we imagined her awed appreciation for the safe, cluttered lives that we led.

One of the review quotes from my paperback editions, taken from the venerable children's literature publication *The Horn Book*, says: "Laura Ingalls of the 1870s and '80s has stepped from pages of the past into the flesh and blood reality of a chosen friend." I don't know if the desire to take that chosen friend to McDonald's is quite what *The Horn Book* had in mind, but Amy sure wanted to do it.

As for me, I wanted to take Laura to North Riverside Mall. In my mind I ushered her onto escalators and helped her operate a soda machine. I took her with me on car trips and reassured her when the station wagon would pull onto the expressway ramp and accelerate to a speed three times faster than the trains she rode, faster than she would have ever imagined a human could travel. *It's okay, Laura,* I'd tell her.

So Laura was my friend, and it's perhaps a testament to the utterly solitary nature of my relationship with her that for the whole time I was enthralled with the book series as a child, I didn't know that a TV show based on it was airing Monday nights during prime time. How could I have missed this? Two major reasons as to why:

1. While I *was* dimly aware that a TV show called *Little House on the Prairie* existed, somehow my eight-year-old mind clung to the specious idea that the phrase "little house on the prairie" was simply a general expression, like "home on the range" or "humble abode," and thus there was little reason to believe that a show called *Little House on the Prairie* was in fact about *that* little house on the prairie, the one that I adored, as opposed to just some *other* house on some other prairie someplace where this Michael Landon guy (who *of course* wasn't Pa, I mean, *look* at him) lived. I suppose if I'd tuned in even once, all these mistaken assumptions would have been cleared up for me, but for the fact that:

2. *WKRP in Cincinnati* ran in the competing time slot on CBS in the late 1970s and my parents and brother and I watched it every week. Because Holy Howard Hesseman, that show was *funny.*

It wasn't until a couple years later, long after I'd gotten through my mooniest phase of Little House love, that I found out that the book and TV show were indeed related. By then I didn't care much, though it was a little disconcerting to watch *Battle of the Network Stars* and occasionally see some of the Little House cast members wearing tiny shorts and swimsuits. (You mean that woman with the Cheryl Tiegs legs was *Ma*?) Even if my family hadn't been watching another channel I doubt *Little House on the Prairie* would have been regular viewing in our household, which tended to favor smartass sitcoms and gritty cop dramas over heartwarming family programming.

Not that it hasn't been sometimes confounding to have this parallel TV universe. More than once, a friend or acquaintance has gushed, "you mean you're a Little House fan, too?" only to discover that we have two very different sets of memories. One of us is thinking of the time Laura taught a calf to drink from a bucket. The other is thinking about the Very Special Episode when some kid named Albert got hooked on morphine. The ensuing conversation often ends awkwardly, with one of us a bit disappointed that the real Laura Ingalls did not have an opiate-crazed adopted brother and the other feeling, well, just depressed. (Though she *would* like to know if the Very Special Episode perhaps also guest-starred First Lady Nancy Reagan as the head of Walnut Grove's Just Say No Temperance Society. Because that would have made for an awesome show.)

So maybe we don't all remember the same prairie, but I'd like to think that there's still a kinship. Just as pioneers kept relics from their distant homelands, the TV show holds on to plenty of the little things from the realm of the books: the calico dresses and the pigtails and the girls running through tall grass.

※

Eventually I would love other books: I'd swoon through my lit classes, major in English, collect thin books of poetry, feel very close to Margaret Atwood and Elizabeth Bishop. But only with the Little House series was I ever truly a *fan*, with wide swaths of my imagination devoted to the prairies of Laura World. A couple years later I became enthralled with *Jane Eyre*, and then, as junior high loomed close, the novels of V.C. Andrews (yes, I know: they're creepy), but the fascination felt different. Instead of losing myself in a fictive world, I read my favorite books with the awareness that I was one reader among many, peering over everyone's shoulders until the story came into full view. It was less intense that way. More normal.

And so I moved on from the Little House books. I know that for a time—when I was ten, maybe—I'd reread most of them, feeling that I wasn't finished. Then, at some point, I was. I left my claim behind, so to speak, back on the shelves of the Oak Park Public Library. (I can still mentally trace my steps through the floor plan of the building and find the aisle where the Little House hardcovers lived.) I'd gotten to an age where the future was more interesting. I went to junior high and high school and college and I mostly forgot the books.

In some ways they stayed with me, in little twinges of recognition. I lived in Iowa for six years when I went to college and graduate school; by my last year in Iowa City I lived in the upstairs of a drafty old frame house with an ancient porcelain sink in the kitchen. It was the first time I lived alone and I loved it. The place was at the end of the street near the river. And, okay, instead of prairie I had a parking lot surrounding my house, a weedy expanse of crumbling asphalt, but there was something, I thought, exquisitely forlorn about it all. I had to sweep the floors constantly—they were painted wood with wide cracks between the floorboards, and whenever I did it I would think, *Draw the broom, Laura; don't flip it, that raises the dust.* Ma had said that somewhere; I remembered that much.

The spring I lived in that house there were lots of storms—it was tornado season, though they never came very close to town—and I kept stopping whatever I was doing to go outside and stand on the front steps and watch the brewing sky over the parking lot. Or I would drive out on the two-lane highway into the cornfields until I couldn't see the town anymore, which took all of fifteen minutes.

I'm making it sound kind of lovely, like I wore simple cotton dresses with cowboy boots and grew sunflowers and baked bread. But I smoked menthol cigarettes and occasionally was so broke I ran up my credit card buying microwave sandwiches from the QuikTrip convenience store. I was twenty-two. I was in Iowa to write poetry in the university's writing program. There was a joke about how everyone who came to Iowa to write poetry wrote a poem about the endless expanses of the Iowa landscape, so then everyone made it a point to avoid writing a poem about the endless expanses of the Iowa landscape. Most everyone wrote postmodern poems instead. An awful lot of them were titled "The New World." I wish I could say that was just a joke, but it wasn't.

⚘

Unlike the Ingalls family, mine had stayed put throughout my childhood. We spent nearly twenty years living in the same house, an early-1900s stucco two-story in Oak Park, Illinois, just outside Chicago. My mother, who had been an army brat and had moved all over the country during her childhood, used to marvel at how settled we were, though of course it seemed perfectly normal to the rest of us. My father had grown up in Oak Park; my grandparents lived a mile or so away. Our house was on a street lined with giant old trees whose massive roots buckled the sidewalks, and I grew up with the understanding that everything around me had already happened, already been built and already grown.

The exception was my mother, whose life was a work in progress and constantly under repair. As I grew up, I watched her go back to school to finish college, then to graduate school, then to work as a psychiatric social worker in parts of the city that seemed to me as legendarily treacherous as Indian Territory. As hard as she worked, she also had a remarkable knack for physical calamity. She'd had knee woes, weight problems, hearing trouble, multiple surgeries, and a tendency to lose her balance so often that on family trips she'd joke that we weren't truly on vacation until she'd had a good fall or two. (The scene in *Little House on the Prairie* where the log falls on Ma's foot felt utterly familiar to me; didn't things like that happen to everyone's moms?)

I was in Iowa when my parents finally left the Oak Park house, in part because my mom had broken her leg on the stairs. They moved to a one-story ranch house in another suburb, where they lived for the next decade. But they still had a notion of settling elsewhere. For years my dad obsessively browsed New Mexico real-estate listings on the Internet; my mom picked out bedsheets in Southwestern-themed patterns. They wanted to retire to a house in Albuquerque, some place with a view of the Sandia Mountains.

I moved to Chicago after I'd finished school and settled down in my own way, living alone with my laptop and TiVo. I became a children's book editor, and I wrote and published two books of my own (for grown-ups). The night after my first book came out I read from it at an event at the Double Door Lounge and met a guy there named Chris, who had a penchant for experimental music shows and hosting epic film fests out of his apartment.

He came to my book signing a few days later to ask me out and brought an Esperanto guide for me to sign. (Later he explained he just wanted to get my attention. By then he already had.) Laura Ingalls realized that Almanzo Wilder was a worthy suitor when he drove his sleigh twenty-four miles across the prairie in sub-zero temperatures to bring her home from her teaching job on the weekends. I knew Chris was The One when he came to meet me at the airport even though we'd been on only two dates. It was a ten p.m. flight home from a business trip, and there he was in the baggage claim with flowers. Nobody risked freezing to death, but come on, that takes *guts*.

During the same summer that Chris and I moved in together, my parents were getting ready to move to New Mexico at last. By this time they'd found their dream house with the view of the mountains. By this time, too, my mother had been diagnosed with ovarian cancer. They wanted to move as soon as possible.

"We're still pursuing the dream," my dad said matter-of-factly one night when he called to ask for help with their moving sale. "We're just, you know, dreaming faster."

"I know," I said. Though, really, I didn't.

"You still want that TV cabinet for your new place?" he asked.

"Yes, and don't sell anything else until we get there," I told him. Chris and I drove out to their place in the suburbs first thing in the morning. I wanted to help with the sale, of course, but I also wanted to grab whatever I couldn't stand to see sold to strangers. Which, as it turned out, was nearly any object I hadn't seen in twenty years, be it a scratched Pyrex bowl or a macramé owl or a *Reader's Digest* home repair encyclopedia with a bright yellow cover that my brother and I had somehow found fascinating. (The Ingalls family loved to pore through Pa's big green book of animals; we had Dad's big yellow book of power tools.) All these things had emerged from a set of boxes stowed in the basement crawl space and were now strewn across tables in our garage, everything mundane but acutely familiar.

I showed the yellow book to Chris. "Maybe we can use this," I told him hopefully, even though it was our new landlord's job to make home repairs.

"If you're going to take books," my mom said, "you probably need to claim those, too." She pointed to a box on one of the sale tables. She couldn't get up from her chair to bring it over to me. At least now her hair was growing back.

I went over to the box, which was full of my children's books. They included *The Adventures of Mole and Troll*, a scuffed-up assortment of Little Golden Books, an etiquette book my grandmother had given to my brother and me, and a yellow-bordered paperback of *Little House in the Big Woods* that I'd forgotten I'd owned.

I brought it back with me with a few of the other books and tucked it into a bookcase in the front hallway of our new apartment. I kept meaning to read it.

❧

Months passed, during which time Chris and I set up housekeeping and built up a rhythm of routines around our jobs, our chores, and the novel I had started writing, or was trying to write. The stuff I'd brought back from the moving sale became ordinary again, absorbed into the background with the rest of the normal clutter.

I flew out to New Mexico twice that year: once with Chris, to see my parents' new house and to celebrate Christmas, and then a second time on my own, to be with my mother as she died.

When I flew home, Chris met me at the baggage claim and I sobbed uncontrollably into the shoulder of his down coat. In my carry-on I had a plastic Ziploc bag full of my mom's silver jewelry. I kept it all in the bag for weeks—constantly untangling the necklaces that kept getting wound around the other pieces, checking to make sure the earrings were matched up, wondering where I could possibly keep these things that clearly belonged someplace else.

For the next few months after my mom died, I kept telling people, "We knew it would only be a matter of time before she went," which was my way of saying that I was okay: I'd known it was inevitable. In a way, I thought, it was already a long time ago.

A year went by. I had gone back to trying to write the novel. Chris had a new job. The apartment had become home, filled with our things, our books on the shelves—so many books, really, that we could forget which ones we had. Even though we'd had them for years, and always in plain sight in order to tell us who we were, or at least who we'd been.

And so I noticed the yellow spine of *Little House in the Big Woods* again and took it out from the bookcase.

I started reading in the late winter, on weeknights before bed. It was perfect comfort reading: the big print and generous leading of the book's pages were the readerly equivalent of the deluxe pillow-top mattress we'd just bought. But as I read, I found myself wanting to stay awake.

"How's it going in the Little House?" Chris would ask when he'd come to bed. "Is it like you remembered?"

"Exactly," I told him. Meaning that right away I found everything where I'd left it in the log cabin in Wisconsin—the pumpkins stored away in the attic, the nails in the hollow smoke-log where the deer meat hung. Laura's long-gone life had woken up in my head, all her thoughts playing back faithfully. "It's all coming back," I said.

"So does that mean it's good?" Chris asked. He got that there was a difference. Obviously, this is why I live with him and allow him to see me in enormous plaid pajama pants.

Yes, I told him. It was *so* good. But that was all I could express. I mean, I could have gone on and on about all the wonderful stuff—the *bears*, the *fiddle*, the roasted pig's tail!—but it was more than that. I got to the end of the book, the part where Laura lies awake in bed listening to the world around her and thinks to herself, "This is now."

> She was glad that the cozy house, and Pa and Ma and the firelight and the music, were now. They could not be forgotten, she thought, because now is now. It can never be a long time ago.

I experienced the same thing I'd felt the first time I read those lines: suddenly, all the *nows*—mine, Laura's, the world's—aligned with each other and made a clear, bright conduit, and then my mind sped up and down it, and then I came back to myself. *Now* I remembered.

❀

A month or so later Chris came home with a box that he held behind his back, though it didn't take more than a glimpse for me to recognize what it was. It was a complete set of the books—nine paperback volumes with matching blue spines lined up in a cardboard sleeve, a Reader's Digest Book Club set with the '70s-era design. They were in near-mint condition. He'd found them at a record store in Lincoln Square, a place that had an eclectic selection of used books—pulp sci-fi novels and comic strip collections, kitschy old cookbooks and nostalgic children's books.

"I didn't know if you wanted the whole set," Chris said. "But they were too cheap not to buy."

I started with *Little House on the Prairie,* reading it, like the one before it, in bed.

"So are the Ingalls family horrible racists?" Chris asked me, because I'd been telling him about the history of the books.

"Ma is, a little," I admitted. "She's racist the way some people's grandmas are racist." Which makes it all pretty awkward, of course, especially when you love your grandmother. At least the book itself acknowledged the uneasiness: Ma really was sort of a jerk, the way she sang wistful songs about vanished mythical "Indian maids" but then couldn't stand to be in the same room as a real Indian. And Pa, for all his sympathies, had to stop himself from calling the Osage "screeching devils." As a child, I'd known *Little House on the Prairie* to be about an uneasy coexistence with Indians who were alternately fascinating and terrifying. Now as an adult I could see that the fascination and terror were embellished with "glittering" Indian eyes and other dismaying details, a whole pile of cultural baggage. As I read on, I found myself willing to take the bad with the good. Though when the bad was Pa in blackface during a minstrel show in *Little Town on the Prairie,* that *was* a little much.

"Oh, no," I said, showing Chris the illustration. "Pa's, uh, a 'darky.'"

"You're worried that these books are going to turn *you* into a racist grandma, aren't you?" Chris joked.

"Go to sleep," I told him, which is what Pa says to Laura in *Little House on the Prairie* when she asks him difficult questions about the Indians.

There were things I would always take issue with, of course—awkward moments in an otherwise happy reunion. Everything had come back so vividly that I learned to stop worrying and love the books as much as I had when I'd first read them. After *Little House on the Prairie,* I moved on to *On the Banks of Plum Creek,* then took a quick detour away from the books about Laura to read about Almanzo Wilder's childhood in *Farmer Boy.* Then it was back to the Ingalls family in *By the Shores of Silver Lake* and *The Long Winter* and, finally, *Little Town on the Prairie* and *These Happy Golden Years.*

I took to carrying the books around. For the next four months I always had a Little House book in my purse. I could never remember whether or not my cell phone was charged or if I had any quarters for the parking meter, but if I needed to suddenly immerse myself in a passage about making button-strings, I was set.

It wasn't just that I was getting old feelings back from revisiting the books, or that they transported me to some sunny and comforting kind of place. At first the books were just an escape, but after a month or two of reading, Laura World had started to spill into other areas of my waking life as I began looking up Laura and the history behind the Little House books on Google and Wikipedia. At some point it wasn't enough to revisit the familiar memory landscape I'd known; now I had to know what the twisted haysticks the Ingalls family burned during *The Long Winter* looked like. I knew what year the Long Winter actually happened (1880–81), and that for years afterward it was known to locals as "the Hard Winter" and "the Snow Winter." Now I knew exactly where *On the Banks of Plum Creek* took place (near Walnut Grove, Minnesota) and that it took about eight hours and thirty-seven minutes to drive there from my apartment.

The accumulation of knowledge began to radiate outward into the rest of my personal universe. Either that or it was a black hole sucking everything else in. I found out that Laura's daughter, Rose Wilder Lane, helped found the Libertarian Party, and that there was some big lawsuit about book royalties nine years ago, and that the series is really big with homeschoolers, and that you can buy a special Christmas ornament depicting Jack, the brindled bulldog, and that there was a TV movie about Laura starring that actress who'd played the crazy girl on Season Two of *Dawson's Creek*.

I mean one minute I'd be looking up the years the Ingalls family spent living near Independence, Kansas, and then the next I was on TV.com poring over a page listing all twenty-six episodes of the 1975 Japanese anime series *Laura, a Girl of the Prairie* (also known as *Laura the Prairie Girl*). Who knew that such a thing existed? The episodes had titles like "A Cute Calf Has Arrived!" and "Dreams and Hope! Departing for the Prairies" and "Wheat, Grow Tall!" The series never aired in the United States and to my eternal frustration I have never seen a full episode, save a few clips on YouTube, one of them in Italian. I still search to this day. Dreams and hope!

I even started a secret Twitter account, @HalfPintIngalls, where I pretended to be Laura Ingalls Wilder and wrote posts like: *What a day. I curled my bangs with my slate pencil for this?* and *Today was a pretty good day until blackbirds ate the entire oat harvest.*

And thus for much of the summer of 2008 I was as frenzied and all-consuming as a grasshopper in a wheat field. My mind buzzed with the exhilaration of worlds colliding. *Twitter! Anime! Laura Ingalls Dawson's Wilder Creek!*

I went back and forth this way for weeks and weeks, going from the yellowed pages of the books to the Web in constant escape and re-entry, though of course looking up everything I could about the books was a kind of escape, too. I'd click and click and sometimes I'd really get somewhere.

Or was I getting anywhere? The books were comforting, but they had started to unravel something in me, too.

As I read my way through the series, I followed Laura and the Ingalls family as they move farther west—and then stop. While in some ways it's satisfying to see the family get their homestead and help settle De Smet, South Dakota, that yearning to keep going stays deliberately and maddeningly unresolved. I wasn't sure if I liked that Laura had traded in her old reckless adventures (poking badgers with sticks! riding horses bareback at railroad camps!) for the social dramas of town life, with all the spelling bees and organ recitals and engraved name cards.

It's not that I didn't love those things, too—I never fail to be enthralled by the copious descriptions of parlor furniture in *Little Town on the Prairie* and hearing how the classier citizens of

De Smet lived—but I noticed for the first time how the books enact the effects of civilization and adulthood: old impulses get thwarted and life gets cluttered with those china lamps.

I'd barely gotten into *These Happy Golden Years,* the last official book in the series, when I began to dread finishing it. I was gradually remembering, after thirty years, how it ended for me the last time.

Which is to say: not well. Laura marries Almanzo Wilder in *These Happy Golden Years,* just like the back-cover copy of my paperbacks said she would, a thrilling little oracle in fine print. But then the happy wedding-day final chapter is followed by a wobbly wagon train of three posthumous books, all of them deeply frustrating to me as a child. I'd read them dutifully—or rather, tried to—since their titles were listed in the front matter of some of the Little House books, implying they were almost part of the series.

There was the novel *The First Four Years,* published in 1971 from a draft Laura had written in a notebook discovered long after her death. It had appeared to be a continuation of the Little House series—a story of Laura and Almanzo as newlyweds—and had been published as such, although Ursula Nordstrom, Laura's editor at Harper and Brothers, admitted there was "a faint air of slight disillusion in it" that set it apart. Critics now believe that Laura had intended it to be an adult novel—the characters not quite the same as the ones in the earlier books—and a solo effort, unlike the books that had been edited (and sometimes enhanced) by her daughter, Rose. *The First Four Years* is now included as a ninth volume in the Little House series (it was in the box set Chris gave me), but anyone who reads the book expecting to return to the world of the earlier books will find it much changed. The couple suffers crop failures; they lose a baby; they get diphtheria. The book was oddly paced and hard for me to follow as a child, so I'd had almost nothing to go on except for the sparse illustrations, the final one an image of their little house burning down.

The next two books didn't destroy the world of the books for me—they simply lost it altogether. *On the Way Home* was Laura's diary of the journey that she, Almanzo, and daughter Rose made in 1894 when they left South Dakota for Missouri. *West from Home* was a collection of Laura's letters home from her trip in San Francisco in 1915 to visit Rose, now an adult, and to see the Panama-Pacific International Exposition. Had I first read them when I was older, I probably could have connected the dots between the Laura of the Little House books, with her braids blowing in the wind, and the older woman who traveled across the country, writing about weather and hotel rooms.

As an eight-year-old kid, though, I couldn't make sense of any of it. I was bored by *On the Way Home,* with its logbook descriptions of fields and roads, and its murky old photos of the middling towns the Wilders had passed through. And *West from Home* just confused me. What was this Panama-Pacific thing? Where was Laura? I'd finally figured out that she went by the adult nicknames "Bessie" and "Mama Bess," and at last I managed to glean two bits of information about her. One: that she was "growing fat," or so her daughter, Rose, said, in a letter home to Almanzo. According to Rose, Laura ate multiple buttered scones "without a quiver!" At the time I read that I was growing up in a household full of diet books, so I was mortified. Two: Rose reported, in the very next letter, that Laura had fallen off a streetcar and hit her head. I couldn't un-know these sad facts, that the little Half-Pint I knew and loved had become some kind of embarrassing middle-aged person who got into stupid mishaps in the big city.

In my mind, the world of the Little House books just went up in smoke at the end, their heroine disappearing into clumsy ordinariness and ignominy. It had always trailed off with a vague, unspoken disappointment. It's the kind of story we learn over and over again about everything in the world: your life starts out as a wild open frontier that you explore until the forces of time or history or civilization or nature intervene, and then suddenly it's all gone, it all weathers and falls down and gets built over; everyone dies or moves away or becomes a grainy photograph, and yes, at some point you just get fat and fall off a streetcar. Progress—it dumps you on your aging and gigantic ass!

Maybe that was another reason why I didn't come back to the Little House books for a very long time. But here I was again, coming back to this place where the path through Laura World seemed to end and disappear in the grass. Only this time I wanted to go further.

I could see Laura Ingalls Wilder everywhere. Really, she *was* everywhere. She was no longer just a person but a universe made of hundreds of little bits, a historical fictional literary figure character person idea grandma-girl-thing. I knew there were poems about her and picture books; I found out there were festivals, pageants, plays, websites, weblogs, authorized spin-off series books, unauthorized spin-off series books, dresses, cookbooks, newsletters, fan fiction, albums, homeschool curriculums, aprons, craft items, figurines, dollhouses. Also, a guy in Minnesota believes she is God. No, really, he was running for mayor of Minneapolis and he has this whole religion called "Lauraism" and he wholeheartedly believes she has appeared to him in visions and that she created the world. And after spending a dozen hours online looking for Laura and finding her in these endless kaleidoscopic configurations, who was I to doubt him?

※

I wanted to go to Laura World: I wanted to visit the places where Laura Ingalls and her family had lived, in Wisconsin and Kansas and Minnesota and South Dakota and Missouri. All these years I hadn't quite believed that the places in the books existed, but they did, and house foundations had been unearthed, and cabins reconstructed, and museums erected. I'd even met a few people who'd been to them. My friend Brian, for instance, had claimed that his wife's knees had buckled—*buckled!*—at the sight of Pa's fiddle while visiting the Laura Ingalls Wilder museum in Missouri. The sites were all tourist destinations now, with gift shops and annual festivals and pageants. I learned there was even a "lost" homesite that Laura hadn't written about in the Little House books, a town in Iowa where the Ingalls had lived in the years between *On the Banks of Plum Creek* and *By the Shores of Silver Lake.* To me this discovery was as astonishing as a breakthrough in physics. Imagine it, a wormhole to another Laura dimension!

But in a way all these homesites seemed otherworldly to me. How could you not want to go to a place that you remember but have never been?

It was fall when I started thinking seriously about exploring Laura World and all it entailed, which naturally involved seeing all the Little Houses or their facsimiles thereof, but there were other things that I found myself itching to experience as well. What *was* it like to wear a corset, or tap maple trees, or twist hay? The details of the books were in such sharp relief that I had the urge to grab at them, the way Laura in *Little House in the Big Woods* had wanted to taste the blackberry-shaped buttons on her aunt's dress at the sugaring-off dance. This past life, which I knew was not really mine, kept surfacing, bubbling up in my head. It seemed to insist, the way past lives do, that there was something I needed to remember, and if I just found the right place or the right motions, I would know what it was.

Chris and I always go somewhere else for Christmas—to Michigan, where his family lives, or else New Mexico to visit my dad— so we always have our own Christmas beforehand. This year he gave me *The Little House Guidebook,* a paperback travel guide to all the homesites. No more furtively looking up maps of rural Minnesota online; this was official now. I flipped through the pages of the guidebook and mentally subtitled it *Everything You Always Wanted to Know About Driving Out to Remote Locations in the Upper Midwest to Find Your Childhood Imaginary Friend but Were Afraid to Ask.* And I was still afraid to ask: what kind of person would I become if I just went with this, let my calico-sunbonnet freak flag fly?

I hugged Chris to thank him and then thought of that moment in *By the Shores of Silver Lake* when the Ingalls family has just made it out to Dakota Territory and Laura says, "Oh, Pa, let's go on west!" She doesn't get to go farther, of course, which made it seem all the more important for me to act, to do, to *go.*

As soon as it was spring, that is. Just then it was winter in our Chicago neighborhood near the river; in the deep snow you could see the delicate little tracks of rabbits right alongside the huge dirty craters where neighbors had dug out their cars. (The city has a winter street parking policy that's very much in the spirit of the Homestead Act of 1862, in that anyone who can dig out his own spot can claim it with an old lawn chair.) Above all this was our apartment, on the top floor of our building, three stories up from the reliably plowed slush, high enough to see nothing but trees and sky and snow out the windows if you stood or sat in the right spot in the front room, the room where we were having our Christmas. At that moment it was the right spot, and a good place to start.

2.

Whose Woods These Are

IT WAS THE MIDDLE OF WINTER when I started to explore this whole Laura business in earnest. I started ordering more books—biographies and academic stuff and even a collection of poetry about the Little House books called *The Love Song of Laura Ingalls Wilder*. By late January my "winter provisions" consisted of a stack of stuff to read and a bag of horehound candy that Chris had included in my Christmas stocking. He'd listened to me describe a scene in *On the Banks of Plum Creek* where Pa comes back from town and brings a couple of pieces of it for Laura and Mary.

"It's not bad," I'd told him truthfully. It came in dusty lozenges and tasted sort of like an off-brand Diet Dr Pepper. Then I remembered when Laura tried it she decided it tasted "brown." "You know, it really *does* taste brown," I said to Chris. "Brown in a good way, I mean."

"Let's not think about the other ways," Chris said. "Ever."

I even started programming the TiVo to record episodes of

Little House on the Prairie—which aired about four times a day on my cable system, between the Hallmark Channel and a local station that showed late-night vintage reruns.

It would be months before the weather was decent enough to go see any little houses anywhere. Thus I spent three weeknights in a row staring at northwestern Wisconsin on Google Maps. I was supposed to be planning a road trip that Chris and I would take in the spring to see Laura's birthplace near Pepin, the "little town" mentioned in *Little House in the Big Woods*, but I wasn't really looking at the roads.

Part of me wanted to believe the Big Woods still existed the way they had in the book. I'd study the very first page of *Little House in the Big Woods*, the Garth Williams illustration. These woods are where Laura World begins, this place where, as the first page reads, "there was nothing but woods. There were no houses. There were no roads. There were no people." The Big Woods were a perfect place to get lost and become someone else. And those trees, they were *huge*, right? If you looked at the illustration on that first page, you could see that the tree next to the log cabin had about the same circumference as a concrete sewer main.

I'd find Pepin on the online map and then scroll up toward the north. I'd use the "satellite" feature to see the aerial photo view of the land, and then I'd zoom in as close as I could to the nubbly green expanses between towns, until I was situated above whatever forests were still there. I could never get close enough. At some point the photo would become illegible, a smudgy quilt of pixels. But I'd still try to see. I'd click around the Mississippi River Valley where Pepin was, or else I'd go farther north and search, floating over the indistinct treetops, wondering what was down there, wishing I could just slip beneath the surface.

Somewhere on YouTube there's a video of a girl giving a 4-H Club speech about the life of Laura Ingalls Wilder. The girl's name is Shelby Ann and she's fourteen. In the video she stands in front of an unseen classroom audience, wearing the best approximation of prairie garb that she could put together, a peasant blouse, a skirt, and an apron. She looks just a year or two too old to be wearing her hair in pigtail braids. She reads from index cards. Shelby Ann makes my heart melt.

"The life of a great writer," she begins. For the first two minutes she reads off the names of Laura's family—her grandparents, parents, and siblings; her husband and her children—and the dates and places of their births. Then Shelby Ann lists the places where Laura and her family lived and the years they lived there.

Beyond the names, dates, and places, the marriages, births, and deaths, only a very few details are mentioned: Almanzo courted Laura with buggy rides; they endured bad crops and diphtheria. Really, it's as much as any of us might know about our great-great-grandparents. But Shelby Ann appears more than happy to tell us where the Ingalls family moved to in 1877 and 1879; who was born in 1870, who died in 1946. She can recite the facts and hardly has to look at the index cards. Maybe she loves that she's memorized something *real* to go alongside everything she's absorbed from the books. Maybe to her all the years and towns and names are the currency of *her* Laura World, valuable things worth collecting.

Until then, I had never thought to wonder if the Little House books were a factual account of Laura's life. As a kid, I never kept track of dates: unlike Shelby Ann and her time lines, I was content with the simple, romantic notion that *there once was a Laura.* That was enough for me. Plus there was something sort of mystical about reading the books and feeling a connection to her long-ago existence, her once-life. With that kind of enchantment, who needed facts?

And yet, I couldn't quite abide by the idea that the books were fiction, either, even though that was the section of the library where they were shelved. But then, what was nonfiction to us kids, besides the World Book Encyclopedia and *The Shaun Cassidy Story?* I wouldn't have put the Little House books in with those, either. I think ultimately I considered the books as having a category all their own—fiction but with a secret true world lurking behind the stories, somewhere in the trees beyond the trees.

Over two dozen biographies and scholarly books about Laura Ingalls Wilder and her family have been published over the last forty years, for practically every reading level, from picture book to dissertation. Now that I was deep in the woods of my Little House obsession, I wanted to read them.

I started in on the copiously footnoted three-hundred-page biographies and critical books published by university presses. Sometimes, though, I couldn't resist reading the cute little fifty-page biographies cranked out by school library publishers for grade school kids, too. *Laura Ingalls Wilder (A See & Read Biography)* and *Laura Ingalls Wilder: Growing Up in the Little House*—the sort of things I would've read at the age when I first fell in love with the series.

And then a copy of *The Little House Cookbook: Frontier Foods from Laura Ingalls Wilder's Classic Stories* arrived mysteriously, a surprise from my friend Jen in Utah. *MAKE VANITY CAKES!!!,* read the note she'd included. I actually shrieked a little as I flipped through the pages. I'd been hoping to find an old cookbook that could give me a sense of how to make the bread the Ingallses had made in *The Long Winter,* or even churn butter, but I'd had no idea that back in 1979 a woman named Barbara Walker had taken up the task of compiling recipes to replicate as many of the dishes mentioned in the Little House series as possible, from mashed turnips to roasted goose. There was, indeed, a recipe for the vanity cakes Ma had made for Laura's country party at Plum Creek, astounding confections that sounded as wonderful as they were impossible to imagine. Were they *cakes,* or donuts, or what? But now I could just cook up a batch and find out, couldn't I? There were also recipes for cornmeal mush, pancake men, *fried salt pork.* My mind reeled (like the cast-iron handle of a coffee grinder) as I considered the possibilities.

I showed Chris the book. "I'm going to make vanity cakes!" I told him.

"What are those?" he asked.

"They're these *things,* and Ma made them, and they're supposed to melt in your mouth, and they're . . ." I found the page where the recipe was and started reading. "They're, uh . . ."

"They're good?" Chris suggested.

"They're made with one to two pounds of lard," I said, staring at the page.

I had a Marxist feminist critique of the Little House series to get through, as well as a lengthy biography of Rose Wilder Lane and the way she influenced her mother's books, but maybe some of the headiest reading would be coming from *The Little House Cookbook.*

⚘

I was pretty sure I could pick Pa Ingalls out of a lineup by now. Not like he would have ever been in one—not Pa!—but still: the old cloudy photos of the Ingalls family that had seemed so disorienting and strange when I'd seen them years before had become a lot more familiar after seeing the same dozen or so photos throughout the books I read. Pa was the easiest to recognize since his looks were so unsettling; I'd never expected Charles Ingalls to be a barefaced pretty boy like his TV counterpart, the way some people had, but I still had to get used to the sight of a thin-necked guy with squinty pale eyes peering out from behind a formidable wedge of frizzled beard.

Caroline Ingalls, aka Ma, looks as solemn as a soldier. Mary always appears a little disappointed. Carrie's a bit pinched. Baby Grace, in her slightly blurry portrait, seems to show some trepidation in her face, as if someone had just tried to explain nineteenth-century government land policy to her. If you were using only the photos to cast one of the Ingalls as the protagonist, the one at the center who would tell the family's story, you would likely still pick Laura, whose face seems a degree or two brighter and more expressive than everyone else's.

I have two favorite images of Laura (besides Garth Williams's depictions of her in the Little House books, of course). The first is a photo I hadn't seen until recently, of Laura together with Mary and Carrie in a photographer's studio. It's actually the first photo ever taken of any of them, sometime around 1881, after the Long Winter. Mary is seated and Carrie and Laura are standing, and all three of them are facing in different directions, and I suppose back then there wasn't quite the sense that you should look toward the camera, or that in doing so you were looking back at the world.

But of course three girls in rural South Dakota in 1881 wouldn't have had a reason to think that there was anything at all beyond that camera, couldn't have possibly foreseen that the world and a hundred years would be pressed up against the other side. Instead each girl is positioned as if she's alone. Laura has her arms at her sides and her long hair is unbraided and pinned back from her face. She's facing left and thus appears to be looking west, the same direction from which all those winter storms and prairie fires and clouds of grasshoppers came. She has strong, high cheekbones and a stoic set to her mouth and eyes. Really, she looks exactly as you'd imagine her.

It's no wonder that the illustrators in a number of the children's biographies I read loved to draw her exactly as she appeared in that photo; invariably they'd take her out of the dim, draped surroundings where she stood with her sisters and place her instead, alone, in the middle of a prairie, where of course it looked as if she'd been standing all along.

My other favorite image of Laura is the back cover illustration of the paperback edition of *Laura* by Donald Zochert, the most well known of the adult biographies, published in 1977, around the peak of the *Little House on the Prairie* TV show's popularity. The front cover artwork shows a beaming pioneer family not unlike the NBC Ingalls clan, complete with '70s hair (little Carrie's Dorothy Hamill bob is kind of cute), but the real magic happens on the back, in the romance-novel-styled vignette meant to depict Laura's young adulthood and her courtin' days with Almanzo, who holds a big straw hat and looks impressively studly with his cleft chin and sideburns. He exchanges what can only be called a "smoldering glance" with Laura, who not only has neglected to wear her sunbonnet but has clearly moved on to leaving her blouse unbuttoned. Like, all the way. Ahem.

Despite the cheesy cover (which I wanted to hide while reading the book on the subway), *Laura* turned out to be a highly enjoyable read. Clearly one reason it's been such a best seller is because reading it feels a lot like reading the Little House series all over again. Zochert drew heavily from *Pioneer Girl*, the unpublished adult memoir Laura wrote a few years before the Little House books, and recast everything in a soft, nostalgic focus with sentences like: "Then the sun began to drop toward the summery land. It was time to turn for home. Pa swung his little half-pint up onto his shoulders and took hold of Mary's hand, and together they began the long walk back across the prairie to the little house." Blizzards and crop failures are quickly dispensed with in a page or two, and there's never any question that the spirit of the Ingalls family will prevail and Pa will fiddle the bad memories away.

Then again, all Zochert needed to do was confirm to a new generation of readers—including the scores of people who'd come from the TV show totally enthralled by weekly prime-time visions of prairie dresses and cozy hearths and sunlit fields in full color—that Laura had really lived once.

Here are some things that actually happened, both in the books and in real life: A black doctor, Dr. Tann, truly did save the Ingalls family from malaria; and Pa indeed drove the covered wagon across the frozen waters of Lake Pepin. Pa walked east to find work after the crops were destroyed because he couldn't afford train fare. The prairie fires happened, and so did the relentless marching grasshoppers, and the months of extraordinary blizzards of the Long Winter.

I also found out plenty of things that weren't in the Little House books: When Laura was twelve, she was hired to live with a neighbor woman who had "fainting spells," in order to keep an eye on the woman and splash water on her face whenever she passed out. Laura once ditched school to go skating at the roller rink in De Smet (the fact that there even *was* a roller rink in De Smet blew my mind a little; how did the town progress so quickly from nearly starving to death over the winter to building teen hangouts?). Not too long after the disastrous events recounted in *The First Four Years*, Laura and Almanzo and their daughter moved to Florida for a short time, thinking the climate would be good for Almanzo's health, but they hated it and returned to South Dakota a year later.

But despite what I was learning from reading all these books, all these biographies and critical studies, some things were becoming more mysterious the more I read about them, growing stranger with each interpretation. It didn't help that a few of the children's biographies of Laura simply rehashed the Little House narrative when covering her childhood, making it harder to distinguish truth from fiction.

I kept trying to get to the bottom of one part in particular: that moment in *Little House on the Prairie* when the Ingallses were in Kansas and stood at the door to their cabin watching a long line of departing Indians. In the book, Laura, herself just a young child, has an odd, inarticulate tantrum after she makes eye contact with an Indian infant riding along on the procession and wants the child to stay with her. "Oh, I want it! I want it!" Laura begged, the book says.

The use of the word *it* makes me cringe when I read the scene now, but I still find the moment moving in other ways. When I was much younger, reading this part made me uncomfortable, in the sense that it always felt terrible to witness another child's breakdown, even when it took place in a book. And when I read the scene again as an adult, it seemed so primal and weird that I was convinced that it was based on a true experience. I wanted some kind of proof that it was true, so I looked for references whenever I could. In *Constructing the Little House: Gender, Culture, and Laura Ingalls Wilder,* for instance, Ann Romines says, "Laura's assertive, imperative, desirous demand for the baby taps an impulse that her Euro-American upbringing has offered no way for a girl to express . . . her outburst is a female child's explosive critique of the languages offered by her culture; it *voices* her yearning for a life of expansion and inclusion."

Then I read Gwenda Blair's *Laura Ingalls Wilder (A See & Read Biography),* which says: "Finally the Indians decided to leave the camp. The day they rode away Laura saw a papoose. She cried because she knew she would never see an Indian baby again."

What an awful explanation. After a while, I began to believe everything and nothing at the same time. Yes, Laura was a nexus of white patriarchal ambivalence, and yes, so sad to see the papoose go bye-bye! I was of all these different minds—all of them, it seemed, of different ages as well, all the time trying to follow a girl whose face kept fading in and out of recognition in endless drawings and photos.

❊

There were other ways to look for truth. Smaller truths, at least. I turned to the *Little House Cookbook*.

"Laura Ingalls Wilder's way of describing her pioneer childhood seemed to compel participation," says Barbara Walker in her foreword. Oh, what an understatement *that* was. She describes how she and her Little House–reading daughter began with making the pancake men described in *Little House in the Big Woods*. They moved on to drying blackberries, buying a coffee grinder to make the rough flour for "Long Winter" bread, and eventually Walker embarked on the exhaustive, unpasteurized odyssey of researching and compiling the cookbook.

That winter, I, too, became "compelled." I began bidding on old hand-cranked coffee grinders on eBay. I bought a jar of molasses— at Whole Foods, oddly enough, since it was the only place I could find it. (The irony of going to a place with an olive bar and an artisanal cheese counter just to find the humblest pantry staple ever, practically the official condiment of *The Grapes of Wrath*, was not lost on me. Who knows what Ma would've thought of organic Swiss chard that probably cost more per pound than all the fabric of her green delaine dress?)

Since the weather was still snowy, it seemed fitting to start with the syrup-on-snow candy from *Little House in the Big Woods*. The recipe was inspired, of course, by that incredibly appealing passage where Laura and Mary pour squiggles and spirals of heated syrup into pans full of snow, which cool into candy. In my childhood imagination I had tended to conflate the hot sugar-and-molasses concoction with maple pancake syrup; I was at least half convinced that I could go outside in the snow with a bottle of

Mrs. Butterworth's and come back inside with the candy. And I had some idea the end result would be soft like gummi worms and taste like waffles. (Truth be told, I *still* thought that.)

Chris deemed the experiment a reasonable success. I wasn't so sure. When I poured the hot syrup into the pie tins full of snow, I'd tried to make squiggles and spirals but more often than not wound up with blobs and clots.

"I don't know if you can really call it candy," I explained to Chris, as he sampled one of the globs. "They're more like sludge nuggets."

"That's a good name for them," Chris agreed. They were definitely sweet on first taste, with the distinct tang of the molasses, though after a couple pieces the flavor became sort of cloying. Plus the candy tended to fuse your teeth together, so much so that you had to keep chewing on new pieces in order to disengage your molars, which led to several cycles of sad, desperate mastication.

After pouring another batch, I began to wonder whether snow was really the best medium for cooling the candy, which constantly threatened to melt into brown, watery puddles. It seemed to cool much more tidily everywhere else it spilled—on the wax paper I'd spread out to hold the finished candy, the counter, the glass lip of the measuring cup.

"So," Chris asked, "did you have a Little House true moment here?"

I looked around. I had a kitchen sink full of brown slush. "I don't think so," I said. But I was just getting started.

When you read biographies of Laura, one of the first things you find out is that the Big Woods weren't really the uninhabited never-never land the books led you to believe they were.

In the book *Becoming Laura Ingalls Wilder*, for example, John E. Miller points out that the Chippewa River valley region where Laura's family lived was home to a bustling lumber business district; he cites a local newspaper editorial, written a few years before Laura's birth, that describes Pepin, the town only a few miles from the Ingallses' log cabin, as having a "busy hum": "The air was alive with the sounds and voices of intelligent and independent industry," the editorial claimed. Miller thinks that was likely an exaggeration, too, but you can't help but think that even if the industrious hum wasn't *that* loud, Pa Ingalls and his family might have been close enough to hear it, so to speak, in between the sounds of the whispering trees and the howling wolves.

Soon you find out that the Ingalls family didn't even quite live *in* the Big Woods proper, that the woods were "just north a ways," and the area where they lived (the Medium Woods, perhaps?) was at least populated enough to have a schoolhouse within walking distance, and Laura attended the school for a few months when she was four. Pa was even the treasurer of the local school district, so in between making bullets and tanning hides with brains, he must've found time every now and then to wipe the bear trap grease from his hands and attend some boring meeting like an 1870s soccer dad.

Little House in the Big Woods betrays itself a little even within its own pages: you only have to read further along in the book to notice friends and neighbors popping out of the Big Woods woodwork with a little more regularity than those first pages would have you believe. That Swedish woman across the road who gave the Ingalls girls cookies, where did she come from all of a sudden? What about Laura's little boyfriend, Clarence, who came to visit in his fancy blue suit with gilt buttons and copper-toed shoes?

What was that kid doing wearing a sissy getup like that in the middle of the wilderness instead of buckskin breeches?

As you get further into the biographies, you discover the real story diverges even more from the fiction. There are significant omissions: there was another Ingalls child, Charles Frederick, nicknamed Freddie, who was born after Carrie but who died in infancy a year or so before Grace, the youngest, came along; the family sometimes lived with relatives or friends; Mary received a government subsidy to go to college at the Iowa College for the Blind, so that all Laura's odd jobs and underage teaching gigs were only for paying part of her sister's tuition.

The biggest doozy of a difference between the books and real life has to do with the path the Ingalls clan took in their eleven-year journey from Wisconsin to South Dakota. It turns out that Pa and Ma and Mary and Laura and Baby Carrie didn't simply up and leave the Big Woods and drive their covered wagon straight into the events of *Little House on the Prairie*, the second book in the Ingalls family chronicle.

In reality, what happened is that the family sold the Wisconsin log cabin around 1868, years before Carrie was born and when Laura was too young to even remember, relocating to north-central Missouri with Ma's brother and Pa's sister and their children (yes, they were married to each other, and additionally one of Ma's sisters married Pa's brother, and all of this no doubt made Laura's extended family tree look less like a *tree* and more like the chemical diagram of glucose or something). Anyway, the two families settled in Missouri very briefly, and then Ma and Pa and offspring parted ways with their siblings/in-laws and subsequently headed down to the Kansas prairie, where they built the log cabin, uneasily coexisted with Indians, were stricken with malaria, et cetera, et cetera, all of it much like in the second book, except Laura and Mary were much younger, and also Ma gave birth to Carrie there; then the family headed *back* to Wisconsin, where they were able to move into the same log cabin in the Big Woods (or just south of the Big Woods, in the Moderately Large, or whatever they were, Woods, okay?), because the guy who bought the place from them couldn't keep making the payments on it, and there, upon resettling, much of the pig-butchering, butter-making, corncob-doll-playing cozy activities that Laura recollected in the *first* book, *Big Woods,* ensued. Got it?

Oh, and *then* there was Burr Oak, that Iowa town I'd found listed as a Laura tourist destination. The Ingalls family had spent a rocky couple of years there, between the events of the *Plum Creek* and *Silver Lake* books: instead of moving constantly west, as in the Little House books, the Ingallses were forced to move *east* to Burr Oak, where, instead of relying simply on themselves and their inner fortitude, they'd had to board with other people and work as servants at a hotel (yes, even Laura), and Pa eventually had to schlep the whole family out of town in the middle of the night to avoid paying a landlord.

Given this uncharacteristic turn of events, it was easy to guess why the book series skipped Burr Oak. "The fictional Ingalls family always looks forward, not back," says Pamela Smith Hill in *Laura Ingalls Wilder: A Writer's Life.* (Obviously, when the real Ingalls family got the heck out of Burr Oak, they didn't look back, either, but for much different reasons.)

So, okay: Pa couldn't quite hack it sometimes, and there was more to the family's misfortunes than the books let on. And when you did the math and reconciled the chronology with Laura's age, it meant that she couldn't have possibly remembered the events of *Little House on the Prairie,* the book I considered to be the strongest in the series. When the Ingalls family settled in Kansas, Laura wasn't even three years old.

In other words, the real-life Laura couldn't have possibly been the Laura of the book, who was big enough to help Pa put up the cabin door and ask pointed questions about why they were settling in Indian Territory.

Even though I'd always known the book was a novel, I nonetheless realized that all this time I'd truly, wholly believed that all the details of this book were from memory—the perfect circle of the sky around the wagon as it traveled on the desolate land, the prairie fire, everything. That it had all been *lived,* and that purity of recollection was what made *Little House on the Prairie* such a great book.

Why, exactly, had I needed to believe that this book was a true record of Laura's experiences? I couldn't even say. I felt, really, like Laura did in the book, when she wanted to keep the Indian baby who was riding by, though she wasn't able to say why, just that she'd looked into his eyes and felt a connection.

Somehow, through the books—especially *Prairie*—I'd always felt like my mind had made some kind of direct contact with this other world and could go through the motions of living there by the sheer power of Laura's memories. I thought the memories were what made Laura World the kind of place it was, some place I'd inhabited in my mind. Now it felt just as disputed a territory as that one lonely stretch of Kansas prairie.

Making the Long Winter bread had suddenly become important. Deeply important.

I had an antique coffee grinder now, and a jar full of seed wheat that I could grind into a primitive flour the way the Ingalls family had in *The Long Winter*. Now all I needed to make an authentic loaf of Long Winter bread was "the dish of souring"—sourdough bread starter.

"If you want to make a starter exactly as [Laura] did, without such helps as sugar, yeast, or milk," Barbara Walker warned in *The Little House Cookbook*, "you may have to try several times."

Of course I wanted to make a starter exactly as Laura did! I *had* to, now that so much of what I thought I knew about Laura World was wrong. The Big Woods were not what they seemed, and the Little House on the Prairie was built on something other than recollection. I needed something real, even if it was only the taste of the improvised bread the Ingalls family ate every day for months during the Long Winter. Couldn't you understand, Barbara Walker? This bread was *all I had*.

And so I was prepared to try as hard as possible to make sourdough. And try I did over the course of three weeks, making half a dozen batches of flour-and-water batter, which I'd leave in a jar somewhere around the apartment in hopes that the Fermentation Fairy would visit and turn it into bread-making mojo. The jar would start out looking like milk gone bad, and after a day or two it would smell like it, too, always failing to rise or bubble. I went through most of a five-pound bag of King Arthur flour with my failed attempts.

The batter needed to be near heat for fermentation to work (Ma kept her batter under the stove). I tried putting the jar directly beneath a lightbulb, near radiators, and in sunny spots, all to no avail. The whole process began to feel superstitious and weird. Why did I have to get rid of half the batter once I'd added more batter to double it? Couldn't it just *stay* doubled? This thing that I was trying to make happen depended on so many different factors: water quality, temperature, humidity, improper covering, lack of patience. Making sourdough is about capturing something from the air, literally, and I began to imagine that this elusive element wasn't just wild yeast particles but the residue of a lost world. It kept failing to materialize and I was making myself miserable over it.

Chris noticed the jar on the windowsill one day. I'd left it near one of our radiators, which in the wintertime clanked and hissed and blasted heat, since the boiler in our building wildly overcompensates during the deep winter months. It was an ideal temperature for growing sourdough, except that it tended to turn the top layer of batter into plaster. "Are you supposed to just let the stuff dry out like that?" Chris asked.

I thought for a minute. In *The Long Winter* Pa brings home a sack of seed wheat and doesn't know what the heck to do with it—boil it?—until Ma has an idea and takes out the coffee grinder.

"I don't know what I'm *supposed* to do," I said. "But I'm going to try something." I went to the closet and got out our portable humidifier, which I filled with water and placed next to the radiator. Then I set out a new jar of batter.

The next day when we got home from work the apartment smelled like bread, and the jar was filled with something that looked like alien spit. *Beautiful* alien spit, I mean. My own Scotch ingenuity had paid off.

I held up the jar. "Let's get grinding!" I said.

Chris and I took turns grinding a whole pound of wheat that night on the couch in front of the TV.

"I feel like I'm sharpening a great big endless pencil," Chris said. "The dull, relentless pencil of winter."

"The Ingalls family did this every day," I pointed out. "And without *French and Saunders* to watch on DVD."

When at last we'd produced a bowl of coarse, brown flour, I mixed it with the sourdough starter, salt, and baking soda and kneaded the resulting dough. It made a round little loaf the size of a small hat, and it barely rose in the pan.

Almost as soon as it had come out of the oven we had to try it. The bread was steaming as I cut two wedges. It was coarse and a little crumbly, like soda bread. I blew on my wedge to cool it and then put it in my mouth, this tiny bit of time travel.

In *The Long Winter*, Laura notes that the bread had "a fresh, nutty flavor that seemed almost to take the place of butter." The bread we'd made did not taste like it needed butter, either, at least not while it was warm and soft. It was good enough that Chris said he'd eat it even if he wasn't starving, but not so good that we'd be tempted to finish the loaf, even as small as it was.

Somehow, it didn't seem right to eat the whole thing and it didn't seem right to waste it. And then, by the next day, it didn't seem right to keep it. I took it to work and left it in the break room with a little note that said *Long Winter Bread*, for those who knew the story.

❀

"If I had a remembrance book, I would surely write down about the day we came to Plum Creek and first saw the house in the ground," Melissa Gilbert–as-Laura was saying in voice-over at the beginning of "Harvest of Friends," the first episode in the TV series after the pilot. It was the one where the Ingalls family first comes to Walnut Grove. I was watching it one day in early February when I was home sick. I'd been trying to fight off the symptoms all that week, taking doses of some stuff everyone was recommending lately, some kind of homeopathic preventive thing that came in vials of sugary granules that I had to dissolve on my tongue. (It hadn't been part of my occasional pretend-I'm-in-the-1800s plan to have faith in dubious remedies, but it was sort of turning out that way.)

I watched as TV Laura came skipping out of what was apparently supposed to be the dugout house in *On the Banks of Plum Creek,* though it looked less like the lovely green grassy dwelling with flowers around the doorway shown in the books and more like a bomb shelter. But no matter, because it was never shown again anyway, and the story completely changed from *Plum Creek* to this whole other kooky plot where Pa fell out of a tree somehow, and the guy he worked for at the feed store was suddenly a big jerk and repossessed Pa's team of oxen, and wow, this was nothing like the books, I thought. I kept watching, even though I was feeling tired and sort of feverish. Maybe I had fever 'n' ague, though I wasn't sure what ague was. Was it like feeling achy, only quainter?

Meanwhile TV Laura kept babbling in voice-over about things she wrote down in her remembrance book, or else would write down if she had one, I couldn't tell which; maybe there was a continuity problem in the script, but of course it didn't matter, did it, because this wasn't really Laura, and none of this had ever happened.

But I was still watching, and now TV Laura was trying to help her pa stack bags of grain in the shed of the feed store, and then all these other townspeople came to help them, too, and well, it was sweet. Sappy as it all was, I slouched back in the couch cushions and let it wash over me. I felt like I was eight years old again and trying, the way I know I did at that age, to hold everything in my mind all at once—everything I saw and felt and wanted to keep close with me.

Like one day, when I was around that age, I actually took a piece of paper and wrote, *If I should ever have a daughter, I will give her the name "Laura Elizabeth," in memory of my favorite author, Laura Ingalls Wilder.* It felt very important to write the words *in memory of*, aware that remembering was a sort of magical act. I had the sense that I was entrusted, perhaps even single-handedly, to carry the very fact of Laura's existence to a future generation. Oh, I know it's hilarious now, but I put the piece of paper with this solemn inscription into an empty wooden jewelry box that I had and closed it up with its little brass latch. Then I waited for life to flow past and become part of Days Gone By, presumably carrying the wooden box with it on its invisible current until the moment I discovered it again. Which, I'm sure, had to be no more than a week or two later, when I'd decided I had better things to put in that box besides sacred intentions.

I hadn't thought about that in years, until this television Laura and her stupid hypothetical remembrance book reminded me. I wondered if maybe lately I'd been more like my eight-year-old self than I realized; maybe I'd been trying too hard to *believe* in everything I loved about the Little House books, trying to fit it all in precious little truth compartments: bites of bread, authentic memories, and so on.

I mean I *knew* what was real (the year 1867, Wisconsin, two pounds of lard, those gray people staring up from their photographs) and what wasn't (various myths about the American frontier, gigantic trees) and there was a lot of stuff in between that I wasn't quite sure about (moments of deep connection with Indian babies). But maybe those distinctions ultimately didn't matter, as long as I recognized them; maybe I didn't need to sort truth from fiction from exaggeration in order to go further into Laura World.

If I had a remembrance book, I'd write down the time I let myself be completely deluded about the size of the trees in the Big Woods. And then I'd go look for them anyway.

3.

Going to Town

YOU DON'T NEED a churn to turn cream into butter. I knew this. My friend Cinnamon, who writes cookbooks (and yes, that is her real name), has told me that an electric mixer can make the inverse emulsification process (aka "buttery goodness") happen in a matter of minutes. This is also why you commonly hear about people who accidentally turn whipped cream frosting into butter by letting the KitchenAid run too long. And then there's always the most basic butter-making method, the choice of classroom demonstrations everywhere, which is to simply shake a jar of cream vigorously until the butterfat separates and the class learns an important lesson about frontier labor and/or dairy science.

For me, though, the appeal of making butter the Little House way wasn't so much about the butter as it was about the *churn*. The churning scene in *Little House in the Big Woods* had always mystified me: it was wondrous and absurd that one could make butter just by rooting a pole around in a big crock of cream. I grew up watching commercials for Ronco kitchen gadgets, and our brand-new Amana Radarange microwave oven could turn a slice of American cheese into bubbly orange goop before my very eyes, but these things were never nearly as amazing as Ma's butter churn shown on page 31 of my vintage *Little House in the Big Woods* paperback.

Now that I'd had luck with finding the old coffee grinder to make Long Winter bread, I set my sights on a slightly more advanced Little House home-ec project: I was going to find me a churn and churn it.

Really this had been nothing more than an impulse, and I could have easily talked myself out of it. But I decided to pursue it in order to better understand what kind of Little House fan I was becoming. Already I knew I was the type who was willing to see the Little House in the Big Woods in the dead of winter. When Chris and I planned a drive up to Green Bay, Wisconsin, to visit some friends, I suggested that we leave a day early and visit Laura's birthplace in Pepin on the way up. I tried to make it sound like just a stop along the way.

"But isn't Pepin right next to Minnesota?" Chris asked. Green Bay was on the Lake Michigan side of Wisconsin. The *other* side of Wisconsin.

"Yeah, but it's still *Wisconsin*," I said. I showed him how, on the map, Pepin and Green Bay were directly across from each other. Across the whole state, but still! Somehow, Chris agreed to the four-hundred-mile detour, and we would set out in early March. We would see the little town and, a few miles away, a log cabin built where the Ingallses' little house had once stood.

❀

In the meantime my Laura-related reading had branched out. I'd found a number of online outposts of the Little House/Laura Ingalls Wilder fan community—bulletin boards and blogs and discussion groups—and I had subscribed to *The Homesteader*, a full-color biannual newsletter edited and published by a woman named Sandra in Kansas.

The online stuff ranged widely from beginner's-level message board threads where fans tried to sort out the differences between the books and the TV show (*"Does anyone know if there really was an Albert and did he die of Leukemia??? please answer if you know thanks!!!"*) to extremely thorough and detail-oriented discourse by folks who had thoroughly read the books and the biographies, scholarly articles, and rare archival stuff.

One of my favorite online finds was a website called Pioneer Girl written by a freelance researcher named Nancy Cleaveland. From what I could tell from her site, she knew things like the plot numbers of every Ingalls and Wilder land claim; the origin and function of every obscure tool used in *Farmer Boy*; and the history of every founding resident of De Smet, South Dakota. The breadth of knowledge was amazing and a little terrifying—my own Laura World seemed awfully fuzzy compared to the extensively cataloged universe that folks like Nancy explored. Reading her site made me feel guilty that I wasn't more interested in poring over land records or tracing genealogy. How could I not want to know *everything*?

I did, however, order an archival copy of the *Pioneer Girl* manuscript from the Herbert Hoover Presidential Library in Iowa, which had inherited a collection of Laura Ingalls Wilder–related material along with her daughter's papers. (Rose Wilder Lane had been a friend of Hoover's after she penned a biography of him.) I'd requested the typed version of *Pioneer Girl* that Rose had sent to her literary agent, who had unsuccessfully shopped it around to publishers before it was suggested that Laura try her hand at children's books.

Since the photocopy fees for *Pioneer Girl* amounted to nearly a hundred dollars, I wondered how many people went to the trouble of ordering it. When I called the Hoover Library to request my copy, I asked the librarian on the phone about it.

"Oh, *tons* of people ask for it," he said. He told me it was more popular than Hoover's inaugural speech, by a long shot. When it arrived a few weeks later, I flipped through the old manual-typewriter-typed fly-specked pages, possibly even typed by Rose herself, and felt a frisson of excitement that I hadn't expected and that made me understand why people loved digging up stuff like this. But I was also figuring out that even when it came to Laura Ingalls Wilder lore, I didn't know everything, but I knew that I was pursuing a different *everything* than the hard-core researchers.

Still, I was discovering things that I hadn't even known I wanted to know. I'd ordered all the back issues of *The Homesteader* newsletter, which was full of varsity-league Little House nerd talk. It included articles such as "Did Almanzo and Cap Garland Really Save the Town of De Smet?" (Cap's descendants aren't so sure he actually made the dangerous trip to find wheat during the Hard Winter); a story about the possible medical causes of Mary's blindness, written by an M.D. and fellow Little House fan; and a piece that speculated about the mysterious real-life disappearance of Ma's china shepherdess (had one of the Ingalls daughters inherited it, or had it been lost before then?). I ate it all up like johnnycake and molasses.

After a few e-mail exchanges, I'd become online friends with Sandra Hume, who edited *The Homesteader* newsletter. Sandra was a freelance magazine writer who lived in far western Kansas with her husband, who was a farmer, and their two kids. She'd loved the Little House TV show as a kid, but she said that the books and Laura's *Missouri Ruralist* essays had helped her make the transition from her Boston suburban background to farm life. She invited me to write something for the newsletter, which led to phone conversations. I'd never talked at length with someone who was as preoccupied with Little House as I was, and we started trading obsessive tidbits. It turns out I wasn't the only person in the world who had read *The First Four Years* and noticed the veiled reference to making whoopee. It's when newlywed Laura discovers she is pregnant and wryly smiles as she remembers an old saying of Ma's.

"'They that dance must pay the fiddler!'" Sandra said. "I remember when I first realized what that meant."

"Oh my God—me, too!" I exclaimed.

But even Sandra sounded a little incredulous when I told her I was looking for my own butter churn. "*Wow,*" she said. "That's really . . . dedicated."

"It is?" I asked. "Do you think it's weird that I want to try it?"

"Not if you write about it for *The Homesteader,*" she said.

❀

Years ago, I saw a *Twilight Zone* episode, one from the 1980s incarnation of the series, in which a teenage boy in modern-day New England recovers from a high fever and finds out he is somehow telepathically connected, in some kind of parallel-existence time-warp scenario, with a Puritan girl who has also just recovered from a fever in the year 1700. The two can communicate with each other, as if they're on some kind of mental speakerphone or something, and they can even occasionally see things through each other's eyes, so that the Puritan girl gets to see an airplane flying overhead and she in turn can show the modern boy her reflection in a pond.

But the best part is when the boy happens to take a swig of orange juice and suddenly the girl is all, "Prithee, what is that *flavor*?" because it turns out that she can taste whatever he eats, and of course she's never had anything that delicious before since she probably gets nothing but porridge. The next thing you know, the boy's in his kitchen with the whole contents of his fridge and a bunch of fast-food containers strewn across the counter, and he's sampling it all so that the girl can "try" French fries and ice cream and cookies. It all sufficiently blows her mind until—and I bet you could see this coming—her fellow Puritan villagers accuse her of being a witch because she dares to utter heretical prophecies about the invention of aircraft and Häagen-Dazs. Somehow, though, she manages to avoid being burned at the stake in some twist where the boy runs to the library and digs up some crucial bit of information that can save her.

Whatever the ending had been, it wasn't nearly as thrilling to me as the basic premise that these two people, hundreds of years apart, were experiencing the same things through some kind of sensory interconnection, conveying the taste of ice cream to each other as directly and miraculously as clicks on a telegraph wire.

I was doing these things—making the recipes, planning the trips—to feel that little jolt of connection with Laura World. Of course I knew it wasn't a literal connection, no wormholes or tesseracts or any of those things. All I was trying to do was invoke the same feeling I'd had when I'd read the end of *Little House in the Big Woods* again. How many ways could I pursue it?

❀

The kind of churn I was looking for was called a "crock and dash" churn, which, despite being the most classic type of churn, wasn't so easy to find on eBay. Most of the churns being sold were the early-twentieth-century contraptions known as Dazey churns— each one a set of gears and paddles that mounted on the top of a glass jar. (I'd had no idea home butter making had advanced like this—somehow I'd always been under the impression that we'd all just gone straight from the Ma Ingalls method to buying sticks of Land O'Lakes at the supermarket.)

I would come to learn several things about buying a butter churn on eBay:

1. *Most of the churns are not actually for churning.* I'd thought I was in luck when I saw dozens of listings for charming wooden churns come up on the Search Results page. That was before I realized they were all four inches high and used to hold toothpicks. It turns out that on eBay, churns are far more common as empty signifier than as signified object, with an alarming number of churn-shaped things used to hold plants, cookies, paper towels, and toilet paper. The idea that you might actually want an old-fashioned churn to do the task for which it was named starts to seem kind of strange.

2. *Newer dash churns seem to exist, but nobody wants to admit it.* Apparently every dash churn is an antique, even when it's listed as "never used." How is this possible? Was churn hoarding a popular hobby back in the day? Maybe people received multiple churns as wedding presents and just stuck the extras in closets, the way we do today with stick blenders? It's a mystery!

3. *When talking to friends about buying a dash churn, one must be careful when making hand gestures.* Do not simulate holding the dash in your hands and pumping it up and down, lest it appear you are talking about hand jobs. (Let's not talk about how I learned this lesson.)

4. *The cost of shipping and handling for a dash churn with two-gallon stoneware crock will surprise you.* I think it was enough to pay for one of Mary's semesters at Iowa College for the Blind.

And lo and behold, one day in February I had a butter churn in my home, sitting in my not-even-remotely-country-themed kitchen. The cream was waiting in the fridge: since milk is homogenized these days, Barbara Walker in *The Little House Cookbook* recommended heavy whipping cream instead. I decided to hold off on using Ma Ingalls's milk-and-grated-carrot technique for coloring the butter until I knew if this wacky churning business would even *work*. I mean, I had no idea how hard it would be to churn butter. I'd always had the sense from the *Big Woods* passage that it was a real slog. In the book the dash was heavy; Ma "churned for a long time"; sometimes Mary churned "while Ma rested." Ma had to *rest*? "Rest" as in "give her arms a break," I wondered, or "lie back for a spell on the trundle bed?"

Farmer Boy, which also had a churning scene, wasn't any more helpful. Apparently the Wilders needed to churn butter twice a week in summer when the cows were producing the most milk. "Mother and the girls were tired of churning, and on rainy days Almanzo had to do it." *Had* to! Even though the illustration shows a decidedly more fun-looking barrel-style churn mounted on rockers, churning still sounded tedious. "Almanzo had to [*had* to!] keep rocking the churn till the chugging broke the cream ..." For how long? Hours? I couldn't wait to find out. I was prepared to churn until my hands blistered.

"Each day had its own proper work," it says in *Little House in the Big Woods*, and according to the book, churning was done on Thursday, which of course made it sound like you needed, you know, *the whole day*. So I picked a Monday when I didn't have any plans at all. It was one of those crazy February presidents' holidays that my office took off from work but Chris's office didn't.

"Have a good day off," he said, as I poured him some coffee to take in the car.

"It's not a day off," I told him. "I have to churn butter!"

When I finally had the cream ready to go in the crock (it had to sit for an hour or so to warm up a bit), I slid the churn across the floor into our TV room so I could sit on the couch and churn.

I figured that the only way I could get through a long spate of churnin' was to do it while watching TV. It did feel a little bit like cheating—after all, Ma didn't have any outside entertainment while she churned, and you can only sing "The Blue Juniata" to yourself so many times. (Maybe she had other songs. I hoped for her sake that she did.) As a compromise, I decided I would watch an episode of *Little House on the Prairie* that I'd recorded. It was the one where Laura impulsively swipes a pretty music box belonging to Nellie Oleson, who finds out about the theft and blackmails her into doing her bidding. This better be good, I thought, and I didn't just mean the TV show.

The wooden dash had felt awfully light when I'd first gotten the churn, but it felt a lot more substantial now that there was cream in the churn—it worked with a buoyant, natural motion, and I quickly got used to pushing it up and down, gently rotating the dash as I went.

It didn't take long for things to start happening. After just a few minutes the splashing sound stopped, replaced by an eerie silence. No—a very faint squishing when I moved the dash around. What was that? I picked up the lid and peered inside. At this moment it seemed things had taken a horrible turn, both on TV and in my living room: Little Half-Pint had accidentally broken Nellie's music box, and I had made a bucketful of dessert topping.

I knew I was working with whipping cream, but I hadn't expected to see it *whip*. When you see *that* much whipped cream at once, the sight becomes a lot less delightful somehow. And a lot more perverted.

But I put the lid back on, took a deep breath, and kept churning. Maybe another ten minutes or so, by which time Nellie had discovered Laura with the music box. "You know stealing is against the law?" Nellie said, sneering. "You're lucky I *like* you." Then the sound inside the crock changed again. Back, somehow, to splashing.

This time when I looked, the cream was thinner—though really, it wasn't cream anymore—and there were mounds of thick, curdlike stuff that was yellow, a pale but unmistakable yellow. The taste confirmed it: in the amount of time that it took for an hour-long TV show plot to thicken—about twenty-five minutes, including commercials—I had made butter. I felt like a genius and a complete idiot at the same time.

Churning, it turned out, was the easy part: it was much more tedious and awkward to press all the buttermilk out, rinse it, salt it, and mold it. I had to press a spoon hard against the butter while keeping the bowl it was in tilted far enough to let the buttermilk run. By the time I was finished I'd made nearly two pounds of butter from two quarts of whipping cream. Of course, I'd also wound up with butter that cost almost twice as much as supermarket butter, not counting labor. Only about an hour and a half of labor, but still.

Chris called at lunchtime to ask how the butter making was going. "Oh, it's *done*," I said breezily.

"How does it taste?" he asked. "Compared to store-bought butter?"

I thought about it. "Exactly the same," I told him. I even took my new butter out of the fridge and sampled it again while I was on the phone.

Yes—the taste was good, but no different from the butter that came from the store. Maybe it had something to do with the cream, which was supermarket cream, after all, but for the most part, butter was butter. It was a little disappointing and yet comforting, too, to know that it had such a universal essence. Still, most people were convinced that hand-churned butter *had* to be better.

"I bet it's *incredible*," friends would say. "It's amazing, isn't it?"

Not really, I always tried to tell them. It was *just butter*. I felt a strange pride at this. *I own a butter churn*, I thought. *You want to make something of it?* Butter wasn't even the point.

But nothing in Laura World was just butter. I knew that, too.

Whenever my family went on camping trips, I used to imagine that the contents of our campsite—the sleeping bags, the plastic lantern, the little propane stove—were all we owned in the world. When we'd return home to our house in Oak Park, I'd fantasize that we were coming to our house for the first time, that we had come to it out of some remarkable good fortune, a marvel like the "wonderful house" that Pa was suddenly one day able to build near Plum Creek. And once the station wagon pulled into the driveway I'd take the first chance I could to run upstairs and gaze at my room, describing its details to myself as if I'd never seen them before: *a green-and-white-checked quilt* (I might even have called it a "coverlet") *lay on the bed; on the white dresser sat a little wooden jewelry box.* For a few moments my room felt enchanted, just from the power of observation I'd borrowed from Laura.

It was a power I'd come to recognize. Other books I read had an *I,* a chatty presence who made a point to confide in me. I'd been befriended in my mind by a number of middle-grade novel protagonists, such as Sheila the Great, or else listened to omniscient narrators describe Ramona Quimby's scrapes. But Laura's point of view felt unmediated and clear, as if she were right behind my eyes. The story of the Little House books was always a story of looking.

Everything looks like a wilderness in early March. We were driving through Wisconsin to see Laura's birthplace outside Pepin—also known as "The Holy City of Pepin," at least to that

Minneapolis guy who believes Laura is God. I couldn't help but feel the sense of a pilgrimage as well. We were on our first Little House trip at last.

To get to Pepin from Chicago we had to drive all the way across Wisconsin, cross the Mississippi into Minnesota, and then drive for another hour north along the river before crossing back over. The landscape had suddenly changed once we reached the river, going from gently rolling farmland to high rock formations and craggy hills. It was an overcast day and everything felt wonderfully raw, as if the river and the ice and the wet, chilly weather had been gnawing at this part of the world for a few hundred years. I couldn't see anything that looked like my imaginary Big Woods, but I liked it out here.

The river was still mostly frozen—some stretches of it that we passed were gray mosaics of water and broken ice; in other places there were ice fishermen out on the surface. We crossed back into Wisconsin and turned onto a winding two-lane road with a sign that said *Laura Ingalls Wilder Memorial Highway*.

I asked Chris if the sign meant I could start geeking out now.

"Now?" he said. "What do you mean 'now'?"

You have to hand it to Pa Ingalls for knowing how to pick his homesites. Whether it was due to luck or his aversion to population density, the guy clearly had a knack for settling in small towns that stayed small. I would find over the course of all the trips that none of the homesites were in any danger of becoming lost amid urban renewal or suburban sprawl.

According to the highway sign, Pepin had a population of 878 people. On the map, the town grid appears as just a few cross-hatched lines along the shore of Lake Pepin, which shows up as a bulge in the Mississippi River between Wisconsin and Minnesota.

From all my reading about Lake Pepin, I could tell you that it had been formed just past where the Chippewa River feeds into the Mississippi, where the smaller river's delta made the water back up and widen. Water skiing, of all things, was invented on the lake in the 1920s. Maybe the best thing about Lake Pepin is that it has its own lake monster. Dubbed "Pepie," it was first spotted in 1871, with initial reports describing it as "the size of an elephant and rhinoceros, and [it] moved through the water with great rapidity." It's one of only three known lake monsters in existence, next to the Loch Ness Monster and "Champ" of Lake Champlain in Vermont. (And do you know who was born only fifty miles from Lake Champlain? *Almanzo*. Whoa!)

I know all this is very impressive, especially in the realm of freshwater lake enthusiasm, but Lake Pepin might be best known to most of the world as the place where, more than a hundred and thirty years ago, a little kid picked up too many pebbles.

It happens in Chapter 9 of *Little House in the Big Woods,* where four-year-old Laura fills her pocket with lake pebbles at the shore while the family is visiting town. And then, when Pa tosses her back into the wagon, the heavy pocket rips off her dress and she cries. For me, reading that scene never fails to bring on a brief, scalding instant of recognition in recalling exactly what it was like to be a tiny little kid, your whole sense of being so lumpy and vulnerable that the smallest things were everything, and the everything could be so unspeakably wonderful, and the wonderful could be snatched away in an instant, leaving a big ragged hole in your universe just like the one in Laura's dress.

❀

Now Lake Pepin was in sight, a glimpse of pale between the buildings along the highway.

"I want to pick up pebbles on the beach," I said. "A whole bunch of them."

"Oh, that's not going to end well," Chris said, because I had just made him read *Big Woods* before the trip.

Most of the town was perched on the side of the hill facing Lake Pepin, though the visitor's center and the Laura Ingalls Wilder museum were along the highway. They were closed for the winter, and as we drove down the hill into the rest of the town, we could see that Pepin was a lakefront vacation town in off-season mode, with a handful of brightly painted cafés and a dockside restaurant, all closed. It was not unlike the scene near the beginning of *Little House on the Prairie,* when the Ingalls family is leaving Wisconsin in their covered wagon and they pass through Pepin early in the morning, past all the quiet, shuttered houses. At the bottom of the hill a set of freight railroad tracks ran right along the shore, and across the tracks was a small marina.

We decided that in lieu of the visitor's center, we'd stop at the public library, a modern building with only one room. There we met a very nice librarian well accustomed to giving Little House tourist directions.

"Have you been up the hill yet?" she asked. She meant the Little House Wayside, the replica of the Ingalls log cabin on the original site, which was seven miles from town. We'd planned on going there next, we told her, and we asked if there was anything in particular we should look for.

Her advice, which I will attempt to paraphrase, was: "Well, the county road there is more or less the same route Pa would travel to town, and to get there you turn on that County Road CC, which you'll see the turnoff just past the place that sells gazebos over here, and then when you go up you can stop at Oakwood Cemetery to see where Laura's aunt is buried, and also her first teacher, and the Huleatts, you know the Huleatts, right? And then after the cemetery you just keep going, and if you can you should look for the intersection of County Road I, because *that's* where the school was, that Mary and Laura attended, with Anna Barry, who's in the cemetery, but of course the school's not there anymore, but where you see where it was, you'll be about two miles from the cabin, though that's by the road, because the way they walked to school was much closer. Anyway, then you'll get to the cabin."

"Did you get all that?" Chris asked as we returned to the car.

"No, but let's go up there right now," I said. "While I can still sort of remember."

We turned off the highway as the librarian told us and went gradually uphill through thin woods and farm fields, past farm-houses that were at least a century old. The whole landscape seemed so sleepy and timeless that I had trouble imagining that it had once been different, that the woods—Big or otherwise—were ever there.

I made Chris turn off at the cemetery, which was in a clearing just up the hill from the county road, and we followed the tire ruts through the slush along the main aisle of the place.

"Who are we looking for again?" he asked, as we got out and stomped around in the old snow and mud. There was a mix of nineteenth- and twentieth-century headstones, the older ones thinner and spotted with lichen.

I was trying to remember what the librarian said. "I think she said Laura's aunt is here? And her first teacher? Anna something? Also some of the Huleatts."

"Who?"

"Uh, the Huleatts? They were friends of the Ingalls who lived here, and they had some kids who played with Laura. You know the boy with the copper thingies on his shoes? Clarence? He was one of them," I said. Then I actually spotted a small monument that said *Huleatt.* "Look!" I said. It was a stone for an Elizabeth, age 72, died 1889.

Chris came over. "Wait, so is that the boy with the copper toes on his shoes?"

"Well, no," I said. "But this person was related to him."

"So where's *his* grave?"

"I don't know. I mean, I don't know if he's even buried here." It didn't feel quite right to be here, tromping over other people's graves, just to look at a familiar name. Were you *supposed* to want to see where Laura's aunt was buried? I had to remind myself: it was not *my* everything. "Let's go," I said, finally. We got back in the car and continued up the road toward the cabin.

The Little House Wayside is just that: a wayside, a sort of rest stop with a little parking lot, a picnic pavilion, and a concrete bathroom shed. The cabin is set back from the road, across an expanse of lawn—or, in our case, snow. It was indeed a little gray house made of logs, just as the book said, as well as the historical marker nearby. It was awfully tidy, with a cinderblock foundation and the logs perfectly aligned. Clearly it had been built by the parks and recreation service and not Pa, and more for the sake of picnics than for history. I felt a little dumb, coming out here thinking that all I needed was to see a log cabin. Now I wasn't sure.

"Well, this is it," I said, as we walked through the patchy snow. Stapled to the front door was a plastic-covered paper sign. PLEASE CLOSE DOOR, it read, in text both capitalized and underlined, TO KEEP THE BEES, BIRDS & OTHER VARMENTS OUT!!!

"Did Pa type that up?" Chris asked. "He doesn't seem like an all-caps kind of guy."

"He wasn't, but you had to make a trip to town to buy lower-case letters," I said. "Just like white sugar."

Inside were two little horse-stall-sized rooms off the main room, one with a window and one dark as a closet. There wasn't much else to do inside but just stand there and look up at the roof rafters and peer out the windows and study the things posted on the Plexiglas-covered corkboards along one of the walls: a few photocopied historical documents, a brochure about Pepin, a couple postcards—one had a portrait of Laura in her old age, another a photo of the very cabin we were in.

We read a 1945 letter from Laura, written in that sort of shaky, elderly-looking script that I'd eventually come to recognize from at least four paces away.

I am very glad that you enjoy reading my books, she'd written to a group of schoolchildren in the letter, *but sorry you could not read them in their order. They are all one story, you know, and they are not so interesting when you read the end first.*

"A little cranky of her, isn't it?" Chris pointed out.

I had to agree. At least we were standing in the place where the story began, I thought—or, well, *near* it. Although I really had to think about it, because truthfully, I felt like we were still a very long way from the Big Woods, and nowhere near Laura World as I knew it. Yet despite everything that was clearly wrong with the cabin, with its utterly blank hearth, I refused to feel disappointed.

But then as I stood there and read the letter again, I suddenly felt an odd little pang of chastened helplessness. When it came to the Little House books, weren't we *always* at the end of the story first? Inevitably out of order wherever we went? How could we avoid that? Here I was, standing where the woods had been, where the cabin the little girl had lived in had long since rotted away, where a slightly clumsy approximation of it had been built as a sort of monument to her, long after she'd grown up and grown old and died, and all her letters to schoolchildren kept for posterity, including the one I was reading now—*this* is *now*, lady!—and this *now*, this perpetual too-lateness, was all I had. I was doing the best that I could with it. Weren't we all trying, those of us who drove out here in our cars, who knew "the end" but kept coming back to the story anyway?

I stepped over to the window to look out at the field and the feathery little trees and the diminishing snow. Maybe it didn't look anything like the landscape Laura had known, but it was bleakly pretty, nearly as lonesome as the sound of wolves howling outside.

Before we headed out I looked at the postcard of the cabin again, which seemed to be there as a kind of reminder. Yes, we were here.

❀

Judging from the empty parking lot, we were the only guests at the motel I'd picked in Pepin. The lobby was empty, too, and there was nobody behind the front desk. I hit the bell, the way you do in a movie about being in a deserted motel, but nobody came. I hit it again and we waited. We could see an open door down a dim side hallway—it had a child gate, and the light in the room flickered to indicate a TV was on. Chris started to walk toward the room but hesitated.

"You made a reservation here, right?" he asked.

"Maybe I should just call," I said. "Maybe they forgot." I got out my cell phone and picked up one of the motel's business cards from a holder on the front desk and dialed the number on it. After a moment the phone behind the desk started ringing through the empty lobby. Chris and I stood and watched it.

The manager answered the phone from wherever she was in the back. "Oh, I'll be right out," she said. She came out apologizing. "I just finished giving my kid a bath. I guess I couldn't hear anything over the splashing."

I felt a little sheepish. We were probably the only Laura Ingalls Wilder tourists in town that week, and here she had to accommodate us and our crazy off-season whims. While Chris moved the car—"you can park it right against the side of the building if you want," the manager had said—I told her we'd been to the Wayside cabin.

"Yeah . . ." She seemed to be trying to find the right words. "There's . . . not much there," she said.

I had to agree. I asked her if she read the books. She looked like she was about my age. She was shy and kind and looked like she wanted to be back in her apartment down the hall with her family. I was sure this time of year she didn't have to spend much time venturing out into these carpeted hallways or this lobby with the big lofted ceiling with all its empty space.

"I have the whole set," she said quietly. "Here's your key."

❀

We had dinner at Ralph's Bar/Mary's Kitchen, which appeared to be one of the few places that was open during the evenings in winter. Luckily it was also one of the restaurants *The Little House Guidebook* recommended. It was a small place that displayed team logos for the Packers, the Badgers, and the Vikings; we sat in a booth and had very good hamburgers in red plastic baskets. There was a nice crowd for a Thursday evening—more than half the seats at the bar were full.

"Everyone seems nice," I pointed out to Chris. We could see that many of the people in the room knew each other. Mostly they looked settled—families with teenage kids, older couples. They were all perfectly normal-looking, but I found myself watching them as intently as I could without being conspicuous.

"What are you looking for?" Chris asked.

"Nothing, I guess." But I couldn't shake the feeling that I *was* watching for something in particular, looking and listening. Hoping to overhear something.

"Oh my God," I said. "I just realized something really weird."

"What's that?"

"Somehow I keep expecting everyone here to be talking to each other about Laura Ingalls Wilder." It was true. I'd been sitting there feeling like something was missing and that was what it was.

Chris started laughing. "What, you mean talking like they *know* her? Like, what would they say?"

"I guess I hadn't imagined that far." Though now that I thought about it, I supposed that they would say things like *Have you been by the log cabin lately?* and *Boy, things sure have changed since the Ingallses lived here!* I knew it was completely ridiculous. I'd been trying to cast everyone here in this bar as extras in this secret world of mine.

"I suppose it's just as well that this isn't a room full of people talking about Laura Ingalls Wilder," I admitted to Chris. "Because that would be a little creepy, right?"

"Maybe a little," he said.

That night, back at the motel, I was getting ice from the ice machine near the lobby when the manager's little boy in footed pajamas appeared in the dark hallway. He seemed to have come out of nowhere and didn't look lost in the slightest.

He growled at me, like a little bear. "*Rowr!*" he said, and then he giggled and ran away.

"Just think," I whispered to Chris later, just before we went to sleep. "We're in the Big Woods."

We were out of the motel early the next morning. We'd need most of the day to drive to Green Bay to see our friends. It took us only a few minutes to see the historical marker in Laura Ingalls Wilder Memorial Park and the closed museum and visitor's center, where I got out of the car and peered in the windows at the gift shop and felt a brief, inexplicable longing for a Little House collector's spoon.

"We should look at the lake again," Chris said when we got back in the car. We'd driven along the marina the day before when we first came in, but we hadn't really stopped to look. Now we made our way down the hill again, past the shuttered summer cottages and the rows of little brick storefronts.

Near the bottom of the hill was a tiny garden-shed-sized log cabin with a tiny porch and a sign that said *COMING SOON!*

SINGLE FAMILY YEAR-ROUND LOG HOMES. ("Wow, what a concept," said Chris.) Then we crossed the railroad tracks and parked along a rocky beach. Except for a couple guys who were ice-fishing near the marina, the shore was deserted. The rocks looked boring and brown and dumped off a truck; so much for collecting Lake Pepin pebbles, I thought. But then we looked out at the lake.

"I can't believe it's still frozen," Chris said. I couldn't believe it, either; we'd crossed the river twice on our way in and the ice had broken there. It was March, after all.

It was a gray morning, nearly misty. The temperature was in the forties, almost warm enough to leave our coats in the car, certainly mild enough to not feel the weather at all. Which is why it was so strange to see that the expanse of Lake Pepin that opened out in front of us was still frozen solid. A rough lip of ice was pressed up against the rocks on the shore, and behind it the entire lake stretched motionless for at least a mile. The great bluffs on the Minnesota side were faint in the distance, rising above the soft white line of the frozen lake. There was no wind, and despite the vastness of the lake, everything felt muffled and still.

"Pa drove the covered wagon across here." I said. It wasn't until I spoke that I realized that the fact astonished me.

"In which book?" Chris asked.

"*Little House on the Prairie.* Right at the very beginning. And in real life, too." I couldn't stop looking out across the ice. "I think this is the same time of year they went across."

"Really?"

I tried to remember. The book had said they set out "in the very last of the winter." "I think so. Then the night after they went across the ice started breaking."

This didn't look like it would break, though. I went a little closer to where a ridge of ice met the rocks and considered stepping out over it. The only thing that kept me from doing it was knowing that I'd want to take another step, and another. As solid as the lake looked, there was also something sort of miragelike about it, with the overlay of gray weather between us and the opposite shore. I felt, very distinctly, that if we went across we would follow them. I mean "them" as in *them*, and it seemed to me, too, that the same other side they'd reached in their covered wagon would be there instead of Lake City, the present, whatever. It seemed perfectly matter-of-fact that it would be this way; that just as the winter turns water into roads, it makes the world revert like this.

"I hadn't expected it to be like this," I told Chris. Meaning I hadn't thought I would find something like an opening into Laura World, that I would come this close.

4.

Good Girls and Golden Curls

I DON'T HAVE A SISTER, but for a time, while growing up, I had Laura Ingalls.

I'm the only daughter in my family, the younger of two. My brother, Steve, is four years older than I am, and for much of my childhood his life seemed infinitely more advanced than mine. While I didn't grow up alone, sometimes being a girl felt lonely.

Books often helped. Plenty of them offered surrogate sisterhood through their characters, but none filled the need the way the Little House books did. I enjoyed *Little Women*, but the March sisters were a self-contained bunch, the four of them so chummy together that I could only be an onlooker at their attic plays and Christmas mornings. Anne Shirley in *Anne of Green Gables* was a little more solitary, but she seemed awfully needy. While I had a perfectly decent set of parents, girlhood felt like an unknown territory. I loved that Laura World was full of wide open spaces that expressed the sort of not-alone lonesomeness that I often felt. One frontier seemed to stand for another.

Of course, this is just a personal metaphor, and maybe a hopelessly quaint one at that. So it seemed to me when I walked into American Girl Place in Chicago with my friend Kara on a late winter afternoon. Located on North Michigan Avenue, an upscale shopping district that attracts throngs of tourists, American Girl Place is the flagship store for the American Girl brand, which began as a small line of historical-themed dolls and has become a veritable empire of dolls, toys, books, clothing, and accessories, all for girls from toddler to tween ages. It's a massive place, as big as a department store, with its own doll hospital, doll beauty salon, and restaurant.

American Girl Place didn't exist when I was young, but I can see why an eight-year-old girl would love it, where everything from the pink-accented décor to the slogans on the wall (*FOLLOW YOUR INNER STAR*, read one motto) emphasizes how special it is to be a girl, how powerful. At American Girl Place, girlhood is *not* a lonely prairie. If anything, it's a city, or even an industry. The sense you get when you visit the store and ride the packed escalator is that American Girl girls have places to go, things to buy, important girly work to do.

"Why are we here again?" Kara asked. We'd been out on Michigan Avenue when I'd talked her into going into the store. "Do they have a Laura Ingalls Wilder doll?" she asked. By now most of my friends knew about my recent preoccupation.

"No," I said. "I just really like looking at the stuff sometimes," I confessed.

It's true: while I've never owned an American Girl doll, my fascination with the company dates back to my college days, when one of their catalogs inexplicably showed up at my apartment in Iowa City. While my "thing" for tiny doll accessories has never run as deep as my Little House obsession, I was starting to suspect they were related somehow.

It would be another month before my next attempted foray into Laura World, a trip to both the *Little House on the Prairie* site in Kansas and Laura's adulthood home in Mansfield, Missouri, and I was itching to see something in the meantime. So when I'd noticed the American Girl sign gleaming forth from Water Tower Place, I thought, why not? Maybe American Girl was the methadone to my Little House heroin, good for a fix. And maybe it would help me figure out why I'd gotten hooked in the first place.

American Girl is now owned by Mattel, Inc., but it was created by a teacher named Pleasant Rowland, who founded the brand's original company, Pleasant Company (clearly her entrepreneurial destiny demanded she call it this), and started the doll and book line in 1986. Reportedly she came up with the concept following a trip to Colonial Williamsburg in Virginia; eventually she'd create a doll character, Felicity, whose stories were set there. The very first American Girl to launch, though, was Kirsten, a Swedish immigrant girl who comes to live on the Minnesota prairie in the mid-1800s with a trunk full of calico dresses and sunbonnets. It might be just a coincidence that when American Girl set out to build its empire, it started in Laura's very own neighborhood. Or it could have been a shrewd move based on market research. ("The gingham sunbonnets scored high with the focus group,

Ms. Rowland.") All I know is that if I'd been about seven years younger, I might have encountered the American Girl products firsthand.

As it happened, my first acquaintance was by accident in 1992. "What the hell is this?" I'd asked my college roommate, Kelly, when the catalog showed up in our apartment's mailbox. "Why are we getting this creepy doll stuff?" She didn't know how it had come to us, either; it seemed the catalog had been addressed to a previous tenant or otherwise mistakenly sent. Yet neither of us could bring ourselves to throw it out.

"I can't stop looking at it," Kelly admitted one day.

"I know!" I said. When I wasn't writing English papers, I'd curl up on our thrift-store couch with a Camel Light 100 and flip through the pages studying each of the historical dolls. At the time there were only four American Girls: Kirsten, of course, and Felicity from Williamsburg; also Samantha, the Victorian one, and Molly, the bespectacled girl from the 1940s. The accessories amazed me: little wooden armoires and kitchen chairs, tiny baskets for bitsy golden brown loaves of bread, straw hats, bandanna-sized quilts, mini trunks. Felicity had the snobbiest accoutrements, but Kirsten's things had a folk-art cuteness, and I wanted some of Molly's stuff full-sized for my apartment, especially that retro dinette set.

I wouldn't fully give myself over to it, though. It was decadent, useless, expensive crap. The dolls themselves cost as much as a monthly car payment, and even the accessories were pricier than most of the clothes I bought at Ragstock. American Girl represented a spendy middle-class existence that I didn't want to partake in.

I still felt a little of that as Kara and I walked around the store's first floor, watching the families carrying big red American Girl Place shopping bags along with their bags from Bloomingdale's and Banana Republic. More than once we spotted a little girl whose American Girl–purchased outfit matched her doll's clothes, and group outings where gaggles of well-groomed mothers blocked the aisles.

"A little Stepfordish in here, isn't it?" Kara whispered.

"I know. Sorry," I said. "Let's look at the books." I steered her over to the appropriate section.

As a children's book editor, I've come to grudgingly admire the American Girl books. Their very first books were historical fiction chapter books that accompanied their doll characters. They were full of tidy morals and prefab story arcs that even the boilerplate titles give away: each girl Learns a Lesson and Saves the Day and so on. Imagine the Little House books written by literate robots, and you get a sense of what the early books were like.

But that was then: these days American Girl courts established children's writers to write their fiction titles and have a respectable line of expert-approved nonfiction guides that cover self-esteem, bullying, and other tough subjects (an impressive feat, because, really, *you* try explaining eating disorders to a ten-year-old).

We wandered around the book displays, looking at the rows and rows of novel covers showing spirited heroines getting their skirts muddy in the midst of brave rescues or tomboyish adventures. Across from the wall of the historical books were all the guides and advice books, including *The Smart Girl's Guide to Parties, The Care and Keeping of You, Stand Up for Yourself and Your Friends.* There were books about dealing with boys, siblings, emotions; books about dancing, knitting, food, diaries, hair. It seemed

American Girl had a book for every aspect of girlhood, collectively forming an encyclopedic master guide to being a girl. It made me feel a little jealous, though I think American Girl has a book for that, too.

⚯

A lot of what *I* learned about being a girl I learned from Laura Ingalls. I discovered that it helps if you try to love your own brown hair as much as you love your pa's. Not for nothing, it also helps to know that feeling bad about your looks is apparently such a universal thing that even little girls who live in isolated Wisconsin cabins (as far as one can get from fashion magazines) can experience it. I also have this crazy theory that the scene when Laura gets leeches on her legs in *On the Banks of Plum Creek* is a metaphorical preparation for menstruation, so that when Laura finds it terrifying and gross at first but quickly learns to deal with it, it brings us girls all one step closer to being able to handle *Are You There God? It's Me, Margaret*. Of course you're welcome to disagree.

However, I never agree with those who characterize Laura as a "tomboy." I know it's a widely held notion, no doubt put forth and perpetuated by folks who identify with Laura and who, unlike me, considered themselves to be tomboys in *their* childhoods. While I'm willing to accept many things as matters of interpretation, wherein your Laura Ingalls Wilder is different from mine, I'm holding my ground here: LAURA IS NOT A TOMBOY.

I will not deny that Laura did some decidedly un-girly things in the books, especially in *On the Banks of Plum Creek*. I understand that haystacks were climbed and old crabs were taunted. However,

I refuse to believe these things make Laura a tomboy. I will also cite page 146 of my *Little Town on the Prairie* paperback, which states that Laura "was not really a tomboy," just a girl who sometimes likes to play catch and ante-over (whatever that is) with the younger boys at recess, and is therefore merely "tomboyish" (see page 145), a distinction that I maintain is important. It's enough for her just to be a *girl*, even if she doesn't throw like one, okay?

I suspect a good deal of the tomboy associations come from Melissa Gilbert's rendition of Laura on the NBC television show, with her chirpy voice, spunky demeanor, and occasional tendency (inherited, of course, from her TV dad) to throw punches. I'll accept *that* Laura as a tomboy, I suppose, but not the book Laura. Plus the TV Laura had a sort of string-beany awkwardness to her and stomped around in her tight pigtails as if waiting for adolescence to relieve her from skinny androgyny. (Though in Miss Gilbert's defense, I don't imagine that "as round and strong as a little French horse" is a type much in demand among Hollywood actresses.)

Whereas the Laura who lived in those yellow paperback pages appeared, in those Garth Williams illustrations, much more unabashedly feminine, with her bare feet and the gently rippling skirt she lifted to romp through the grass on the cover of *On the Banks of Plum Creek*. I held that image in my mind constantly while growing up: in all its sensual freedom, it seemed to me the very essence of girlhood.

Maybe what bugs me the most about the tomboy designation is the way it implies that Laura's grubby antics are somehow beyond the realm of ordinary girl experience. Certainly *Plum Creek* never draws that line, and by the time I'd reached that book in the series I understood that Laura did more so-called boyish things because

she was a pioneer girl. Children's book reviewer Christine Hep-
permann, in an essay in *Horn Book Magazine,* describes a typical frontier experience for girls, one that matches Laura's almost
exactly:

> . . . while mothers fretted that pioneer life was turning their
> daughters "wild"—i.e., making them lose all sense of propriety—
> the girls stepped in to do the jobs that needed to be done. . . . They
> spent more time outdoors than their eastern sisters, removed from
> the watchful eyes of their overworked parents, developing a famil-
> iarity with the land that frequently proved advantageous.

These hard-working, nature-savvy girls couldn't have all just
happened to be tomboys, could they? I loved that Laura trapped
fish with Pa and rounded up oxen run amok because she *had* to.
Or maybe I loved that she had to and still got to be a girl.

My earliest years were spent watching my brother Steve's life and
trying to decipher all the ways in which I could or could not follow his example. I was often fascinated with his Cub Scout activities but eventually figured out that my interest could only remain
vicarious: there would be no Pinewood Derby for me. My parents
were fairly progressive and I doubt they ever discouraged me from
so-called boy things like sports and other pursuits, but I could
intuit, the way kids seem to understand, that my brother's world
wasn't quite mine. I distinctly remember sitting in his room and
flipping through one of his magazines feeling profoundly bored
and left out. Never mind that the magazine was *Boys' Life*! It still
didn't seem fair.

This is not to say I rejected "girl things"—dolls and dresses and so on. Rather I pursued them fervently, partly out of the need to distinguish my existence from my brother's, and partly out of the terror that perhaps I wasn't *enough* of a girl.

I was particularly obsessed with both long hair and long dresses. The hair was really the sore point. Mine was cut in a very short pageboy because my mom had found my fine, straight hair difficult to manage; it was different from her own, which was thick and wavy. Sometimes, especially when I wore my brother's hand-me-down clothes, strangers in restaurants would mistake me for male. I thank God and the '70s that maxi dresses were in style, allowing me to own a floor-length pink gingham dress that I would've worn every day if given the chance.

But being the '70s, it also meant I was part of one of the first generations of girls to grow up hearing the message that we could be whatever we wanted. So much well-meaning children's programming, like *Sesame Street* and *Free to Be You and Me*, encouraged us to defy social rules we had yet to fully understand; all the while, the pink and pretty trappings of conventional girliness called to us, too. Years after I wore out that gingham dress I had a college job at a preschool and watched one of the four-year-old girls, whose hair was as short as mine had once been, race around the playground with a skirt on her head to simulate a wig. "Don't tell her to take it off," the teacher told me. "She gets upset."

I found the world of the Little House books to be so much less confusing, not just because it was "simpler," as plenty of people love to insist, but because it reconciled all the little contradictions of my modern girlhood. *On the Banks of Plum Creek* clicked with me especially, with its perfect combination of pinafores and recklessness. (I will direct your attention to the illustration on page 31 of my *Plum Creek* paperback, where you will note how fabulous Laura looks as she pokes the badger with a stick; her style is casual yet feminine, perfect for precarious nature adventures!) At an age when I found myself wanting both a Webelos uniform *and* a head of beautiful Superstar Barbie hair, *On the Banks of Plum Creek* was a reassuring book. Being a girl sometimes made more sense in Laura World than it did in real life.

I must have also appreciated the way the first few Little House books keep boys at the periphery. (The one major exception, obviously, is *Farmer Boy*, but that's a book *about* a boy.) Boys are minor characters throughout the preadolescent chronicles of the Laura books—a cousin here, a classmate there, a younger version of Pa or Grandpa conjured up for the sake of a story. Boys in these early books rank at about the same level as bears: obviously not as dangerous, but like bears, their exploits make for swell anecdotes once in a while, the sort of story that invariably ends with a good whipping. At worst, the boys in Laura World will hurl a few witless taunts ("Snipes! Snipes!") and are promptly told to shut up; at best, they might do something spectacularly stupid, like get themselves stung by a whole hive of yellow jackets. Remember Cousin Charley in *Little House in the Big Woods*? Remember the illustration, page 209, in which the poor kid gets plastered with mud and wrapped up like a sad giant burrito while the other cousins look on with vague disgust? Notice how most of them are girls. Notice how they *clearly* know better.

This is yet another reason why *tomboy* never sounded quite right as a way to describe Laura. Boys are such a remote presence in these early books, the prairie where the Ingalls girls played so empty of them, that it's hard to imagine that Laura would want to emulate them, as the term implies. Only once does Laura ever seem to express jealousy: when her little friend Clarence in the Big Woods, he of the fancy outfit and the shiny copper-toed shoes, comes to visit. She loves his shoes, but, as the book states, "Little girls didn't wear copper-toes." Her one pang of boy envy, and it's about fashion.

But to heck with boys and girls and tomboys, because in the Little House taxonomy of childhood, the most crucial distinctions are between bad girls and good girls, which opens up a whole other can of leeches. It all goes back, of course, to Laura and Mary.

You know Mary's the good one, right? By *know* I mean the fact is seared into your mind from repeated exposure to her endless shining examples: Mary always sits quietly (though really, she does everything quietly). Mary doesn't interrupt. Mary doesn't mind Sundays one bit. Mary decides Baby Carrie can have *her* beads that she found at the Indian camp, even if a certain someone else would rather keep her beads for herself like a selfish little flutterbudget. If that wasn't bad enough, Mary's goodness is like a big blue sponge so absorbent that it passively sucks up all the positive attention, so that all the compliments and the candy hearts with the prettier sayings on them inevitably come her way. You have to wonder if her behavior keeps her hair golden as well, pumping a sort of virtuous Sun-In to her locks on a daily basis.

And yet the characterization of Mary Ingalls as a goody-goody with perfect posture and a soul like a springtime meadow seems to be mostly a creation of the books. The Mary who shows up in some of Laura's pre–Little House writing is bossier, has a "sharp tongue," and lords her age over her younger sister. One story, written in 1917 for the *Missouri Ruralist*, has an account of the blond-hair-is-better-than-brown fight that goes on throughout *Little House in the Big Woods*, but in this version Mary really rubs it in

("Don't you wish your hair was a be-a-utiful color like mine?") and tells Laura she has an ugly nose, too.

We'll never know if this reflects the real Mary, if perhaps she got a personality makeover for the Little House books, where she plays the perfect counterpart to Laura. In that sense she clearly serves a purpose: how else would we know how badly Laura's behaving if Mary wasn't around to give her weak little admonishments? ("Pa said we mustn't!") But Mary is also so insufferably dull that it makes Laura's badness seem quite reasonable, especially to those of us with an inner girl who likes to let down her sunbonnet once in a while. Which is to say, most of us.

And yet don't you think that there's—yes, I'll say it—something about Mary as well, something deeply appealing? Maybe it's not so much that she's good but that she's mastered the act of it so well, what with her folded hands in her lap, all her gestures clear enough for the rest of us to follow suit if we wanted. I know sometimes I wanted to emulate her—and why not, since for the first few books Mary totally wins at life, with high scores in the hair, prettiness, and seam-sewing categories? Wanting to be Mary was a little like wanting to be Miss America: both seemed to offer so much reward in exchange for such a simple performance.

Years later, in a sisterly heart-to-heart talk with Laura in *Little Town on the Prairie*, Mary cops to the truth:

"I wasn't really wanting to be good. I was showing off to myself, what a good little girl I was, and being vain and proud, and I deserved to be slapped for it."

Laura was shocked. Then suddenly she felt she had known that, all the time.

Oh, yes, and so did we.

But maybe the whole goodness thing shouldn't be written off

as just a racket; after all, what of the girls and women who really *do* identify with Mary? They're out there. In my own observations, Team Mary folks are often self-contained older siblings who feel less compelled to rebel, more inclined to prove themselves by their accomplishments: the Marcia Bradys of the world with their shelves full of trophies.

Rebecca Steinitz, in an essay in *Literary Mama* magazine, writes about discovering that her oldest daughter favored Mary, as well as Meg in *Little Women*, despite her own long-held belief that one is "supposed to like" Laura and Jo. Eventually Steinitz concludes that not every girl wants to be the "smart, tormented girl." "[My daughter] is an optimist who prefers life to go smoothly, and, like Mary and Meg, she will do all she can to keep it that way," she realizes.

Anita Clair Fellman, in her book *Little House, Long Shadow*, thinks the Mary proclivities are culturally ingrained: "Whereas the current preference is for spunky girl heroines, previously there was more ambivalence about such female role models, and even today there is still much in female socialization that makes Mary's desire always to do the right thing resonate for many female readers."

In pointing out that the gutsy gal archetype is more the standard these days, Fellman mentions another interesting bit: until the 1960s, the Little House books were often referred to as "the Laura and Mary books." It must be a sign of how much our cultural inclinations have shifted that as a reader from a later generation, I found this hard to believe: how could anyone ever have seen them as anything other than the *Laura* books? And yet the phrase turns up in vintage book reviews, and a Google search confirmed that, indeed, people of a certain age use the phrase when discussing the books online—proof that Mary wasn't always thought of as the boring, pretty also-ran. Instead she was the yin to Laura's yang, the two sisters together forming an ideal girlhood filled with equal measures of safety and danger.

I had to show Kara the historical doll section of American Girl Place, which displays all its expensive accessories behind glass, like a museum exhibit. To buy something, you'd take a tag with a little color photo of the item and bring it to the cashier. We lingered at the display for the doll character of Kit Kittredge, a nine-year-old growing up in the Great Depression. We agreed that Kit had some of the best furniture (*don't worry so much about the hard times, Kit! You can always just sell your stuff to us people who live in the future!*), and Kara, who collects vintage typewriters, fell in love with Kit's tiny one. I found a tag for it and slipped it into my pocket.

"What, are you going to buy that typewriter?" Kara asked.

"No," I admitted. "I just like taking the tags." Something about them, with their images of doll-sized treasure, always buoyed me. I loved the simplicity these miniature things evoked, the way they called to mind uncluttered lives where each carefully crafted object shone with significance. Kirsten's quilt, Molly's locket—they exuded something of the same aura with which things in the Little House books appeared; I could see them with a bit of the charmed sight of Laura World. On some level I recognized that the things on display at the American Girl store purported to be as cherished as Ma's china shepherdess, Charlotte the rag doll, and the butter mold with the carved leaves and strawberry.

Obviously, that was one thing my Little House and American Girl fascinations had in common: the *stuff*. In both instances, I felt like I was glimpsing the lives I'd once desperately wanted. In the case of American Girl Place, it was an indulged and solidly upper-middle-class existence where both me *and* my doll had everything we needed. And yet when it came to Little House, it was sort of the opposite feeling, in that the world I wanted to inhabit was an uncomplicated one, full of sunlight and clean-swept floors.

 There was still another feeling, too, one I noticed as we perused the display cases for Felicity, the Colonial Williamsburg character, whose accessories were by far the most patrician of all the American Girls—china teacups, lacy fans, delicate pretend cakes, embroidered pillows, satin slippers. They were so lovely that to look at them inspired a mildly masochistic delight, the realization that someone (even if it was a fictional-Felicity someone) lived a life that was far prettier than mine. That sickening sensation, I recognized, was none other than That Nellie Oleson Feeling.

All hail Nellie Oleson, New York–born daughter of a Walnut Grove mercantile proprietor, later the most exquisitely dressed country girl in Dakota Territory! With her utterly scrumptious nastiness she completes the spectrum of Little House girlhood types, from good Mary to not-so-good Laura to bad, bad Nellie. From the moment she's introduced she gets right down to her bratty business, wrinkling her nose, sticking out her tongue, and yanking hair.

Fine, so it's not much of a repertoire—even by nineteenth-century school-yard standards these seem like awfully basic moves. What *really* gives Nellie her evil superpowers, though, are the enviable shiny details of her life—her ribbons and lawn dresses and wax dolls and candy sticks—all of it paraded before Laura and Mary when they visit her awesome carpeted house in the "Town Party" chapter of *On the Banks of Plum Creek*. While I'm fond of the swaying prairie grasses of my Laura World, somewhere in my subconscious dwells a Nellie World, too.

Which, well, looks an awful lot like American Girl Place. Though while Nellie Oleson is exactly the kind of girl who would own an American Girl doll, had they existed during her time, she herself could never be an American Girl character. Really, one of the most brilliant things about the American Girl marketing concept is that Felicity, Kirsten et al. are like *nice* Nellies, friendly girls who wouldn't yank their possessions away from you, the way Miss Thing in *Plum Creek* snatched back her doll from Laura (see the page 164 illustration: ooh, the *burn*!). A visit to American Girl Place always satisfies the secret hope that I used to have reading that chapter as a kid—my wish that Laura would just suck up a little and try to work things out with Nellie so she could play with her stuff. (Pathetic, I know.)

I've always appreciated the way Nellie's hatefulness evolved with age. By far my favorite/most dread-evoking Nellie moment is in *Little Town on the Prairie* when, years after her ignominious scene back at Plum Creek (remember the "Country Party" chapter—the crab, the leeches, the screaming?), she shows up on the first day of school in De Smet late, and fashionably so:

> She had grown taller than Laura, and she was much slimmer. She was willowy, while Laura was still as round and dumpy as a

little French horse. . . . She wore a fawn-colored dress made with a polonaise. Deep pleated ruffles were around the bottom of the skirt, around her neck, and falling from the edges of the wide sleeve. At her throat was a full jabot of lace. Her fair, straight hair was drawn smoothly back from her sharp face, and twisted into a tall French knot.

This, along with the illustration on page 130 of the classic old books, inspired both terror and admiration in me when I read them as a kid: terror that in a few short years my worst enemies might turn suddenly, gloriously swanlike, catching me unawares and at the very depth of horsey dumpiness. The admiration, of course, was for Nellie's outfit. The descriptions were a little confusing—I had no idea what a polonaise was, or what color was fawn—but I understood she was clad in a full-body armor of high hauteur. You might wonder what happened to her trademark curls; perhaps her powers enabled her to will her own follicles into whatever form she required. It's also clear she'd stepped up her game and ditched the frivolous ringlets and ribbons for the deep pleats of contempt. As a kid, it made me wish for a first-day-of-school outfit that could make me as impervious. To hell with Gloria Vanderbilt jeans; surely having a jabot of lace at your throat meant nobody would mess with you.

The character of Nellie was based on three different girls Laura knew in real life. One was a storekeeper's daughter in Walnut Grove; the second was the first girl's school-yard rival, a spoiled girl from New York (and like the Nellie of the books, she wound up in South Dakota a few years later). The third, a girl whose family homesteaded outside De Smet, had for a while competed with Laura for Almanzo's attention: she was the one who'd come along on the buggy rides until Laura finally made Almanzo choose, just as she did in *These Happy Golden Years.* The fact that Nellie wasn't any one person but rather a composite of three of the real Laura's antagonists' worst traits makes her even more terrifying, some kind of blond Frankenstein assembled from assorted bitch parts.

Of course, Nellie Oleson's always seemed just a tad unreal in her various TV and theatrical incarnations. When the rest of the cast is wearing their farm duds and sensible calico dresses, you can always count on Nellie to appear in a sort of ruffled drag, a preponderance of frills and bustles and twirling parasols and convolutedly feathered hats. It calls up a brief preschool memory of mine in which I'd decided, during dress-up time, that a hat I'd put on conferred upon me a whole new persona. "I'm a *bad girl,*" I announced proudly. "Because I have a *hat.*" I don't know exactly where I got the idea that Bad Girls Wear Hats (sounds like a Raymond Chandler novel, doesn't it?), but I must have picked it up from one female villain or another on TV, must have intuited that being bad and female came with a wicked and conspicuous sense of fashion.

On the NBC *Little House on the Prairie*, Alison Arngrim as Nellie Oleson goes beyond mere style. Some of the early episodes are queasily accurate portrayals of mean-girlness, like the one where Nellie torments a stuttering girl by pretending to befriend her and inviting her to join her exclusive club, only to demand that she say a tongue twister as her initiation ritual. Arngrim's performance is precise enough to trigger your own old traumatic memories of past cruelties (mine involves a girl named Sabina

Stuven and the question "What kind of jeans are *those*?"), but at the same time you can't help but feel a delight at having survived them.

It's no surprise that Nellie is vanquished on a weekly basis on the show—either by offscreen punishment (you really don't want to know the extent to which *Little House on the Prairie* spanking references have been lovingly cataloged on YouTube), or by any number of hilarious TV comeuppances. After a while, though, you come to appreciate that Nellie gets to be Nellie.

※

At American Girl Place I looked around at all the girls with their parents, especially the ones with their mothers. Had a place like this existed when I was a kid, my mom probably wouldn't have taken me. I likely wouldn't have expected it, either—I considered our family to be above such Nellie Oleson-esque entitlement even as I was slightly envious of it.

When I was the same age as Laura in *On the Banks of Plum Creek*, my mother was in school, writing papers after dinner and after I went to bed. At night she lived behind the noise the electric typewriter made. I knew she was doing important things, understood this with the same unwavering conviction that Laura had whenever Pa said it was time to move. I knew that sometimes you could go to school and discover that you didn't have a jacket when everyone else was wearing a jacket, just like when Laura and Mary found out that their dresses were too short, and I knew that it would be all right in the end.

In my world, my mother was both there and not there the way Ma was a mere glimpse on the cover of *On the Banks of Plum Creek:* there she was in the doorway of the dugout, working away, while right above her Laura was on her own, running through the grass over their invisible house.

If being a girl is a frontier all its own, what is the manifest destiny?

It seems like there are two different kinds of Little House fans: those who claim their favorite book is *These Happy Golden Years* and those, like me, who don't. To be sure, I love the book, in which Laura embarks upon a slow, subdued courtship with Almanzo Wilder and marries him at the end. But I love the other parts more—Laura's stint teaching school out at the miserable settlement where she boards with crazed, knife-waving Mrs. Brewster; the treacherous ride home with Almanzo where both she and the horses risk freezing to death; the terrible and surreal summer storm they encounter on one of their buggy rides. I get the sense that other people find Laura and Almanzo's romance more enchanting than I do. Almanzo's a great guy and all, but he's the *inevitable* guy, biding his time between blizzards and school terms, waiting for the engine of the book's narrative to slowly wind down to the happy golden ending with the brand-new house with the fancy plastered walls and its pantry drawers full of silverware. (Well, okay, I really like the part where she gets to have that pantry.) But somehow there's a feeling that the world gets smaller, narrowing down to the view out the front door where Laura and Almanzo sit at the very end of the book.

Could it ever have been otherwise? I suppose not. Then again, there was Cousin Lena, who let us see other possibilities.

It's a little hard to place Lena if you haven't read the books in a while. She appears for a few scant chapters in *By the Shores of Silver Lake*, when the Ingallses travel out past the end of the train line to a railroad camp in Dakota Territory. They meet up with relatives, and Laura discovers she has two cousins, the children of Aunt Docia's husband. One is Lena, just a year older than Laura but infinitely more experienced at this new life of tents and shanties and railroad men. She says wicked words like "gosh," sleeps in her clothes—"We'd just have to put them on again in the morning anyway," she says—and races at breakneck speeds in the buggy she drives (SHE DRIVES!) and on the black ponies she rides bareback that she can mount while running.

The few days that Laura—and we—spend with her are intense: Laura takes lessons in bareback pony racing and learns new songs about young men who "can very obliging be." That's right, for the first time in Laura's Little House girlhood, males are on the horizon, even if they're distant still: sometimes they're vaguely threatening, if the songs and Pa's warnings are to be believed, and sometimes, if they're Big Jerry, the half-Indian railroad worker, they're kind of beautiful, as Laura watches him ride into the sunset one afternoon. Lena is there through all this heady confusion, part of a world where anything could happen: you could be married off at thirteen, marry a railroad man instead of a farmer, not marry at all.

We hardly need for Ma to explain to Laura, in so many words, that Lena is a bad influence. She's what Ma would call "boisterous" and what a feminist scholar like Ann Romines could call "problematic to the narrative." In her book *Constructing the Little House*, Romines points out that Lena is a threat for showing Laura "that there might be another way to be an American girl." But like so many of the threats throughout the Little House books—wolves, Indians, swift creeks—the danger that a girl like Lena presents is something to be savored briefly, like a piece of Christmas candy.

Once the railroad camp breaks for the winter Lena heads off to parts unknown with her family (and a wagonload of goods swiped from the company store), never to be seen again in the series.

Out of everyone in the books, Lena was the character I wanted to be the most. Naturally I often identified with Laura, but when it came to imagining myself physically in the stories *with* Laura, it was as Lena. I suppose it was because I could tell that different worlds were converging during their short acquaintance, the way it would be if *I* could be friends with Laura. And then, I always sensed that Lena was not from Laura World but another girl protagonist visiting from an epic story of her own, one that was just as vivid as the Little House books, and perhaps even *wilder*, more tempestuous and windswept.

As it turns out, the life of the real Lena Waldvogel was indeed something of a saga. Although she was Aunt Docia's stepchild in *Silver Lake*, Lena was her biological daughter (the relationship was changed in the fiction, probably to explain why she never appeared in earlier books). Lena's father had gone to prison when she was an infant; he'd fired his gun through a closed door at some men he thought were coming to rob him and killed one of them. Docia divorced him and some years later married Hiram Forbes (aka Uncle Hi in the book), an alcoholic, with whom she had several children. The family moved around even more than the Ingalls, and twice—once in Missouri and then again in Minnesota—Docia and Hi tried to leave Lena and her brother Gene in orphanages. By the time Lena was in her teens she was on her own, working in Wisconsin. "She'd learned from life how to take care of herself," says Donald Zochert in *Laura*.

Without knowing any of this I could only guess at what Lena's stories were whenever I read the books as a child. When I got to the Lena scenes in *By the Shores of Silver Lake*, the world—suddenly it wouldn't be just Laura's anymore—would open up; suddenly I'd sense a vast, unwritten expanse, one that my mind could claim. As it happens, *Silver Lake* is the book where the twelve-year-old Laura's imagination starts to flourish, when she starts to see beyond the literal truth in the world she describes to blind Mary—who, in her typical stick-in-the-mud fashion, would rather her sister not take poetic license when describing things like a man riding horseback in the distance:

"Laura, you know he [Big Jerry] couldn't ride into the sun. He's just riding along the ground like anybody."

But Laura did not feel that she had told a lie. What she had said was true too. Somehow that moment when the beautiful, free pony and the wild man rode into the sun would last forever.

The fictional Lena has a foreverness to her, too, though it seems the real-life Lena and Laura had never kept in touch. In her book, Romines mentions finding a letter in the Wilder-Lane archives that Lena, by then married and living in Nebraska, had sent to Laura after reading *Silver Lake* and recognizing herself as a character. "Dear Mrs. Wilder If you are my dear cousin Laura Ingalls—Please just write me a line and I can then write to you in a more personal manner." If Laura ever wrote back, no record exists. Nothing else about Lena except that glimpse across the distance.

I think ultimately what makes the Little House girlhoods so compelling is that they're real girls' lives reimagined. *Silver Lake* hints that the kind of life Lena led was a rough and overworked one, but somehow it seems equally true that she was as free as those black ponies. Laura herself gets to see more of the world as a fictional girl than she ever did as a real one: she goes with Pa to see the railroad grade being built in the "Wonderful Afternoon" chapter, but in her correspondence to her daughter while writing the book, the elder Laura admits she never would have been allowed to watch.

Of course, the fiction allows for other truths to come through. Consider, for instance, the narrative of girlish horse lust that begins in *Little Town on the Prairie* and runs alongside the slowly (*very* slowly) developing relationship between Laura and Almanzo. Oh, yes: long before it's appropriate for Laura to even notice Almanzo, she's digging those Morgans of his. When their courtship finally commences in *These Happy Golden Years*, nothing unseemly ever happens in that buggy seat, but there's plenty of hot action at the other end of the reins, thanks to Almanzo's frisky new team, Skip and Barnum. "They are not as much fun when they behave," Laura says at one point. "It is pretty warm to excite them so much," Almanzo says at another. Whew! If you don't believe me, get the audiobook version of *These Happy Golden Years* and listen to Cherry Jones work herself up reading the "Singing School" chapter. Hear her breathless, mounting excitement as Laura and Almanzo sneak out of the church early to relieve some of Barnum's pent-up energy. "Driving Barnum": so *that's* what the kids are calling it these days. Metaphorically speaking, that is.

As sublimated as things get in Laura's teen years, I think the fact that her character gets to mature at all is one of the unsung virtues of the Little House series, something you can't appreciate until you consider that when Laura Ingalls Wilder began *By the*

Shores of Silver Lake, her daughter, Rose, who edited and helped her throughout her writing career, advised her to make *Carrie* the new protagonist. Since Laura's character was now twelve and presumably too old for the reading audience, Rose reasoned, perhaps younger sister Carrie could be the new Little House Girl, so to speak. You can tell it makes sense from a publishing standpoint. In fact, it sounds downright American Girl, to think of girls' lives as interchangeable components in telling the story of girlhood. Laura objected. "We can't change heroines in the middle of the stream and use Carrie in place of Laura," she wrote in a letter to Rose. She was right.

Back at American Girl Place, my friend Kara and I had finally finished looking over all the doll things. I still wanted Molly's dinette set. Kara is part Lakota Sioux and thought it was pretty stupid that the Native American doll, Kaya, had mostly wild forest animals for her accessories. "Oh please, she's an *Indian*, not Dr. Doolittle," she sighed. We'd both been pretty charmed by the new 1970s doll, Julie, whose stuff included a tiny fondue set and tennis-shoe roller skates. "I *had* those," I'd gasped.

But now we kept stopping in front of the biggest display cases, which didn't have dolls in them or merchandise of any kind. These were chambers a little bigger than a phone booth and each one showed a corner of a room from an American Girl's life, filled with historically correct details and strewn with ordinary things— all of them life-sized, or at the very least, girl-sized. Kirsten's corner had log cabin walls and a quilt-covered chair where she'd left her knitting; Molly's had 1940s kitchen cabinetry. The idea was that you could almost stand in each girl's place and inhabit her life, if you believed enough in her things.

I didn't think any of it would have an effect on me. But Julie's display, showing a corner of a '70s-era girl's bedroom, was pretty uncanny, with a lava lamp and bricklike vintage cassette recorder on the modular side table that was just like the ones my parents had. The little room was full of ordinary things that had already become precious, that I couldn't help but want to have again, to feel like whoever it was I used to be, whether it was my past or someone else's. Julie was just a character, of course, but on the shag carpeting of her room sat a boxed set of the Little House paperbacks, the ones with the blue covers, just like mine. One of the books was splayed open next to her beanbag chair.

I liked this Julie, I decided. She wasn't real, but she was reading *By the Shores of Silver Lake.*

5.

There Is a Happy Land
Far, Far Away

I WASN'T SURE about taking a plane to see the Little House on the Prairie. It felt a little off, somehow not the proper way to get to a spot so closely associated with land—all those trudging, earthbound frontier struggles with their wagon-lurching river crossings and trades of tired-out horses. It didn't seem quite right to just zip down there, all tidy and trackless, with no trace on the land for a faithful brindled bulldog to follow me. If I had a brindled bulldog, I mean.

But the plan was to fly to Springfield, Missouri, and then drive three hours into Kansas. I was renting a car, and figuring out an unfamiliar car stereo system requires something of a pioneering spirit, yes? I would take a day to drive to Independence and back, and then the following day I would take a short trip east of Springfield to Mansfield, Missouri, Laura's adulthood hometown, where she and Almanzo built Rocky Ridge Farm. By all accounts the museum at Rocky Ridge was one of the major Little House destinations, the home of Pa's fiddle and other important relics.

I was going alone this time: Chris had a lot of work deadlines that spring and was going into the office on weekends. It was just as well—he was usually up for anything, but if I was going to see all the Little House stuff there'd be five more places to visit. Wouldn't he have to stand around a lot while I swooned over old quilts? It was probably better to give him a break. It wasn't like he made me go to all the experimental music shows he went to see in Chicago, the ones where guys hooked up microphones to pieces of sheet metal and kicked them around the stage. (Though it really is the sort of thing you have to see at least a few times in your life. Like Almanzo's chores in *Farmer Boy*, it builds character.) Anyway, going by myself meant I'd be free to gaze at Pa's fiddle for hours on end if that's what I felt like doing.

I'd decided to call the Little House on the Prairie beforehand to make sure it would be open, since it was spring, still early in the tourist season. I wound up speaking with Amy Finney, the manager of the museum, who had a gruff, friendly voice.

"Come out first thing in the morning," she said. "Before things get too busy." She asked me if I'd ever been to southeastern Kansas before.

"No, but I was in Topeka once," I told her. "And Leavenworth." I think I went on to name every Kansas town I could remember passing through on the family vacation we took to the Grand Canyon in 1983. Because I am a dork.

"Well, yes," she said. "Those *are* in Kansas."

"I'm sorry," I told her. "It's just that I can't wait to come out."

My guilt about flying all but vanished the moment the plane

broke through the clouds and began its descent over one of the most fabulously bucolic settings I'd ever seen surrounding an airport, with deep green swatches of farmland and tiny barns whose shapes were unmistakable from the sky. I'd almost forgotten that Springfield is in the middle of Ozark country. I kept waiting for the typical airport-surrounding ugliness to show up as the plane drifted in over the storybook landscape, over lush fields and cows—*cows!*—in coordinated little herds. But no, it was pretty much like a Grandma Moses painting right up until the runway appeared beneath us.

A month or so before my trip I'd found myself reading anything I could about the real-life circumstances of the Ingalls family's year or so in Kansas. Once I knew that *Little House on the Prairie* hadn't really been written from memory, it felt like some kind of hole had opened up in my knowledge, a hole I was now trying to fill with history.

The history of the land dispute at the center of *Little House on the Prairie* is a bit more complicated than the book told it. Okay, a lot more. Although the Homestead Act of 1862 granted free land to settlers who could reside on their claims for five years (the proverbial "bet with the government" that Pa Ingalls would make in Dakota Territory), much of the land in Kansas wasn't eligible for homesteading because it had either been sold directly to railroad companies by Indian tribes or was still part of Indian reserves.

The Osage land was the largest and last of these reserves in Kansas, and up through the 1860s big chunks of it had been ceded to the government in exchange for cash or annuity payments. By

1867 only a strip of Osage land remained in southern Kansas, henceforth called the Osage Diminished Reserve, and individual settlers had started illegally moving there in hopes that the land would be opened for homesteading, or at the very least available at prices cheaper than what the railroad and prospecting companies were typically charging. (Remember the Oklahoma Sooners? They were doing the same thing in the 1890s, back before the name became affectionately attached to college football.)

All this just scratches the surface of the situation, by the way. A scholarly article by Frances W. Kaye, with the terrifically scathing title "Little Squatter on the Osage Diminished Reserve," reminds readers that the conflict between Indians and white settlement was no simple thing:

> Rather it was a complex and venal struggle that featured railroad companies, timber pirates, state and federal politicians and civil servants, Indian agents occupying every inch of the spectrum from honest to corrupt, mixed-blood intermediaries, fullblood and mixed-blood traditionalists and accommodationists, illegal Euro-American squatters of all stripes, including army officers, and lawyers for every side. All the negotiations were both blocked and speeded up by acts and threats of illegal violence, charges and countercharges of corruption, and great confusion and hardship.

Just to give you an idea.

Anyway, all this business with the illegal squatters wasn't going over so great with the Osage, who had yet to get their money from land ceded to the government in an 1865 treaty and were feeling pretty screwed over to begin with. They knew they were probably going to have to move anyway, and in 1868 agreed hastily to what would come to be known as the Sturges Treaty, named for the railroad company president who stood to benefit from the deal—which was to sell the Diminished Reserve lands to the LL&G Railroad. The news of the agreement upset rival railroad companies, settlers, and politicians who felt the land should be in the public domain. It also brought even more squatters to the Diminished Reserve. The treaty was hotly debated but never ratified, and in 1870 it was finally withdrawn in Congress. By then the Ingalls family had moved to the Diminished Reserve and Pa had built the log cabin.

By now I'd seen both the TV movies based on *Little House on the Prairie*. The first was the 1974 pilot movie for the NBC series starring Michael Landon and Melissa Gilbert. I'd read about how Ed Friendly, a former NBC executive turned independent TV producer, had bought the rights to the Little House books after he'd seen his daughter reading them. The story seems to be that he'd read *Little House on the Prairie* on a flight from L.A. to New York and as soon as his flight landed he'd raced to call his lawyer to find out who held the rights and set up a meeting.

(While I don't know what Mr. Friendly looked like I imagine this anecdote as something out of the *Airport* movies, full of vignettes of glamorous jet-setters. He'd be the tanned guy in the nice suit at one of those '70s modular phone kiosks barking, "Get that Laura Ingalls Wilder on the telephone! I have an offer she can't refuse! What, she's dead? Well, who's her agent? Get me *her people!*")

Friendly set out to produce the show and subsequently partnered with Michael Landon, who'd recently come off his role as

Little Joe on the long-running Western series *Bonanza.* The rest is, well, television history, intermingled with various myths and rumors, like the one about Landon casting himself as Pa only after the actor who'd been slated for the part failed to show up on the set, which sort of makes Landon sound like he was nobly stepping in for some varmint who deserted his TV family and not just casting himself in the plum role of the show. It was also his vision for the series that won out over Ed Friendly's; Friendly wanted to stick more closely to the story lines of the Little House books, whereas Landon went much more for life-affirming lessons and heartwarming fare. It wasn't too long after the show started that Friendly dropped out and was involved in name only, leaving Landon to produce (and often write and direct) the show for much of its homespun-values-laden run.

But before all that was the *Little House on the Prairie* pilot, which is surprisingly faithful to the book, if not to historical fact. After seeing countless dumb anachronisms in the later seasons of the show (people in small towns in the 1880s weren't *constantly going out to restaurants,* for Pete's sake), I wasn't prepared for the numerous historically correct visual details of this first movie— the misery of the covered wagon in the rainstorm, the cut of Ma's dress, the squat ramshackleness of the cabin.

When I watched the movie on video one afternoon, I had been reading up on all the Kansas history. I'd stopped having daydreamish Laura World visions of soaring prairies and now my mind was swimming from learning about the various treaties and big-business interests, from trying to understand the difference between homestead and preemption land claims. So it was a relief to see that TV log cabin, so earnestly accurate, and all the familiar scenes in the book acted out by exceedingly familiar people,

Michael Landon and Melissa Gilbert and everyone else. The Christmas scene is well done, as is the scene of Ma's stormy-night vigil, where she sits in the rocking chair with the gun in her lap, shakily singing, "There is a happy land, far, far away, where saints in glory stand, bright, bright as day."

Even the Indians are sort of familiar, though not at all in a good way, seeing as how they're the grunting types from countless old Hollywood Westerns, played by swarthy guys in orangey makeup. They come in two varieties: the bad ones, who barge into the cabin one day and stroke Ma's hair in a way that seems both childlike and menacing, and the good one, Soldat du Chêne, who speaks only in smooth French and is only slightly less threatening, like Serge Gainsbourg in buckskins. They all, however, have that good old stoic thousand-yard stare that most Indians of a certain era in TV have. Their stock quality is a reminder that the NBC *Little House on the Prairie* is very much of its time in the early '70s. Watching the movie I could sense that Michael Landon–as–Pa and his TV family set out to bring a bit of civilized warmth to this formulaic Western landscape, to make all that cowboys-and-Indians stuff the kids were watching on TV throughout the '60s have a little more heart and wholesomeness.

The show was staking out its claim of family values on another contentious frontier, too. "TV has embarked on a new era of candor, with all the lines emphatically drawn in," declared *Time* magazine as it reported on the new TV season of 1972, two years before *Little House on the Prairie* aired. "Religious quirks, wife swapping, child abuse, lesbianism, venereal disease—all the old taboos will be toppling." If TV in the '70s was thought to be a wilderness of *Maude* and cynical cop shows, it's clear the producers of *LHOP* sought to establish the show as a haven for any pa and ma who wanted a decent place to settle down with their children for a weeknight of viewing. Certainly this had already worked for *The Waltons* on CBS, the success of which partly inspired *LHOP* to be developed.

And yet if you've ever watched *Little House on the Prairie* long enough to catch some of the more sensational episodes, you've probably wondered how on earth some of this stuff could be considered family programming. Plenty of Internet discussion of the show, in fact, is devoted to recounting all the shootings, fires, fistfights, infant deaths, grisly accidents, and drunken brawls that viewers have witnessed over the course of this ostensibly heartwarming show. I found a blog called *WTF Little House on the Prairie?* written by Mike McComb, a grad student in film and TV studies at Syracuse University. His site consists entirely of highly detailed and often very funny recaps of some of the more traumainducing episodes. (One, for instance, is "A Matter of Faith," in which Ma, home alone with an infected leg and half crazed from blood poisoning, decides to amputate her own leg after reading the line *and if thy foot offend thee, cut it off* in her Bible: "She starts flipping through [the Bible] as if it were a magazine with a really good recipe for gingerbread," McComb writes in his recap. "She gets out of the chair and hobbles over to the drawer to get the dullest knife she can find.")

In my e-mails with Mike he said he was fascinated with the show—among other reasons—for how it exemplifies what "family viewing" meant thirty years ago. He pointed out that it was something much different in the '70s, when families had only the one TV that received only a few network channels; back before VCRs and DVRs, when everyone in the household watched whatever show was on at a certain time, and most likely they watched it together. "If a kid was confused, or freaked out, or unsure of what was happening in Walnut Grove, he could ask the rest of the family about it during the commercial break," Mike wrote.

I suddenly remembered that was exactly how it was when I was a kid. Somehow I'd all but forgotten that we'd be watching something like *Fantasy Island* and my mom would routinely turn to my brother and me during some questionable moment and ask us if we understood what was happening. In those days, then, it wasn't considered too inappropriate to see Ma Ingalls trying to hack her own leg off on TV so long as the story ended on a lesson or a positive note—all's well that ends well, as Ma herself would say!—and presumably an adult would be able to explain what was going on in the meantime. As Mike pointed out, family programming used to simply mean shows that presented opportunities for kids to ask, *Dad, why is Michael Landon punching the blacksmith?*

These days, of course, there's an expectation that something "family friendly" will be made under the auspices of a company like Disney, shown on a family-oriented channel (like the Disney channel), and released on DVD as "something the kids can watch." Which is exactly what happened when Disney produced its own *Little House on the Prairie* miniseries in 2005.

It was also Ed Friendly's *Little House on the Prairie*—his second go at adapting the book. After he'd parted ways with Michael Landon on the NBC show, he'd continued to produce frontier-themed stuff for television in the '70s, such as a short-lived ABC series called *Young Pioneers*, based on the novels of Rose Wilder Lane, Laura's daughter, and a TV movie about the Pony Express, starring Leif Garrett. When he finally returned to the story of the Ingalls family, he and Disney did it in a big way: a four-hour, six-episode epic filmed on breathtaking locations in rural Canada with a considerable budget. This production wasn't anyone's star vehicle—the cast was made up of skilled actors, Native Americans among them, who seamlessly became their roles. (Pa looked a little too much like a bearded Kevin Federline for my tastes, but he played him well and at least he *had* a beard.) One of the online reviews I read said that this version of *Little House on the Prairie* had more in common with HBO's *Deadwood* than with the Michael Landon version. Another review said that it was suitable for children ages six and up. Gritty *and* kid-appropriate? I had to see this!

You can't help but be impressed by the 2005 *Little House* movie. The production values are fantastic, with wide-screen prairie vistas and amazing sound editing that insists on capturing all kinds of rugged aural verisimilitude, from the rumbles of wagon wheels over packed dirt to the roar of the prairie fire in the distance. I watched it on DVD, and during the scene when the covered wagon crossed frozen Lake Pepin and the ice cracked, the speakers on our home theater system boomed appreciatively.

Often the movie seems to go out of its way to prove that it's Not Your Mother's *Little House on the Prairie,* with plenty of pioneer grunge and a level of authentic detail that makes the NBC TV movie's well-meaning attempts pale in comparison. Here the well-worn chronicle of Laura and her family trundles along as usual, but this time all kinds of frontier wretchedness is strewn around the edges of the story: On their journey the Ingallses see wrecked wagons by the side of the road; their horse gets bit by a rattlesnake and has to be shot; they hear rumors of crazed rogue soldiers wandering the wilderness. They ride through the new town of Independence, which is a squalid and grim assortment of shacks, filthy tents, and crude saloon signs, and even glimpse some extremely disheveled-looking women swaying outside a makeshift brothel. (That's right, this Little House version is so dedicated to frontier veracity that they're willing to put *whores* in a Disney movie. It's rated PG for *history*, folks!)

But where the realm of the white settlers is all seamy misery, muddy roads, and unwashed, whiskey-smelling creepiness, the Indians in this version are magnificently clad, well organized, and occasionally a little magical. The Indian path that runs near the cabin, while vaguely ominous in the book, is portrayed here as a kind of portal into the wonders of the Native American world: Laura visits it furtively, and when she does, a strange wind blows over the prairie, things start moving in slow motion, and soft New Agey music starts playing as she peeks through the grass at carefree Indian children playing. Sometimes one of them, a boy nearly her age, peeks back and smiles.

You can probably guess that this recent cinematic return to the prairie is an attempt to render the Indian-related conflicts of the original story in a more enlightened fashion, wherein the Ingalls family is even more decidedly on the side of the Osage than not. This is accomplished largely through the mystical, friendly Indian-kid sequences and also by making Mrs. Scott, the neighbor lady, into a piggish, child-hating racist who invites herself to tea and says of the Indians, "Why bother with treaties? Why not kill them all?" She's so horrible that even *Mary* would like her to shut up. "I don't think that's right!" Mary shouts at Mrs. Scott. (Yes, Mary's the good girl in the family, which used to mean that she was polite and quiet. But these days we tend to assume that a truly good girl would also despise bigotry, so she pipes up.)

In something of a departure from the book, the tensions between the Indians and the settlers escalate until the Ingallses and

Mr. Edwards retreat to the Scotts' house and barricade the windows; in the midst of the all-night vigil, Mrs. Scott has a paranoid meltdown of sorts. But no attack comes, and in the morning Dr. Tan, the black doctor, rides by and delivers the same fortunate news that the Ingallses heard in the book: that Soldat du Chêne— yes, that "good Indian"—convinced the other Indians to leave the white settlers alone. "You dumb-ass white fools lucked out this time," Dr. Tan says. Okay, so he doesn't say it, but his tone strongly implies it. Really he says, "You should thank Soldat du Chêne!" as he rides off.

This latest *Little House on the Prairie* movie, the NBC TV movie, and staunch defenders of the Little House books all take great pains to draw lines between racist and tolerant, greedy and sympathetic, good Indian and bad Indian, good white settler and bad white settler and good-black-doctor-somehow-not-quite-so- bad-as-white-settler. And yet the lines everyone always seems to ignore are the most fundamental ones, the ones that would have been on the map in 1869.

Neither the book nor the movies ever make the land situation particularly clear, and, of course, few kids—and probably not many adults—would even know where to start asking questions. Not when there are so many other things one could ask during family viewing. (*Dad, why is Mrs. Scott so mean? Mom, who are those ladies in town who are dressed all funny?*)

Then again, the family that lives inside the book and on the TV screen have their share of awkward questions, too. "Why do they go west?" Laura asks Pa at the end of chapter 18 of the book. She asks, in so many words, that if the land Pa has moved them to is Indian Territory and the government makes the Indians move just for the white people, isn't that, well, wrong?

Pa doesn't answer Laura. "Go to sleep," he says.

There are renditions of this scene in both the movies, too—in the 2005 one Laura points out that the Indians are peaceful, which ratchets up the sense of unfairness a notch—but in every version, including the book, there's a sense that it's somehow too late for a question like Laura's, but the fact that she asks counts for something.

Historians think the real-life Pa, Charles Ingalls, probably knew what he was doing when he moved the family to the Diminished Reserve, even if Laura Ingalls Wilder never quite knew. In an article in the journal *Kansas History*, researcher Penny Linsenmayer points out that the timing of the family's move from Missouri, where they'd lived only briefly, seems to indicate that Charles Ingalls sold his land there because he thought he could get a better deal elsewhere. Not the legal land claims in other parts of Kansas, though—those were more expensive, thanks to the blasted railroad companies. But squatting on Indian land that might one day soon have the Indians removed? *That* he could afford. It didn't hurt that plenty of local newspapers encouraged the illegal settlement in 1869, right around the time the family made the move.

So while *Little House on the Prairie*—the book, as well as the movies—gives the impression that the Ingalls simply settled on the wrong side of the line between Indian land and legal settlement territory, Linsenmayer points out that "the Ingalls family settled so firmly in the bounds of the Osage Diminished Reserve that it is doubtful they were unaware they were intruding on Indian lands." Oh, *Pa*. Though if he'd ever passed any of this awareness on to Laura or anyone else in the family, it seems to have been either forgotten or misunderstood over the years; as it was, Laura had been misinformed about where they'd even settled, thinking that it was in Oklahoma instead of Kansas.

After the Sturges treaty fell through, Congress scrambled to come up with another solution to address the growing tension between the Osage and the illegal settlers that had led to crop burnings, threats of hangings, and assorted other ugliness, and in mid-1870 finally passed legislation to remove the Osage and sell the Diminished Reserve lands. If there had been an Osage who'd persuaded his tribesmen to remain peaceful, as the book says, it was highly unlikely to have been the chief Soldat du Chêne, who had been known to French settlers in the early 1800s (somehow Laura had been given his name when she'd consulted researchers for the book). At any rate, the Osage tribe agreed to the removal deal and left Kansas that fall for Oklahoma. Not too long after that, the Ingalls family left, too.

It's not entirely clear why Pa decided to pack up the family and leave. In fact, had they stayed they would've been able to file a legal claim on the land less than a year later. The family might have been misinformed in all the confusion that ensued while the Osage removal legislation was still being decided (lots of troops sent in to keep the peace, frontier newspapers jumping to conclusions, etc.) and believed that soldiers were coming to kick them off the land. But Pa had also gotten word that the buyer of the log cabin in Wisconsin had defaulted on payments, and he may have decided it was easier (and cheaper) to just return to their Little House in the Big Woods. Considering how many of Pa's decisions to move involved money, this makes sense, too.

This isn't in the book, of course. Laura—and, it must be said, Rose, who worked closely with her mother on the Little House books—left out the part about the house in Wisconsin, and they were likely never certain about what had happened with the land if they'd had the location wrong in the first place and only Pa and Ma's (possibly disgruntled) stories to go on.

At any rate, it's all the government's fault in the book. It's never stated whether the Indians are leaving under government orders or just nobly moving on because, as Ma says, "That's what Indians do," but they do, just like they're "supposed to," and after that spring comes, the fields start growing, and everything is just peachy until the government shows up with the news that the land is still Indian Territory, even though there aren't any Indians around. Confusing? Well, that's the government for you!

Some scholars believe that it was probably Rose's notion to blame the Feds at the end of the novel, what with her proto-Libertarian ways. Anita Clair Fellman, whose book *Little House, Long Shadow* argues that all the Little House books are infused with this kind of conservative sentiment, says of *Little House on the Prairie* that "Wilder and Lane took the array of family lore, information and misinformation that they had and formed it into a particular shape that suited their emerging politics." Much of Fellman's book depresses me, mostly because I hate thinking that when I read these books as a kid I was merely a half-pint half full of ideology. But regardless of whether or not her point is true, making those blasted politicians in Washington the culprits works out nicely in a storytelling sense, since it takes everyone else in the story off the hook. Good Indians and good settlers can still be good as long as we all agree that the government is full of jerks, right?

I can't help but wonder why *Little House on the Prairie* has been adapted as often as it has (three times, if you count *Laura the Prairie Girl*, the Japanese anime series), since the book is really the story of a failed venture. The Ingalls family comes out to pursue a dream of building a new home; they contend with Indian tensions, sickness and fire, wolves and panthers, and then they give it all up. Whenever I read the book as a kid, the part where they pack up the wagon again and leave always took me by surprise. *That's it?* I'd think. I'd forget the ending every time until I got to it again.

But maybe that's what makes it so perfect for the screen. The plot of *Little House on the Prairie* is the most self-contained, after all: a family travels to a new place; they build; they go. The story wipes itself clean so it can be told over and over again.

Things were a little rough the morning I set out for the Little House on the Prairie site. The night before there'd been thunderstorms so severe they'd knocked out the Wi-Fi connection at the Baymont Inn, where I was staying in Springfield, and the lightning flashing outside my room kept me awake, and the pouring rain gave me a slight anxiety attack from worrying about whether I'd completely closed the power windows of the rental car. Then the next day I couldn't figure out how to start the rental car again, because instead of a key it had a button, and even though I kept pushing it the engine wouldn't start, and this odd little lumpy icon would light up on the dashboard with the word *BRAKE*. After about ten minutes of fiddling with the parking brake, I looked closely and noticed that the lumpy icon actually depicted a *foot on the brake pedal*, indicating what I was supposed to do when I started the car, which of course I *would* have done automatically if I'd just had a key and not this weird *button* completely confounding my intuitive knowledge of how to start a freaking car. But finally I started the car and headed west on Interstate 44 toward Kansas.

I do realize how this all sounds. I realize that in this account of my journey to the Little House on the Prairie, a journey that in Pa's time would have taken at least ten days, my litany of misfortunes contains words like *power windows* and *Wi-Fi*. I realize, yes, that one of the greatest hardships I had to contend with involved a car that starts with the push of a button. Even then I knew what an insufferable feeble-hearted dope I was, as I hurtled along changing lanes and counted the exits.

It was an overcast day, the sky resolutely steely. Probably it would rain at some point. The bucolic Ozark hills I'd seen while flying in gave way to a duller, flatter landscape. I swigged coffee compulsively and scanned the radio stations.

Then there was an incline on the highway, going over a slight rise, and when I got over it I could see a storm cloud in the sky ahead. I turned off the radio. The thing ahead was not so much a cloud but a canopy, so inky deep gray it was nearly black. It jutted over the field like a shelf and I was driving into its shadow. The fields on either side of the road were suddenly enormous now, pressing up back at the sky. I drove on into the dark and held my breath, and finally a burst of rain slapped against the hood and windshield, and then another. And then it was behind me.

Everything felt different after that. I remembered where I was going.

⚛

Of all the ways in which the NBC show betrays the Little House books, the one that gets me the most is that the show kept the title *Little House on the Prairie*, taking the name of one of the darkest books in the series and forever altering the associations that come with it, linking it to a cloying mélange of family-friendly sweetness and homey values. I'll grant that a good deal of that mess works well enough with other books in the series, with their cozy Christmases and country-girl yearnings. *Little House on the Prairie*, though, stands apart as a masterfully creepy book, its terrors completely unlike the familiar fairy-tale shadows of *Little House in the Big Woods*.

In *Little House on the Prairie*, everything lurks in plain sight under open sky—the creek bottoms with their strange atmosphere, the deadly well, the panther with its scream that carries across the night distance, the circle of wolves that surrounds the cabin. The book has its cheery moments, like when Pa plays a fiddle duet with a nightingale, but it's the dark stuff that really stuck with me, gave my Laura World its depth and shadows. Nearly everything and everyone in the world of this book shows a malevolent side: Laura discovers her beloved bulldog has the power to kill Indians, her mother has the capacity to hate them, and both the little house *and* the prairie burst into sudden, encroaching flames.

This was the kind of stuff that I used to think Laura had faithfully recalled, but ever since I'd discovered that the book was mostly fiction (though I continue to believe maybe a few fleeting primal memories are in there somewhere), all of the story's nightmarish turns felt even more charged somehow, now that I knew that much of it was imagined. It was as if that unrecalled landscape was a place where Laura and Rose could project anything they wanted, and so they brought to life a repository of both family and historical uncertainties, things Laura may have sensed from hearing her parents' stories about that year down near the Verdigris River.

Apparently Laura and Rose conjured up other specters on that prairie as well. One of the drafts of *Pioneer Girl*, Laura's unpublished memoir, begins with a pretty familiar account of the Ingallses' time in Indian Territory, only to launch into an astonishing episode in which Pa joins a posse to hunt down a family of mass murderers—the Benders, who had operated an inn some distance away, and who'd been discovered to have killed and buried dozens of travelers. According to the manuscript, Pa had stopped at the deadly inn a few times on his trips to Independence, but he could never afford to spend the night. When the horror is discovered, Laura and Mary overhear Pa telling Ma about the bodies that had been found. "I screamed," Laura's account says, "and Ma told Pa he should have known better." Then Pa rides off into the night with the other vigilantes, and when he returns he never tells what happened but hints that justice had been served, though in real life the mystery of what became of the Benders was never officially solved.

The case of the "Bloody Benders," as the killers came to be known, was an infamous one in the late 1800s, and they'd lived just one county over from the Ingalls settlement. The account of the Benders had been left out of *Little House on the Prairie*, but Laura would bring it up again—complete with the bit about Pa's involvement—during a speech at a book fair in Detroit in 1937. It's sort of a kick to read the text of the speech now and visualize the seventy-year-old Mrs. Wilder, beloved author, standing at a podium in her best hat as she sweetly intones, "In the cellar underneath was the body of a man whose head had been crushed by a hammer." I presume the audience was made up of adults and that Laura, unlike Pa, *did* know better.

"You will agree it is not a fit story for a children's book," she told the crowd in conclusion.

Uh, you think?

(And yet, it doesn't sound all that far from the sensational plots that Michael Landon would come up with on the NBC show, where children were routinely kidnapped and occasionally the Ingalls crossed paths with the likes of the Jesse James gang.)

It's just as well that this Frontier Motel Hell version of *Little House on the Prairie* was never published, though, because it doesn't hold up as a true story. The Bloody Benders were for real, but by the time the murders were discovered and the Benders had disappeared in 1873, the Ingalls family had moved back to the Big Woods of Wisconsin, and there was no way Pa could have been part of the band of vigilantes. Which means that either Laura and/or Rose made that part up, or else Pa could tell some whoppers. Most speculation these days points to Laura and Rose, who'd likely long been intrigued that such a sensational crime happened so close in time and place to their family's sojourn in Kansas Territory, and they decided to take advantage of it by weaving it into the revised *Pioneer Girl* manuscript, which Rose's literary agents had initially found to be a little too grandmotherly and dull. Nothing like a serial-killing family to liven things up, right?

I couldn't believe it when I heard about this whole Bender business. The idea that Pa could be a footnote in the annals of true crime was stunning enough, but then the whole thing was just cooked up? You mean Laura Ingalls Wilder was bullshitting? I e-mailed Nancy Cleaveland about it, since I figured she'd know more about this than anyone else. She pointed out that *Pioneer Girl* is vague about dates, and Laura and Rose probably didn't think anyone would know that the Ingalls family story didn't quite overlap with the Benders.

"I guess Laura never figured that there'd be people sitting around and able to look up every little detail of her life," Nancy said. She also thought that it had been Rose's idea to include the Benders. "Maybe Rose had always told the story to impress the town girls in Mansfield," she said. No doubt Laura had thought it would impress a book fair crowd, too. She couldn't have known that years later the world would be so phenomenally full of information that anyone could read her speech, look up census records, or find where the Little House on the Prairie had really stood, something she herself had never known for sure.

For a while on my drive I didn't know where the damn place was, either. There are no major interstates near Independence, Kansas: to get there I would travel a succession of small highways. I didn't have a real map, only a Google Maps printout of my route. Somehow I'd thought that would be enough. The roads went in mostly straight lines, after all, and it was *Kansas*; did I really need anything more detailed?

As it turns out, yes. Especially when there is rain involved. It was April, so throughout the drive the pouring rain came and went and came again, sometimes in great big gully-washing torrents. I quickly learned how to turn the windshield wipers up to full speed on the rental car (though it would've helped if *that* had been a great big button on the dashboard). At one point I found myself on a two-lane road driving through a vast grove of pecan trees; the ground was flooded on both sides, with water stretching as far as I could see. Yet somehow I didn't even wonder if any of the roads would be flooded until I tried to get to the last stretch of highway, a turnoff near the Verdigris River. It seemed a very Pa Ingalls kind of problem to have, though. Ah yes, flooding along the Verdigris River! We'll just take this county road, then! All's well that ends well!

But after another forty-five minutes of driving, I began to suspect that it *wouldn't* end well. Somehow the highways weren't connected to each other in the way I thought they'd be, and I didn't know any of the tiny towns I'd passed. The printout map was pretty useless, especially now that I'd left the road that the wobbly little highlighted line represented and was driving somewhere in the empty space above it. Except, of course, it wasn't empty; it was filled with rain. Lots and lots of it.

For the past few months I'd been trying to figure out how people managed to find places back when there weren't roads or odometers or Rand McNally maps or online directions (for all the good they were doing me) or GPS systems. How did Pa know when he'd traveled a mile? Did he have a watch that let him estimate the pace? Later I'd read that when people needed to be more exact with distances, they'd tie a cloth to a wagon wheel spoke and count how many rotations it took to go a mile. It sounded awfully tedious to me, but what else are you going to do in the middle of the prairie? But for the moment, driving through Kansas in the rain, I had no idea how anyone ever found anything out here. How did I ever think I could find where I was going using Internet wizardry and fancy pictures taken from outer space?

I dialed 411 on my cell phone. The rain was getting heavy again, and I was grateful that directory assistance had the direct-connect feature, which I knew from past experience worked pretty well as long as you used a really loud voice to tell the computer the name of the place you were looking for.

"Independence, Kansas," I told the automated system. *What listing?* it asked me.

I had to think for a moment and then I took a deep breath.

"LITTLE HOUSE ON THE PRAIRIE," I yelled.

There was a pause, and finally the phone started ringing. A woman answered. It sounded like Amy Finney. It *was* Amy.

"You're on *what* road?" she said. I wasn't sure. "What town did you just pass?" she asked.

"Um, Dearing, I think?"

"Okay, here's what you'll do," she told me. She gave me directions that would take me through Independence and then onto the highway that led to the site south of town. Something about a traffic light by the Walmart, and a left turn, and signs for the local airport. "Got it?" she said.

"Sure thing," I said, though I didn't get it at all.

The idea that I could even visit where *Little House on the Prairie* took place thrilled me a little more deeply than the prospect of seeing the other Little House sites, because I never imagined that the site could be found. When I read the books as a kid, I knew that the places with names—Pepin, De Smet—could be looked up somewhere, using the encyclopedias and maps of my world, but the cabin out on the prairie didn't seem quite real, was deep in the most remote regions of Laura World for me. Certainly the book implies the cabin was bound to be lost forever, once the family had emptied it out and left it behind.

"The little log house and the little stable sat lonely in the stillness," the book says, when the family takes one last look back from the covered wagon. I could barely stand to read those lines whenever I read the book. Yes, the latch-string in the door was left out, a detail that had always called up a completely different kind of visual association for me, so that instead I imagined a thread coming loose from a stitch, or else slipping out from the needle. (This is probably a result of my embroidery attempts around the same age that I read the books.) It was an extremely frustrating notion for me: the latch-string was left out, just *hanging* there, somewhere.

It didn't help that nobody seemed to know where the Ingallses had lived in the first place. The back copy on the 1970s paperback editions I checked out from the library read, "They traveled all the way from Wisconsin to Oklahoma," but other sources said they'd been in Kansas.

This confusion had come about partly as a result of Laura's faulty memory: in the book she states they'd lived forty miles from Independence, Kansas, which would have put them in Oklahoma, known at the time as Indian Territory. She and Rose had even gone on a road trip to try and find the spot in the 1930s, with no luck. A few years later, in 1947, when Garth Williams was assigned to illustrate the new editions of the Little House books and set out across the country to research all the homesites, he followed Laura's erroneous directions. He thought he'd actually found the place after he'd talked to an elderly man driving a two-horse wagon who claimed to remember where the cabin had been. (I imagine old guys driving wagons around probably get stopped and asked if they remember So-and-So from the past all the time.)

It turns out the Ingalls settlement was actually about *fourteen* miles from Independence instead of forty. Researchers believe Laura may have simply misheard this bit of Pa's account, or else wasn't aware that Indian Territory had once included part of Kansas along with Oklahoma. It did make me feel a little better to consider that if Laura didn't know where the family had settled, then she couldn't have known what an opportunistic jerk Pa had been and how far over the line into illegal territory he'd gone. The only clue as to where the Ingallses had really lived was in the family Bible, which, in its inventory of births and deaths and marriages, listed Carrie's birth in Montgomery County, Kansas. Somehow Laura and Rose weren't aware of this record (as to why, one theory is that during the writing of *Little House on the Prairie* the Bible was still back in South Dakota, in Carrie's possession) and instead went careening around northern Oklahoma.

But amazingly, a couple of Kansas researchers in the '60s and '70s managed to find out where the cabin was located—even though Pa hadn't been able to apply for the homestead—by checking the census and then comparing it to land claim records, looking, by process of elimination, for an area that hadn't had a claim filed on it when the area opened for homesteading in 1871. Donald Zochert's book *Laura* manages to give a surprisingly breathless account of the meticulous research. Researcher Margaret Clement made a map of all the claims on file and found that she could trace the path the census taker had taken in 1870! She narrowed her search down to two quarter-sections of land, went out to visit both of them, and found out that one had "a beautiful hand-dug well" on it and knew she'd found where the Ingalls family had lived.

(Zochert really is good at this kind of thing. If the words *beautiful hand-dug well* don't give you just a little bit of a charge, I don't even want to know.)

❈

I had to call Amy two more times before I finally found the turn-off, marked by a sign ("Go just a little ways *past* the sign," she said. "Don't try and turn at that road right *at* the sign."), and went along a series of tiny roads.

When I finally found the place, it looked like an ordinary farm at first, with a vintage red barn and a clapboard farmhouse. It wasn't until I parked along the rail fence at the edge of the road that I saw the log cabin just beyond the windbreak row of trees west of the house. I'd imagined it nestled deep into the prairie, but here it was, front and center. It hadn't been built on the site of the original cabin; instead it had been placed close to the road.

A little ways beyond to the west were two other buildings that were part of the exhibit, little houses as well, both white clapboard. One was a tiny post office, the other a one-room school-house; both had been moved from their original locations in nearby towns. The three of them stood in a row, a sort of odd little town. Behind them was the open land. I supposed it was prairie, but everything growing was so new and green I couldn't tell.

The farmhouse serves as the office and gift shop, and Amy Finney was at a desk near the front door. "Glad you made it here," she said. She was in her fifties and had a round face; she wore no-nonsense short hair and a denim shirt with an embroidered *Little House on the Prairie* logo on it. She looked like someone you'd want around in a crisis, and it was no wonder she'd managed to navigate the last twenty miles of my drive for me over the phone.

The house was cozy; Amy told me that a bachelor farmer had lived here before the museum had taken it over. The front two rooms were filled with shelves of books for sale, standard souvenir fare such as postcards, mugs, and magnets, and an assortment of homey merchandise like rag dolls and sunbonnets. When I'd gone to Wisconsin, the museum shop in Pepin had been closed for the season, so this was the first homesite gift store I'd seen. Finding myself in a room—nearly a *whole house,* even!—full of Laura Ingalls Wilder stuff was such a trip that for a moment or two I sort of forgot about the cabin outside. There were calico aprons, and charm bracelets, and jars of honey. You could buy a tin cup with a peppermint stick and a shiny penny taped to it, a tribute to the Christmas gifts Laura and Mary had received from Santa Claus by way of Mr. Edwards.

On the wall near the door was a literature rack filled with dozens of photocopied pages. Each one sold for twenty cents and featured some bit of Little House lore—Laura's family tree; a map of the Ingalls' travels across the Midwest; a form letter Laura sent to fans; a collection of Laura's favorite Bible quotes. I knew it was all the sort of information you could find for free online, but there was an appealing authority somehow to these slightly wavery photocopies. They contained facts, answers, things one might not have known before, and I liked that this had a specific value, that they shored up a low-tech defense against God knows how many people who thought that *Little House on the Prairie* was just a TV show.

Amy told me folks like that still come in all the time. "I can remember the first time someone came in and said, 'Wait, you mean Laura *wrote books,* too?'" she said. She pointed out the large framed photograph of the Ingallses that hung over the merchandise shelves. It's the only portrait of the family together, taken when all four of the daughters were grown; everyone is dressed in somber, high-necked clothes, their faces vacant and unsmiling.

Amy said that a couple months ago a woman had come in and had been so appalled by the photo that she actually refused to look at it or acknowledge that it depicted the real-life Ingalls family. The woman claimed to be such an avid fan of the TV show that she watched it for six hours a day.

"She went and sat right over here"—Amy pointed to a window seat—"and she crossed her arms and had her back turned to that photo and she kept saying she would *not* look at that picture of those ugly people and that was *not* Ma and Pa." She laughed. "I guess some people get so used to Michael Landon they can't accept anything else."

Amy looked pleased when I told her I loved the store, since she had been responsible for expanding it from a small selection of postcards and books. "Well, I guess the store at the museum over in Mansfield is bigger—they have more money over there—but people tell us we have a pretty good collection of stuff over here," she said. "Of course, not everyone likes that we're selling stuff."

I had some idea what she meant by that. On a table in the middle of the front room of the gift shop was a tall plastic jar: DEFENSE FUND DONATIONS, the label read. HELP US DEFEND LAURA'S LITTLE HOUSE ON THE PRAIRIE HOME SITE AGAINST FRIENDLY FAMILY PRODUCTIONS INFRINGEMENT ACCUSATIONS. I'd heard about the lawsuit. Back in the fall of 2008 many of the Little House fan blogs and message boards had been posting about it. Basically, the company who'd created the TV *Little House on the Prairie* was suing the Little House on the Prairie site here in Kansas over the use of the trademark "Little House on the Prairie." It sounded absurd, really. And I didn't understand: wasn't *this* the Little House on the Prairie? I decided I'd ask Amy after I'd gone out to look at the Little House for myself.

The Little House on the Prairie replica cabin gets an *A* for authenticity. *A*-plus, really. The Big Woods cabin we'd seen in Wisconsin had been a tidy, splinterless affair constructed by professionals; the Kansas cabin looked like it had been built by—well, Pa. The walls were made of spindly, unstripped logs with peeling bark, the corner joists were ragged, the cracks between the logs were filled in with crumbling clay.

I'd read it had been built following Laura's descriptions as closely as possible; certainly the door looked like it had been made per the directions in the book, with its elaborate latch descriptions that to this day I can never figure out: "First he hewed a short, thick piece of oak," the book says. "From one side of this, in the middle, he cut a wide, deep notch. He pegged this stick to the inside of the door, up and down and near the edge. He put the notched side against the door, so that the notch made a little slot." Somehow it's so specific it's disorienting: One side, in the middle? Up and down and near the edge? Every time I read this passage I follow along as best as I can and then get completely lost. But to look at the door, or its facsimile thereof, you'd never guess it could sound so complicated. I felt both stupid and relieved to see how it works: you pull this little rope, and then this thing goes up.

The doorway was low; I had to duck a little to go inside. The cabin was furnished somewhat: there was a primitive bed with a quilt, some rough wooden furniture, a table with a red-checked cloth on it (just like Ma had used), and a guestbook for visitors. The mantel held a glass oil lamp and a china shepherdess (both of them glued in place), and there were a couple of enamelware pots on the hearth. None of it felt terribly lived-in—something like this could only gesture toward hominess—but I liked being there; it felt, in fact, like a playhouse. I wanted to just sit there for a while; maybe it would rain again and I could listen to the rain on the roof.

But the rain had stopped, for the most part, and I could see out the door that two other cars had pulled up along the fence. I went back to explore the rest of the place. Behind the tiny post office (which I found out had once served Wayside, Kansas) were a couple of little printed signs on slightly crooked posts, and beyond them lay the open space of the prairie. One sign indicated that Dr. George Tann, the black doctor who'd treated the Ingalls family during the "Fever 'n' Ague" chapter of the book, had lived somewhere off in the distance across where the highway now ran.

The other sign simply said *Look north and visualize covered wagons coming over the Kansas prairie.*

The one-room schoolhouse seemed the most forlorn of all the buildings, since it looked just the same as it had been when it was last used in the 1940s, with the old linoleum in the cloakroom vestibule and warped paper maps pinned to the walls.

On one wall hung a collection of laminated letters and drawings from elementary schoolkids around the country. A girl named Amanda from Virginia had written on both sides of her paper and the front of her letter ended mid-sentence: *My favorite part was when Laura sees all the wolves. My other favorite part was when Laura looks right into a baby Indian's eyes and he—*

I read the other essays but I kept going back to that truncated little sentence, written in pencil in that curly-lettered grade-school print. The letter was solidly stapled at the corners so I couldn't lift it up and see what the rest of the sentence said, as if a second-grader's book report held the key to what had actually transpired in that literary portrayal of white settler/Native American relations.

The TV movies had only vaguely referred to this scene. Near the end, the Ingalls family would watch the Indians ride off and the expressions on their faces would indicate that the mood was poignant. In the Disney version, Laura watches the procession and sees the boy she'd sort of befriended on her trips to the Indian path. He sees her and waves with a sweet smile. Laura waves back. It's a scene anyone could watch and understand. In the book, though, the moment is one of sheer id, a flood of crazy impulses and unexpressed emotions. "She could not say what she meant," the book says, and doesn't explain further.

But never mind why Laura cried in this scene, whether it was "because she would never see an Indian baby again," as that See & Read biography stated, or any other explanation you decided to believe. It was the papoose kid I was still wondering about. Laura looks right into his eyes, and he *what?*

Somewhere outside the screen door of this schoolhouse, I kept reminding myself, was where, in *Little House on the Prairie,* that long procession of the departing Osage people had passed the Ingallses' cabin.

Or maybe they hadn't yet been departing. I had been reading the *Pioneer Girl* manuscript the night before and now I remembered, curiously enough, that the novel had said one thing and the memoir another. "The Indians came back," Laura wrote in *Pioneer Girl.* A few pages earlier she'd reported they'd disappeared following a suspicious prairie fire; then came Christmas and the spurious episode with Pa and the Benders, and then, she says, the Indians returned: "I sat on the doorstep one day and watched them coming on their ponies. . . . As far as we could see, in both directions on the flat land, were Indians riding one behind another." If this was based on something the family had really seen, it's possible the Osage were returning from one of their seasonal hunts. Here, as in *Little House on the Prairie,* she saw the Osage women riding by with their papooses and she cried when Pa wouldn't let her have one. And shortly afterward, as in the novel, the soldiers came to order the white people off the Indians' land.

But in *Little House on the Prairie,* the chapter describing the same procession (complete with papoose tantrum) is called "Indians Ride Away," and Laura and her family watched as "that long line of Indians slowly pulled itself over the western edge of the world. And nothing was left but silence and emptiness."

So where was that baby's family headed anyway? Were they returning or leaving? It was easy enough to look out the windows across the schoolroom and see the bluffs and hills along that western edge and imagine something had just vanished beyond it, pretty much just as the sign outside had entreated visitors to *visualize covered wagons.* I knew there'd been countless times when I'd been encouraged to wistfully consider that aforementioned silence and emptiness, the absence of Indians who'd "once roamed" prairies and forests but somehow were never described as actually having homes in those places.

Every fall during my childhood the *Chicago Tribune* ran a creepy but venerated cartoon that had appeared annually in the paper since 1907. It was called "Injun Summer," and it depicted an old man and a young boy raking leaves and looking out on a field in which the corn shocks looked like teepees in the moon-light and ghostly war-dancing figures appeared in the smoke of a bonfire. "There used to be heaps of Injuns around here—thousands—millions, I reckon," said the old man in the accompanying text. "Don't be skeered—hain't none around here now, leastways no live ones . . . They all went away and died, so they ain't no more left." If the text was to be taken literally, the entire Native American population had simply withered away and only came back once a year in ghost form to entertain hillbilly-talking folks doing yard work.

Of course, as a kid I knew that wasn't true, though for a time that Keep America Beautiful commercial might have given me the impression that modern Indians did nothing but skulk around littered highways shedding single tears, which wasn't much bet-ter. I'd also had some vague sense that a lot of people disliked the "Injun Summer" cartoon (the *Tribune* finally stopped running it in 1992), but it wasn't until I was older that I could smell the casual racism along with the nostalgia and burning leaves. And I had to admit that even that most sympathetic scene in *Little House on the Prairie,* where the Ingalls family feels depressed after watching the Osage procession, has a whiff of this stuff as well. It became even stronger once I'd remembered the earlier version in *Pioneer Girl* and realized the extent to which Laura and Rose were telling a story, and how it was the lousy old sad-Indian story our country has loved to tell. Of course, there are other variations now—like the magical Indians in the Disney version—but it was all still a story.

Later in the gift shop I noticed that there were only a couple Indian-related items. One was a booklet speculating about the real identity of the Osage Indian in *Little House on the Prairie* who'd persuaded other tribes to leave the white settlers alone. The other was a dreamcatcher. I asked Amy if she ever got any flack for not having more Native American merchandise.

"Honestly I've never heard anyone mention it," she said. "I mean, we try to include the Indian stuff." Every summer they hire tribal dancers to perform during the Prairie Days Festival, though she admitted they were awfully expensive. "But you know, you gotta have them come." I knew what she meant: it seems necessary to show that we all know better—better than Ma, and better than the Scotts, the neighbors who'd uttered some of the most egregiously racist lines in the book; by now we also know better than Laura and Rose. But how could we know better *and* know what really happened when the Laura of the book looked into an Indian's eyes? Maybe that Amanda kid's paper, with its cut-off sentence, said it best.

I went back outside and walked toward the farmhouse. A family with five kids had come out of the cabin and was headed for the other buildings, filing across the lawn like a scout troop. I passed a twentysomething couple who'd stopped to read the sign outside the cabin. I was about to return to the gift shop when I realized I had almost forgotten about the well. *The well Pa dug.*

It was behind the farmhouse, with a sign that said *Hand Dug Well.* You pretty much had to take the sign at its word, since you couldn't see down it: a little square stone wall had been built around the edge and a wooden cover fitted over the opening. It didn't look like much, but I walked all around it, again and again. I felt a little silly in my obsessiveness. By now I had stopped taking for granted a lot of things in *Little House on the Prairie*—who knew, for instance, if there'd really been a neighbor named Mr. Scott who'd helped Pa dig the well and collapsed from the toxic underground gas, or if the whole episode was just a fictional bit borrowed from the perils-of-pioneer-living grab bag? I knew I couldn't know beyond the very educated guesses of researchers whether this well at my feet was really dug by Pa—the sign stopped short of saying so.

For various reasons—all the history, all the confusion—this place hadn't felt like Laura World to me; it still didn't, but this little wooden door in the ground made me feel like I'd at least reached its threshold. I stared at the ground and remembered the scene in the book where Laura and Mary and Pa visit the deserted Indian camp and see all the evidence of lives lived there; the places where people had cooked, where their horses had grazed, where a woman had leaned forward as she'd stirred something cooking on the fire. That detail especially—those moccasin footprints with the deeper toe imprint—had always captivated me far more than the beads the girls discover scattered among the grass. Now I tried to conjure up the Ingallses the same way, with this one spot in the ground. Pa had to have stood *here* and *here* and *here*, I thought, as I kept pacing a little ring around the well.

The rain hadn't started again in earnest, but the wind felt wet and chilly. The young couple had made their way over to the little restroom building right across from the farmhouse. The woman was pregnant and she stood under the eaves just out of the drizzle, looking cold in her light skirt. We just waved to each other; the wind was strong enough that you'd have to shout above it to say hello.

I stood out by the road and looked around in all directions. I'd wanted to explore the area, see the creek bottoms to the north, get a sense of the "high prairie," as they called it. But I felt earthbound and small. After reading the book so many times, I'd felt like I could float above the landscape, but now that I was here all I could feel was the sensation of being in a big wet field in Kansas.

There weren't any visitors left in the farmhouse by the time I went back in to talk to Amy. I hadn't realized how cold I was until she asked me if I wanted some tea. She brought it to me in a souvenir mug. "Pull up a chair if you want," she told me, and she started telling me more about the lawsuit.

I already knew it involved Friendly Family Productions, which was the most recent incarnation of Ed Friendly's entertainment company. After Ed Friendly's death in 2007, his son Trip Friendly (aka Ed Friendly III) had taken over the company and was now suing the Little House on the Prairie homesite and museum for trademark infringement.

According to Amy, both Little Houses on the Prairie, the Kansas site and the Hollywood entertainment franchise, had coexisted for decades without any incident. The homesite hadn't really had a relationship with the Friendlys, but they did have one with Michael Landon, who had visited the site. (Amy still thought well of the late Mr. Landon. "He was why folks of any age could sit down and watch that show and not ever be bored," she said.) Now, though, the production company had an issue with merchandising rights. In his complaint, Trip Friendly contended the homesite museum was using its website to sell merchandise that had nothing to do with promoting tourism and infringed on Friendly Family Productions' copyright.

Amy thought that the complaint was a lot of fuss over a few prairie dresses that were sold on littlehouseontheprairie.com, mostly to Japanese fans. "We have only about six international sales a year," she said. While the homesite had registered various trademarks in the "Little House on the Prairie" name for toys and clothes, Trip Friendly had a trademark claim to the name, too. Somehow the issue had prevented Friendly from closing a merchandise deal with the producers of the new musical stage production of *Little House on the Prairie* that was currently in development. I did my best to follow Amy's explanation of the case, but it was sometimes confusing, and my knowledge of trademark law is about as basic as my understanding of nineteenth-century public land laws.

The lawsuit called for restitution of Friendly Family's lost income, which made Amy especially bitter. "We can hardly pay our bills," she said. She told me the "Little House on the Prairie" site makes just enough to break even with its operating expenses. All the Laura Ingalls Wilder museums are off the beaten path, but this place is one of the more struggling homesites, in part because its Kansas location is too far from the other destinations to be part of a vacationing family's Little House pilgrimage. Independence, fourteen miles away, is just a little too far away from the cabin and a little too, well, independent: as the commercial hub of southeastern Kansas it's nearly ten times bigger than De Smet, South Dakota, and doesn't need to bill itself as a Laura Ingalls Wilder hometown.

"We're just out here by ourselves," Amy said. The isolation that Pa had valued so much and sought out on purpose was now something of a problem.

According to Amy, Friendly Family had originally offered the homesite $40,000 to buy the trademarks and give up the website address, but they'd refused. "I mean, we didn't give this place the name, it's just the name of the place," she said.

I knew what she meant. After all, what else could you call it? Then again, was the place really the same thing as the book that was written about it? It was and it wasn't. But of course I knew that wasn't the issue here.

After their offer had been turned down, Friendly Family filed their lawsuit against the homesite. The case had been allowed to stand in a recent hearing, and now, Amy said, the Little House on the Prairie site was trying to raise money for its legal fund. Hence the collection jar on the table.

In the meantime it was business as usual, though not without some rancor. The farmhouse gift shop no longer carried DVDs of the *Little House on the Prairie* TV show, except for the pilot movie, the one that purported to take place somewhere in the fields just outside. "We used to sell the other seasons of the show, but we don't anymore. I mean, why should I help *him* make money?" Amy said. She meant Trip Friendly. The store also carried the video for the 2005 miniseries that Ed Friendly had produced for Disney, though Amy had mixed feelings about it, too: "It looked nice and all, but they tried to advertise it as 'the real thing,'" she said. "But they didn't even have Carrie in it! So it wasn't the real thing, and they shouldn't have said it was." I almost pointed out that Carrie actually wouldn't have been around at first, since she was born in the log cabin, and Laura and Mary would have been much younger than they'd been portrayed in either the 1974 or the 2005 movies. But then I realized that by "the real thing" she meant the book rather than real life. In a way I couldn't argue with that.

The young actress who'd played Laura in the Disney movie,

Kyle Chavarria, had been a special guest at the site's fall festival a couple years ago, and Amy seemed proud of how thrilled the girl had been to visit the real-life location. She'd been given a painting a local artist had painted of the log cabin, the Little House itself, Amy told me. "And you know, her parents thanked us and told us that when she'd filmed that whole movie up in Canada, she didn't even get a souvenir. Nothing. She was so appreciative," Amy said. "It meant so much to her just to have something from this place."

I'm sure it had partly to do with the rain, but I didn't want to leave the farmhouse. After everything, it felt to me like the realest thing about *Little House on the Prairie* aside from the book itself. You could lament that the name "Little House on the Prairie" meant too many things now—that was the point of that lawsuit—but even before all that it had been a story about a place that nobody could fully remember or even find. The fact that that place was *here* was sort of incidental; after all, even in the book it had turned out to be the wrong place to have settled.

The real story had once been about land, but there wasn't really any land anymore, just an idea that everyone built on again and again—a movie, a TV show, a musical, a story of good Indians and even better settlers who become wiser every time their covered wagon arrives at the beginning once again.

This place where I was now wasn't in the middle of that perfect circle of sky or story. Once, somewhere in the distance, there'd been Indians and soldiers and squatters and Bloody Benders; maybe one of those photocopies on the rack by the door could tell me everything I needed to know. But at the same time, I didn't feel like I could ever truly know what had happened here. There had been a cabin and someone had dug a well.

I liked this farmhouse, though. The rain flung itself against the west window while Amy got more hot water for my tea. I picked out some souvenirs—a few books, a jar of local honey, a handmade sunbonnet. Amy and I talked some more and I told her I'd tried churning butter.

"You mean you've never *done* that before?" she asked incredulously. She thought it was pretty hilarious since she'd grown up on a farm—"We had our garden, we raised our own meat, we did everything," she said—and she couldn't imagine why someone would want to make their own butter if they didn't have to.

"I know," I said sheepishly. "It's just something I tried to do, just for the experience of it."

"Just like coming out here," she said. I could tell she understood. She told me about a young couple who'd come from Spain, who'd watched the TV show there, and when they came to the States the man had planned a special trip out here, and he hadn't told the woman where she was going until they were here, and when she found out she wept.

"Some people don't understand the passion that goes with these sites," Amy said. "You might think you know, but you don't know until you're here every day and you see these people come in here." She shook her head. I could tell she loved her job and loved helping people find this place. Every day it was being found.

She went back over to her desk to ring up the things that I had bought. I looked out the front door and could see that the rain had let up again. The little farmhouse porch framed the gray sky and the road and fence and field beneath it.

"Wish us luck with the lawsuit," Amy said just before I left.

Months later I read that the case came to an agreement in court that fall. The terms couldn't be divulged, the news story said, but not much would change at the Little House on the Prairie site. And as I read the story on my computer screen I realized after a moment that the image of the place that had come to my mind wasn't of the place I'd seen, the farmhouse and the one-room school and the earnest replica cabin, but of the Garth Williams illustration near the end of Little House on the Prairie. The cabin and the stable stood like toy blocks and the horizon line of the prairie stretched all the way across both pages of the book. I watched for more news about the lawsuit, but the story seemed to disappear after that.

But back at the site I wished Amy good luck, and I walked out to the rental car, and then I drove back the way I had come.

6.

The Way Home

I FELT LIKE I was skipping ahead of things by visiting Mansfield, Missouri, the site of Laura Ingalls Wilder's last home. After all, the place Laura had dubbed Rocky Ridge Farm was where her happy-ever-after was presumed to have taken place, long after all the events in the Little House books; shouldn't I see everything else first? But the place was only an hour east of Springfield, and here I was already.

This was where the Wilder family—Laura, Almanzo (aka Manly), and their daughter, Rose—had wound up after more than a month of traveling by wagon from South Dakota in 1894, about ten years after the events of *These Happy Golden Years,* the romantic happy-ending installment of the Little House books. In the intervening years there'd been drought and economic turmoil; Laura and her husband had endured crop failures, a fire, and a bout of diphtheria that left Almanzo weakened. They decided to start anew in a different part of the country, and with another family they set out for Missouri, which was touted as the Land of the Big Red Apple. Laura had kept a diary of the six-week trip, and this was the account that was published posthumously in *On the Way Home* in 1962 as a sort of epilogue to the Little House series. She hadn't written the diary for an audience at all; it would be nearly twenty-five years before she began writing for publication. The entries are straightforward but descriptive: in them Laura records the towns they passed through, the strangers they met, the daily temperature.

I can't tell how interesting *On the Way Home* would be to a reader unfamiliar with the Little House books. The narrative, plainspoken and in the first person, had confused me as a kid; I couldn't quite *see* Laura beneath it. Nothing seemed to happen in this book; there were no scenes, just dusty towns rolling by. "On the road at 7:45, a nice level road and good farms fenced with board fences," reads a typical entry. "We passed the best field of oats that Manly ever saw."

When Chris decided to read the Little House books for my sake, I figured he'd stop with *These Happy Golden Years*, the official end of the series, because eight books is a lot to read when you're humoring your significant other's obsession. But he was willing to keep going. "Give me the next book," he said when he had finished *The First Four Years* and handed it back to me.

"You know, you're done with all the books in the series now," I told him, as I pushed that last blue paperback into the box set. "You don't *have* to read beyond. It's just journals and letters from here on out."

"I know," he said. "But I want to know what happens next." So I gave him *On the Way Home*. He kept it on the nightstand on his side of the bed when he wasn't reading it. Which, I noticed, wasn't very often. The rare moment I caught him reading it I asked him how it was going.

He sighed. "They're in Nebraska now," he said. "I guess." He read aloud: "'Beatrice is not as large as Lincoln but a nice town, I think. We saw the courthouse, it is handsome.'"

"Look, if you can't handle the excitement, just say so," I told him.

On the Way Home was nearly incomprehensible to me as a kid, but when I read it again as an adult, I could appreciate the glimpses of a shakier and less romantic time in U.S. history, where people crossed the country in search of better circumstances and didn't always find them. More than once Laura mentions passing wagons coming the opposite direction from Missouri, carrying people who hadn't had luck there. There's some great details, too: after visiting a house full of children and pigs, Laura notes, "They looked a good deal alike." But wry moments notwithstanding, there's, well, a lot of looking at oat fields.

Where things get interesting is when Laura's daughter gets involved. *On the Way Home* is where many Little House readers first encounter the ambivalent presence of Rose Wilder Lane, who wrote the book's preface and afterword in the early 1960s, a few years after her mother's death and when she herself was in her old age. In the preface she provides a bit of helpful historical context, mentioning the droughts and the nationwide economic panic in 1893, and then describes her life in De Smet just before her family set out for Missouri.

Rose's first-person perspective in these pages is considerably more knowing than Laura's girlhood point of view in the Little House books. Unlike young Laura, little Rose is so devoid of wonder that even when posing for a photo at the age of two she thinks the photographer's watch-the-birdie trick is a "stupid pretense." At seven, Rose can read well beyond her grade level and stoically understands that her family is in crisis, with her father disabled by illness and her mother with "me on her hands," she says. The way they live in a rented house nearly empty of furniture really isn't "like camping," as her mother tries to cheerfully assert, but Rose knows she's supposed to pretend that it's fun. Rose comes off as very much the sad, wise kid in her narrative, like Tatum O'Neal in *Paper Moon,* only even more sullen.

Her account leaves off for a while to let Laura's entries tell the story; then it continues where the diary ends, with the family camped outside Mansfield and looking for land to buy. In the preface, Rose's recollections have a cautiously hopeful tone, but in the afterword the mood is much stranger. She recalls the day her parents get ready to go into town to buy the place they've picked out, and reverently describes the outfit her mother puts on for the occasion. If you're a Little House reader, you'll recognize it as the black Sunday-best dress from *These Happy Golden Years,* and in the midst of all the rapturous detail of basques and sleeves and ribbons and braids and bangs you can suddenly see Laura again, the way she appears in those past books. After trying as hard as I could to recognize Laura through her brusque diary entries or as the beleaguered mother in the introduction, I remember, as a kid, getting to this part in the book and feeling relieved: here she was at last. "She looked lovely," says Rose. "She was beautiful."

A moment later, though, the scene turns ugly. Laura looks for the precious hundred-dollar bill that they've brought from South Dakota in a wooden lap desk, the money that represents all their savings for a down payment on a new farm. It's missing. Rose's parents look everywhere, desperately riffling through the

desk's contents; finally her mother asks her if she's taken it. Rose's
reaction:

> NO! I felt scalded. . . . I was angry, insulted, miserable, I was
> not a baby who'd play with money or open that desk for fun,
> I was going on eight years old. I was little, alone, and scared.
> My father and mother sat there, still. In the long stillness I sank
> slowly into nothing but terror, pure terror without cause or object,
> a nightmare terror.

Not the sort of thing you'd expect to read after sixty pages of oat-
field observations and weather reports, is it? The money turns up
a page or two later—apparently it had fallen into a crack in the lap
desk—but if there's any relief or jubilation Rose doesn't mention
it; the family simply hustles over to the bank and buys the land,
and from then on Laura refuses to ever discuss the incident. After
reading eight books in which the phrase "All's well that ends well"
is oft repeated, it's kind of a jolt to find that in this post–Little
House world, all that ends well is also deeply traumatic and emotionally unresolved!

Plenty of Little House fans have wondered what motivated
Rose to cap off her mother's understated travel journal with such a
primal scene. *The Homesteader* editor Sandra Hume blogged about
it on the fan site Beyond Little House, venting in the form of an
open letter to Rose. "What were you thinking?" she asks Rose
hypothetically. She thinks Rose wanted to show Little House
readers that her mother wasn't always "Laura Ingalls," the beloved
figure in the books, but doesn't feel *On the Way Home* was the
place to do it. "In what was essentially a companion Little House
book, all I was left with was an overwhelming sense of disrespect,"

she wrote. Other readers chimed in as well: "Rose's epilogue has always left a bad taste in my mouth," one commenter said.

"She was crazy," said another.

�֎

On the road from Springfield to Mansfield I passed billboards for stage shows in Branson, various country-themed craft and souvenir emporia, and armadillo roadkill. This was Ozark country, and although most people, myself included, consider Laura Ingalls Wilder country to be the land of big skies and empty prairies of the upper Midwest, you only have to do the math to realize that Laura had really lived most of her life here, more than sixty years. In that time she and Almanzo had worked to turn the land they'd bought into a working farm and built the house, bit by bit, until it had become one of the most impressive houses in the area.

She'd been here nearly forty years by the time she started working on the Little House books in earnest, writing them in pencil in the orange-covered notebooks that she'd bought at the drugstore in town, as all the biographies attest. As a kid, I loved this detail; I myself had steno notebooks from Walgreen's and wrote stories in them while lying across my bed on my stomach. Naturally I imagined her doing the same thing. Of course I didn't quite get that she would have been in her sixties.

Many of the biographies have a photo of Laura's writing desk, a charming narrow antique thing with a hinged lid—my grandmother had one like it. Laura's desk stands in a room with vintage wallpaper: her den in the farmhouse at Mansfield. Although I know better, sometimes I still imagine her sitting down casually, as if to write a thank-you note, and just dashing off a Little House book or two in the midst of a long reverie about the prairie days.

Actually, that wasn't too far from the basic story I'd grown up with. Now that I'm older I know that there must have been much more to it than that. And I know that sometimes Rose was there, although that part is all too easy to leave out.

Most of what's known about Rose today is in a thick book by William Holtz called *The Ghost in the Little House,* an extremely detailed and academic autobiography that's notorious for its argument that it was Rose, not Laura, who was the real writer, the true creative spirit behind the Little House books. That's actually only a small part of the book, though; the rest of it relates the events of Rose's life, at times on practically a month-by-month basis. Rose, it seems, left one hell of a paper trail—reams of letters and often deeply personal journals, all in addition to her numerous books and articles. (Given how prolific she was, it's ironic that a mere forty or so pages of narrative in *On the Way Home* is probably her most widely read work these days.)

By all accounts Rose was a pretty miserable kid, growing up both poor and extremely bright in the small town of Mansfield. If that sounds like a perfect recipe for despair, it was. Rose was tormented by the town girls; her one recourse was to defeat them regularly in the weekly spell-downs. "They might laugh at my clothes," Rose wrote in a journal years later, "but they couldn't laugh at my spelling." As an adult, she felt she'd been stunted, both physically and emotionally, by her impoverished childhood; she had bad teeth she blamed on malnutrition. In an essay published in *Cosmopolitan* she'd written, "No one knew what went on in my mind. Because I loved my parents I would not let them suspect that I was suffering. I concealed from them how much

I felt their poverty; their struggles and disappointments. These filled my life, magnified like horrors in a dream."

Even beyond Rose's anguished perspective, the story of the Almanzo Wilder family has a grimness that the story of the Pa Ingalls family does not, though they have plenty of similarities— hard times, moves across the country, the struggle to establish a home. No doubt part of the difference is that Laura's childhood was transformed into idealized fiction in the Little House books, whereas the most vivid memories Rose shares about her childhood are of the things that scarred her for life.

Of course, the reason that we know anything at all about Laura's pa and ma in the first place is that her family narrative, with all its frontier details, fit the contours of an especially romanticized historical era. Rose, on the other hand, grew up in a comparatively murkier time in history, during an economic slump folks would have preferred to forget. We always regard the log cabins where Laura lived in the Big Woods and on the prairie as two of the coziest places on Earth, but the windowless cabin where the grown-up Laura and her family first set up house at Rocky Ridge Farm seems more depressing than anything. Even when I read this as a kid I could sense that there wasn't any pioneer glamour here, just hardscrabble poverty. *Another log cabin?* I remember thinking. It seemed to me that they should have been *done* with cabins. After all, I'd followed along with the Little House books and watched the Ingalls family gradually become more comfortable, practically middle-class by the end of *These Happy Golden Years*. Weren't people supposed to make progress, build more rooms on their shanties, and buy parlor organs to put in them? It was jarring to find out it didn't always work out that way.

But back to Rose. At first, the more you read about her, the more tempting it gets to think of her as the Anti-Laura. You get the idea that *she* wouldn't have found living in a sod dugout to be very magical at all: in one of her short stories, a wary mail-order bride gets her hoopskirts "squeezed into a grotesque shape" when she goes through the narrow doorway of her new sod home. And while the teenage Laura preferred the homestead shanty to town life, Rose preferred getting the hell out of that backwater Mansfield the minute she was old enough. She was seventeen the year she took off for Kansas City to live a "bachelor girl" lifestyle as a telegraph operator. From there she went to San Francisco, into marriage and divorce, and then on to a career as a journalist that took her all over the world, on travels through Europe and the Middle East, with stints living in Paris and New York City and Albania—a country she especially loved.

After a while you have to simply stop comparing Rose to Laura at all, because the inventory of her life experience is so overwhelming. Her story is an inevitable detour that serious fans come to in the course of exploring Little House books further: once you go down that road you quickly find yourself in a dizzying new realm of literary, intellectual, and political history. God help the casual reader who picks up *The Ghost in the Little House* expecting homey anecdotes about Laura and Rose working diligently in their country kitchen and instead finds herself trying to figure out the political situation in Albania in 1922. Some fans manage to go down the Rose rabbit hole and are able to love her and appreciate her career, but it's a process, to be sure.

I hate, for instance, that I have to leave out so much about Rose's later life here—the way she dodged bullets amid civil war in Europe, drove with a girlfriend across Europe in a Model T Ford (the friend was nicknamed "Troub," the car, "Zenobia"), won

the O. Henry Prize for one of her short stories, served as a corre-
spondent in Vietnam when she was nearly eighty. Really, she was
kind of a rock star.

At the same time I find I'm all too willing to skip over other
things about her life: her wretched bouts of depression, her prickly
politics, the controversial role she took in working on the Little
House books (questions of authorship aside, scholars at least seem
to agree that Rose could be overbearing as all get-out when she
edited her mother's work, sending multiple pages of single-spaced
typed criticism, even for magazine articles), and especially the
complicated relationship she had with her mother, fraught with
resentment and the kind of deep-seated bitterness that surfaces in
parts of *On the Way Home*.

And yet elsewhere in that same book, Rose makes it clear to
readers that although they must go through her to get to their
beloved Laura, they *do* get there eventually. Her afterword goes
on to relate the gorgeous seasons in their first year at Rocky
Ridge Farm. "Winter evenings were cosy in the cabin. The horses
were warm in the little barn, the hens in the new wooden coop,"
she writes. "A good fire of hickory logs burned in the fireplace."
She describes her father oiling harnesses while her mother knits
and reads poems aloud by the light of the kerosene lamp. Ah,
Little House–style contentment at last! When I read this scene
as a child, I was reassured by how familiar this sounded, just as I'd
been relieved, earlier in the book, to finally see Laura in her best
dress. While Rose's door opens to a whole other universe far too
extensive to ever fit into Laura World, moments like this make
it clear that Rose was as in love with that world as Little House
readers. Why not, since by all accounts she had a role in shaping it?

On the Way Home ends with Rose listening to her mother

describe the kind of house they'll one day build at Rocky Ridge, with a fireplace, porches, a water pump just outside the kitchen, and a parlor filled with books. It's here that I think I can understand why Rose chose to put together and publish *On the Way Home*: she wanted to portray the long trip as the link between the Laura of the Little House books and Laura Ingalls Wilder, the woman who would one day live in the very dream house described, write her story in those orange notebooks, and live the proverbial farm-wifely existence that helped characterize her fame in her later life and became part of her legacy after her death. (Maybe it's no coincidence that at the time Rose published *On the Way Home*, the Laura Ingalls Wilder Memorial Society in Mansfield was working to establish the farmhouse as a museum.)

Of course somewhere in there, amid all the various Lauras of story and legend, was the mother who presided over Rose's terrible childhood. Rose was trying to make that clear, too.

Chris finally finished *On the Way Home* before bed one night. "I don't get why you have such a problem with that stuff Rose wrote," he said.

"Come on, she published this book for Little House fans but felt the need to dump all her weird mother issues on us," I told him. "You don't think that's weird?"

"But it was her experience," Chris said. "I don't know; I liked that part. You could tell it was what she remembered."

"But it's not about *her*," I protested. "It's supposed to be about Laura." But maybe for all of Rose's litanies it really *was* about Laura and all her different personas. I remembered reading in Holtz's book about the way Rose insisted—vehemently—that everything her mother had written in the Little House books was true. In the early '60s, when those census records on the Ingalls family's stint in Kansas were being unearthed, researchers did the math with the dates and realized that Laura had been much younger than her counterpart in *Little House on the Prairie*. It was the first substantial evidence that parts of the Little House novels really were fiction. When a teacher's magazine published an article about this discovery, Rose's response, according to Holtz, was swift: she wrote the author to insist Laura really *had* remembered things from when she was three, she said, and it had been the publisher's idea to advance the girls' ages in *Prairie*. The Little House books "were the truth, and only the truth; every detail in them is written as my mother remembered it," she wrote.

She even got on the case of a teenager named William Anderson, who by the age of fifteen had researched and published the very first biography of Laura and her family, a booklet called *The Story of the Ingalls*, that's still in print and began his career as one of the leading authorities on Laura Ingalls Wilder (and, you'd hope, earned him a few thousand extra-credit points in his tenth-grade history class). When Rose read a draft of his booklet, she took offense at a detail that differed from the account in the Little House books. It had been something about how many neighbors the Ingallses had had in their first year in De Smet; it seemed the books portrayed the family as more isolated than his research indicated. Rose actually wrote Anderson back and accused him of trying to publish "a statement that my mother was a liar." Yikes, kid.

The obvious irony is that Rose, of all people, knew how the details of her mother's life had been shaped to make the Little House books—ages had been changed, neighbors erased, events omitted, composite characters created—and of course Rose had been there all along, offering advice and even helping with the work.

Nobody really knows why Rose stuck to her contention that

the books were the truth and only the truth, though Pamela Smith Hill suggests, in the biography *Laura Ingalls Wilder: A Writer's Life*, that Rose may have felt there was room for only one fiction writer in the family—herself. Late in her life it had become clear that mother's literary legacy was enduring; her own wasn't so certain. But as long as people believed the Little House books were straight autobiography that hadn't been crafted or shaped, then Laura could be the accidental artist and Rose the real one. It's worth considering that of all her mother's writing that Rose could have published posthumously—dozens of polished newspaper essays and especially the manuscript of *The First Four Years*, which would have been of obvious interest to Little House readers—she'd chosen the most artless work, a travel diary.

Rereading *On the Way Home* made me wonder if Rose's claim to the "truth" perhaps included another bargain she'd made with herself, one whose terms she expressed in the afterword: if the Little House books were true, then so was Rose's own wretched childhood. It's all real, she seemed to be saying, whether it's fiction or myth or nightmare. You'd better believe it.

Mansfield hadn't been one of the Little House sites I'd been dying to see. It wasn't really part of the world of the books, after all, so I could only hope to feel stirred by the famed relics in the museum—things like Pa's fiddle, the glass bread plate Laura and Almanzo had bought from the Montgomery Ward catalog, the orange-covered notebooks Laura wrote the books in. But wasn't that a lot to ask from a bread plate?

I started to feel a little differently when I got the cookbook. Not the one Barbara Walker had written, but *The Laura Ingalls*

Wilder Country Cookbook, which a friend of mine had sent as a gift (she insisted I make Laura's gingerbread). This one was a collection of Laura's recipes that she'd compiled during the 1930s and 1940s, classic old-fashioned fare like scalloped corn, lima bean dishes, and meatloaf, not to mention ham, chicken, and liver loaf.

 Maybe I don't have to tell you that aside from the gingerbread, I wasn't exactly compelled to cook anything out of *The Laura Ingalls Wilder Country Cookbook.* But I'd become fascinated with the photos in its full-color glossy pages. Almost none of the photographs were of the recipes (because how thrilling can a salmon casserole look, anyway?); instead, they showed appealing little glimpses of the Mansfield farmhouse and still-life arrangements of its antique housewares. Glass canister jars gleamed on a shelf beneath a sunny windowsill; the paint of the front porch railing was lightly crackled as it held an earthenware bowl of lemons: all of it so perfectly shabby chic it looked like it had come straight from back issues of *Martha Stewart Living.*

You could probably argue that Laura really *was* something of an early-twentieth-century Martha, for a regional audience at least, back when she wrote for the *Missouri Ruralist* and other publications during the 1910s and 1920s. The *Ruralist* was a regional newspaper that provided agricultural news, farming advice, and general-interest articles to readers twice a month. In 1911 Laura had started writing for the paper after a speech she'd written for a local farm group about raising chickens (she'd become something of an expert on the subject) impressed the editor. For the next decade or so she wrote dozens of articles about family life, home-oriented values, and matters of farm business; eventually she had her own column titled "As a Farm Woman Thinks."

I feel a bit faithless when I confess I'm not really a fan of Laura's *Ruralist* writing. I suppose it's partly because I've never much gone for that kind of journalism—the life's-little-observations, common-sense wisdom stuff full of anecdotes and aphorisms. Almost anything in that genre feels musty to me, even if it was written last week, much less ninety years ago. The *Ruralist* columns are also where those well-known Laura quotations come from—the two or three slightly hoary, interchangeable lines about the value of "sweet, simple things" that I see endlessly quoted.

I know in these columns she spoke on behalf of farm wives, who were shrewd businesswomen and equal partners with their husbands, and I appreciate that she was opinionated, but my eyes get heavy every time I read more than a couple starchy paragraphs about the values of hard work and neighborliness and moderation and so on. The Laura who wrote these things isn't quite the Laura I know, more like a know-it-all aunt droning on and on: "It may well be that it is not our work that is so hard for us as the dread of it and our often expressed hatred of it," she says in a 1920 column. "Perhaps it is our spirit and attitude toward life, and its conditions that are giving us trouble instead of a shortage of time." I suppose she's got a point there, but zzzz.

And yet even in this non–Little House era of Laura's writing career there are things that I love about her. One of my favorite articles is a magazine piece, written with Rose's help, called "My Ozark Farm Kitchen," in which she describes (and shows in photographs), the ingenious cabinetry and shelves Almanzo had custom-built for the Mansfield farmhouse; she made it sound as wondrous as anything Pa had ever put together, only with a distinctly grown-up sense of delight that for me is every bit as satisfying as flipping through the Container Store catalog. I am also fond of a *Ruralist* column called "The Home Beauty Parlor," which includes advice like "Washing in buttermilk will whiten the hands and face. Fresh strawberries rubbed on the skin will bleach it, and rhubarb and tomatoes will remove stains from the fingers," all of which makes Laura's Ozark farm kitchen sound like some kind of wonderful organic-chic retro day spa.

Never mind those old chestnuts about self-reliance in the *Ruralist* columns; if Laura launched a home décor/lifestyle magazine called *Simple Things* I would totally subscribe to it. But I'd settle for visiting the house in Mansfield.

It was impossible to miss the farmhouse from the road. It was perched high on a green hill surrounded by giant old trees, a simple but stately white clapboard house with two porches and a stone chimney. I'd expected the Laura Ingalls Wilder Historic Home and Museum to be a sleepy kind of place, as tranquil as the house always appeared in pictures, but as I drove up I saw modern buildings alongside the house and realized it was a fairly bustling complex with the museum, the educational center, a gift shop, and a parking lot across the highway.

It was a tight operation. When I went into the museum and paid my admission, the woman at the front desk launched into a memorized spiel: the house tour was forty-five minutes long; visitors must wait for the tour time on their tickets; visitors weren't allowed to take photos in the museum or the farmhouse, only outdoors; visitors could browse in the museum until their tour began.

"Uh, can I come back into the museum after the tour?" I asked the woman, a sharp-eyed woman with salt-and-pepper hair. Her name tag said PAM.

"Oh, you'll have to," she replied. "There's so much you'll really need to come back to see it all," she said, as if I had no choice.

But Pam was right: I only had to glance at the huge room and the rows of glass cases to see that there was more Laura stuff under this roof than anywhere else in the world. The other home-sites might have a few of the Ingalls family quilts or a couple of Laura's china place settings, but clearly this was the mother lode, a lifetime's worth of possessions. It was almost too much to take in at once—all the cases of yellowing handkerchiefs, gloves, letters with faded handwriting, bits of needlework, everything labeled with little typed cards. So much of it was unremarkable at first glance but utterly precious once you looked closely. Here were Laura and Mary's school slates and the china jewel box that Laura had received for Christmas in *On the Banks of Plum Creek*! So many of the photos I'd seen over the years were here, too, in their original form: Ma and Pa's wedding tintype, the Ingalls family portrait that the woman at the Little House on the Prairie site in Kansas couldn't bear to look at. Mary's artifacts were particularly poignant: one case held the beadwork trinkets Mary had made at the Iowa College for the Blind, her Braille books, the letters she'd written on the special slate that kept her handwriting straight.

Certain pieces were iconic; Pa's fiddle was in a display case all its own, its tuning screws ancient. Every so often it was carefully taken out and played at festivals by professional musicians. The bread plate from *The First Four Years* was heavy and chipped. The infamous lap desk where the hundred-dollar bill had been misplaced was in its own case, too; lest anyone forget the lap desk's significance, a fake bill was sticking out from under its lid.

There was a white lawn dress that Laura had made and worn in one of my favorite photos, one where she's standing at the edge of a spring at Rocky Ridge Farm. It was taken at a distance and the dress made her a pale figure in the deep shade of the trees. Now it hung on a dress form in a glass case, small but life-sized. I stared down at its shoulders and its high pretty neckline trying to sense what Laura's physical presence would have been like. The figure I imagined had enough substance to be a real person but was still somehow slight, ghostly and remote enough to live in the world of a story.

When it was time for the house tour, about a dozen of us gathered at the museum door. The woman waiting in front of me seemed vaguely familiar; from the way she kept glancing back, she seemed to think that about me, too.

"Didn't we see you yesterday?" she asked me finally. "At the Little House on the Prairie?" I suddenly remembered the family of seven who'd driven up in the minivan; I'd seen them filing out of the cabin in Kansas. They were following the same course I was. As soon as we made the connection, she turned and announced it to her family. "Guess what, this lady is seeing all the Laura things, too!"

Her name was Karen, her husband was Keith. Their children ranged in ages from about five to preteen: two boys, three girls, including seven-year-old blond twins. The family hailed from Houston. Here, as in Kansas, they seemed to give off the sort of exuberant team spirit that would no doubt make them an excellent casting choice for one of the friendlier reality shows; they'd be the folks you'd root for.

I also struck up a conversation with a woman named Catherine Pond, who was especially excited to see the kitchen. It turned out she was a writer and architectural historian who had written a book about the history of pantries in American houses. When she mentioned this, it launched us both into an excited recollection of the various pantries in the Little House books. Catherine's favorite was the one described at the end of *These Happy Golden Years*, in the house Almanzo built.

"With all the little drawers for the sugar and the flour?" Catherine said. "I loved that!"

"Yes! And remember the one in the surveyors' house?" That was from *By the Shores of Silver Lake*, when the Ingalls family spends the winter in a well-stocked house owned by the railroad company; I lived for the description of the neat shelves full of abundance.

"You have to read this article Laura wrote about the kitchen in the house here," Catherine told me.

"Oh my God! 'My Ozark Farm Kitchen'? I loved that!" I was practically squealing like a fan girl. I was beginning to feel at home here.

We were all led into the educational center to watch a short introductory video, a brief history of the Ingalls and the Almanzo Wilder families. You could hear audio of Pa's fiddle being played and even of Laura herself speaking in a rare interview. Although her elderly voice was unlovely—sort of flat and jowly—I loved hearing it and delighted in discovering, when she mentioned Mary's education, that she pronounced "Iowa" with a long *a*, as in "Ioway College of the Blind in Vinton, Ioway."

Then we went on into the house, led by an older lady with a pulchritudinous Ozark accent. (She referred to the home's residents as "Lawra" and "Almayanzo.") Although the kitchen didn't have a pantry, it was every bit as retro fabulous as I'd hoped: we all admired the gleaming enamel cookstove, the patterned wallpaper, the cheery yellow-painted cabinetry. My new friend Catherine approved. Even the "modern" refrigerator, installed in the 1950s, was now charmingly vintage. The counters and cabinets and even the ceiling were low, since Almanzo had built the whole house to fit Laura and himself, both short-statured. My friend Justin had visited the house on a field trip when he was a kid and had warned me that the place would look like "a freakin' fun house," but it was really enchanting. Everyone in our group seemed to agree, including a retired contractor. "A place will still sell if you customize it," he said, as if he were giving Laura and Almanzo free advice on their remodeling decisions.

The guide pointed out a calendar that hung by the kitchen window. It was open to February 1957. "That calendar was hanging there the day Laura died," she said, and a hush came over our group. Laura had passed away just a few days after her ninetieth birthday. To emphasize this point, the table in the dining room displayed a carefully strewn arrangement of birthday cards from schoolchildren, as if to show when time stopped for Laura, and moreover that it stopped contentedly.

We learned that the Wilders enjoyed their radio but never owned a TV. In the bedroom a 1956 Montgomery Ward catalog rested on a side table. It was a long, narrow room with two twin beds that faced each other, foot to foot, which seemed unromantic until the tour guide mentioned that Laura slept in Almanzo's bed after his death in order to feel closer to him, and then it seemed breathtakingly sweet and sad.

Everything about the house tour, in fact, felt like an homage to the bittersweetness of old age or the vanished past. In between the tour guide's segments we all had begun to talk to one another in the group, we adults at least, talking about anything we might have remembered and that connected us to a place like this.

"I just keep thinking about how much changes in a lifetime," said the wife of the retired contractor. "We didn't have TV yet when I was little and I remember thinking that was a big deal, but I mean Laura, she saw the railroads get built," she marveled.

Keith said that the house reminded him of his grandparents. "My grandma would never throw anything away," he said. "Breakfast was whatever was left over, and they were happy to have it."

"I really want to find kitchen canisters like the ones Laura had!" I said to Catherine the Pantry Lady. I couldn't say anything more profound than that, though of course I'd been moved by everything I'd seen so far. The house seemed to embody everything I loved about the Little House books—the kitchen built for dozens of daily rituals, the big windows that let you see the landscape (Laura hadn't had them curtained). I couldn't get enough.

Even the linoleum, original to the house, seemed like a tribute to the past. "We get forty thousand visitors walking through here every season, and look how it's held up," the guide said. "They just don't make this stuff like they used to."

⌗

The museum seemed to have a tractor beam like the Death Star: it sucked us back in after the tour. None of us could resist the big magical building full of old-timey things. There were buttons Laura had collected; the notebook with the draft of *By the Shores of Silver Lake;* the engraved name cards that had been so fashionable in De Smet in *Little Town on the Prairie.*

"Are you going over to see the other house?" the retired contractor asked me as I studied a display of Little House books that had been published in Slovenian.

"It's part of the tour, but we don't know what's there, do you? Was that where Rose lived?" his wife asked.

Between the rapturous nostalgia of the farmhouse and the tractor-beam effect of the museum, I had all but forgotten there was *another* house here—a small newer one that Rose had had built in 1928. It was an English cottage-style house built with Sears Roebuck plans and called the Rock House. It was on the farm property but farther down the road, out of sight of the rest of the museum complex. Now I recalled hearing that we could drive or walk over to see it.

"No, I think Rose had built it for her parents as a little retirement house or something," I told Mr. and Mrs. Contractor. I'd remembered this from the biographies. "But I don't know what's there."

At the moment all I could do was take in as much as I could here in the museum. While I'd loved seeing the site in Kansas the day before, there hadn't been much to see besides the land and the well and the cabin; here, though, I could gorge myself on artifacts. Like Laura's gun. *Laura's gun!* The card next to it in the case said that she carried a revolver during the journey from South Dakota to Missouri and often used it to shoot "small game." I liked how spunky that made her seem, though I was wondering if perhaps younger children would be troubled by the notion of Half-Pint taking out bunny rabbits and birdies like Dirty Harry.

I was still contemplating this when Karen came down the aisle with her twin daughters.

"We're looking for Charlotte," she said. "Do you know if it's anywhere?" She meant Laura's rag doll that she'd gotten for Christmas in *Little House in the Big Woods*. I told her I didn't think so; the doll would be one of the most sacred Little House relics if it still existed, and I would've seen pictures of it in the biographies.

"I guess you're right," she said. We started sharing our personal histories with the Little House books. She told me she hadn't read the series as a child, but there was a homeschooling curriculum based on them, and now the younger kids were studying under it.

"They play Little House all the time," she said, gesturing over at the girls. "I think they really love the family, how sweet they all were, how simple it all was. And, you know, we just love the faith that was running throughout."

Keith nodded. I noticed just then he was wearing a sweatshirt with a logo of a Christian college. "They're just great books," he said.

Both Karen and Keith were so nice to talk to I hoped they wouldn't pick up on the fact that I wasn't quite the same kind of Little House fan that they were. I know there are a lot of folks who can easily see Christian messages in the books, lessons about trusting and accepting the will of God in times of hardship and relying on the bedrock of one's faith to get through. There's plenty of stuff in the books that can help illustrate these things, I guess. But the Ingalls family in the books didn't appear to be much the praying types, unless the occasional hymn on Pa's fiddle counts. Mary becomes a little godly by the later books, but as for the rest of the family, their reasons for attending church seemed to have more to do with partaking in civilized town life than with religious devotion. I suppose I'm inclined to see it that way because that's how my family did things—went to church (Congregational) sporadically and understatedly. Whenever Ma Ingalls brought out the Bible, it seemed to me to be pretty interchangeable with the other books they turned to for comfort, like the novel *Millbank* and Pa's *Wonders of the Animal World*, only slightly more important.

But in the case of families like Keith and Karen's, their Laura World includes certain aspects that mine does not; in their Little House scenes the Bible is likely always close by and the Lord near at hand watching over the family through the droughts and blizzards.

I don't mind that it's this way for other people, especially if it makes the books more meaningful to them. And yet there's a moment in the 2005 movie version of *Little House on the Prairie* when, after the Ingalls family has found the spot where they would build the log cabin, they all stand in a circle and clasp hands. Pa leads them all in a prayer to thank God and bless the land. Perhaps it was added to appeal to the Karens and Keiths in the Disney demographic. But for me it changed everything about who the Ingallses were supposed to be, even though the real family was long lost under that book's myriad and slippery fictional layers. Suddenly it wasn't enough that they were good people, they had to be the *right* kind of good. I guess I found it presumptuous, but it was deeper than that: what made me uncomfortable was the idea of the prayer as an embellishment, a pious flourish.

Anyway, these were the kind of sooty agnostic thoughts that I didn't want Keith and Karen to know I had, because it would have made things awkward. Of course, it wasn't their fault that a brief moment in a TV movie creeped me out. And like I said, they were swell people. Karen even had the kids tell me what they liked most about the books.

Abigail: "They were always happy."

Anna: "I like Laura and Mary."

Olivia: "They were always together. And Almanzo was a very nice man."

Jacob: "I liked the one about the farmer boy."

"They were all just so content," Karen added. "*So* content. Even in the hard times. And the way Laura portrayed it was all so simple. So . . . simple." She laughed. "I guess I said that before. But it's true. It's a beautiful portrait of a life of contentment and peace and trust."

Sometimes when I hear folks maunder on about how simple Laura's lifestyle was I wonder if they've ever thought about all the hauling and fetching and stowing and stoking it took just to boil a pot of water. But seeing Karen and Keith and Abigail and Anna and Olivia and Jacob and the older kid whose name I didn't catch, I could understand. Surely they were up to all that cheerful hauling and fetching, and wouldn't it be nice to have just a stove fire to think about rather than carpooling to soccer practice? Never mind, then.

Karen went on. "And we love Mary, too. She was so content, you know, and she never complained."

One of the twins, Anna, I think, nodded solemnly at this.

If their photos are any indication, Laura and Almanzo were the cutest old couple ever. They stood side by side in their photos, their poses stiff but matching, and together they smiled faint, gentle smiles that seemed to tell the camera, in the nicest way possible, that they'd rather be alone.

I was nearly at the far end of the museum by now, where the items in the glass cases were getting a little random. They had Laura's glasses on display, her jewelry, her *wallet*. It turns out she was one of those people who actually fills out the little I.D. card that comes with the wallet, but maybe everyone did in those days. Apparently Almanzo never threw out any of his license plates.

And then at the very end of the room, after all the Laura and Almanzo stuff, was a section dedicated to Rose—a very nice exhibit of her typewriters and manuscripts, even some of her furniture. A long glass case displayed copies of her books and mementos from her travels: a well-worn travel bag; native craft knickknacks from Albania, Vietnam, and other exotic locales. While it was an impressive collection—very National Geographic—nobody seemed to be spending any time over on this side of the museum. I noticed people would wander over and peer at a couple of the things in the cases, but once they realized they weren't looking at Laura things they'd simply turn around.

"Mom, what's this stuff?" I heard one of Karen's kids ask.

"I don't think it's anything about Little House on the Prairie, sweetie," she replied. "Do you want to go back? Let's go back." She herded the kids back over to the other side of the museum.

I'd heard that local residents had mixed feelings about Rose, who in her adulthood had lived on and off in Mansfield between sojourns in Europe and elsewhere. For a while, after she'd built the Rock House for Laura and Almanzo, she'd even lived on her own in the farmhouse, with a few of her writer friends sometimes staying as long-term guests. "Even today Rose is regarded with some suspicion in Mansfield," says William Holtz in *The Ghost in the Little House*. "There are hints of visits by 'men' and 'wild parties' when 'she had those women living with her.'" (Sadly, Holtz's biography never mentions any raucous debauchery, literary or otherwise, at Rocky Ridge Farm, though one of the more permanent houseguests was her friend nicknamed "Troub," so who knows.)

It wasn't simply a few parties that gave Rose her iffy reputation—she'd also written books like *Old Home Town* and *Hillbilly*, stories about small-town life in the Ozarks that were often based on local incidents and scandals. (Apparently people in Mansfield were annoyed either because they'd been written about in the stories or because they'd been left out.) And of course the fact that Rose was a hometown girl turned worldy-wise semifamous cigarette-smoking divorcee probably didn't go over so well with some folks, either.

I find myself mostly on Rose's side when it comes to all the nasty little small-town indictments. You go, Bachelor Girl! In fact I'm pretty much with her up until 1932, when she published a story as a magazine serial in *The Saturday Evening Post* and then as a novel a year later. It would become a bestseller, one of her most popular works. Rose had begun writing it shortly after her mother had sold *Little House in the Big Woods*. She worked on it while helping Laura edit her next novel, *Farmer Boy*. And prior to all this, you might recall, Rose had typed and edited *Pioneer Girl*, Laura's adult memoir manuscript.

Anyway, she then wrote this story, *Let the Hurricane Roar*, which takes its title from a line in a popular nineteenth-century hymn and thus is not about hurricanes at all.

Rather, it's about a young couple who set out to establish a homestead on the prairie. They live in a dugout alongside a creek, not too far from both a slough and a railroad camp. Perhaps this sounds familiar. Prosperity seems close at hand as they raise a beautiful crop of wheat, only to lose it, suddenly and astonishingly, when a cloud of grasshoppers descends; subsequently the husband must travel east alone to find work. Oh, and there's a blizzard that freezes herds of cattle in their tracks. Also, the husband plays fiddle. And did we mention that their names are Charles and Caroline, just like Laura's parents, and that they just so happened to be from the Big Woods of Wisconsin, too?

If you've read *Let the Hurricane Roar* and Rose's 1938 pioneer novel, *Free Land*, you would no doubt notice the similarities to the Little House books. (Though I don't think anyone just casually picks up *Free Land* these days, since it's kind of dry and slow going and only available in a small press edition, mostly for the benefit of Wilder/Lane enthusiasts/scholars/geeks who don't even need me to point this out.) But it's Pamela Smith Hill, in her Wilder biography, who really leads the charge against Rose for writing *Let the Hurricane Roar* the way she did. (For those of you keeping score at home, William Holtz is Team Rose and Hill is Team Laura.) She writes that Rose "pulled out the most dramatic, most colorful elements of her mother's autobiography" and furthermore did it in secret. "This amounts to plagiarism," says Hill, who believes Laura had sufficient grounds to take her daughter to court had she chosen to.

Rose's reasons for writing her pioneer novels were at least as idealistic as they were opportunistic: she meant *Let the Hurricane Roar* to be a "reply to pessimists" and hoped it would inspire Depression-era readers with its themes of resilience in the face of hardship and the strength of the American character. Rose had written fiction for much of the first half of her career; later on she'd write the political stuff, the articles and treatises about freedom and individual liberties that would earn her the reputation as Mama Libertarian, so you can see how *Let the Hurricane Roar* would be a turning point. A few years later *Free Land* would be the last novel she ever published, and William Holtz points out that it has so many antigovernment sentiments that Rose was "but a step from pamphleteering." *Let the Hurricane Roar* is less overt than that, though the original cover image, showing the young pioneer couple standing in a field surrounded by an emphatic blaze of light, is appropriately heroic and solemn, practically a propaganda poster.

Whatever their differences, Laura and Rose seemed to have patched things up by the time Laura started working in earnest on *Little House on the Prairie*, assisted, as with her earlier books, by Rose. It probably didn't hurt that this new book was based on a chapter of Ingalls family history that Rose hadn't touched with her sticky literary-appropriating fingers. (And that's yet another instance in which *Prairie* stakes out a metaphorical claim on some sort of contentious imaginary territory. See how it is with that crazy story?)

And whatever betrayal Laura may have felt—or not felt, or repressed behind some sweet motherly façade—this *Hurricane* business is one of those things that probably looks worse in retrospect, now that we know the Little House series as a whole and can see the full scope of the material that Rose had drawn from. In defense of Rose, at the time she wrote *Let the Hurricane Roar* she couldn't have anticipated that her mother would use the same family history as the basis for a multibook epic that would become classic children's literature. But of course you also can't help but think that Rose would never have given Laura that much credit to begin with. Anyway, the whole thing doesn't exactly make people warm up to Rose.

Laura's lived experience has become sacred to us, even to those of us who understand that much of it is fiction. We don't like that Rose borrowed it and got her *ideas* all over it. Plus the more we romanticize Laura and associate her with nostalgia, the more Rose's artistic intentions seem to backfire, so that her vivid portrayals of heroic struggles and frontier adversity just seem dark and trenchant and bitter. So bitter, in fact, that we can't imagine she'd have anything to do with the Little House books.

In my constant quest for all the obscure Laura-related reading I could find, one of the most bizarre things I'd come across was an independently published e-book called *Laura Ingalls' Friends Remember Her* by Dan L. White, a writer who lives near Mansfield. The book consists of a series of interviews with locals who'd known the Wilders, which are pretty interesting. There's also a bit of speculative fiction, attempted in the descriptive style of the Little House books, about Laura seeing the Ozark hills for the first time (typical sentence: "Around her a field of grass lay curled in a basket of rolling knolls, where gentle hills gaily bounced to and fro"), which is a little weird, though I feel I understand the Laura-loving impulse to write stuff like that. And then there are several short essays in which the author gives his opinions on Laura and Rose, which are creepy and dismaying.

Apparently Dan L. White had read *The Ghost in the Little House* and disagreed with the notion that Rose had influenced the Little House books. He argues that whereas Laura was a good Christian who "had a beautiful sense of the beautiful" and made the Little House books "sing with joy," Rose was "loose" and "irreligious."

He asserts that Rose had lovers and that the one child she'd had during her marriage (an unnamed boy, who was either stillborn or died in infancy) may have been born out of wedlock. But the most virulent charge he makes against Rose is that she wasn't *happy*:

> Rose's writing never sang. It usually spat and hissed. . . . Her sentences were choppy and bumpy and anything but sweet. Even when she tried to convey a positive ending, the bitter taste remained. . . . Whether writing stories about her youth in Mansfield or about life on the prairie, Rose always seemed to be complaining. In her writing, there was never just pure out and out Little House happiness.

A woman this ungrateful, ill-natured, and "progressive" (quotation marks his!) couldn't have had anything to do with the Little House books, he says.

It's easy enough to shrug off the more sputteringly nasty assertions in the book as simply the personal ideology of the author, whose other books include *Devotionals with Laura* and *Big Bible Lessons from Laura's Little Books*. But the happiness thing struck a nerve somehow, a chord of truth even. For two reasons: First, wasn't that at the heart of what bothered us fans about Rose, that she seemed so utterly miserable? Even when we appreciate that she struggled valiantly with mood disorders—depression and, some believe, bipolar disorder—we still find ourselves resenting that she couldn't keep her cruddy angst out of *On the Way Home,* or that she could be such a prairie party pooper in her pioneer novels.

Second, I thought of all those sentimental Laura quotes—in the museum bookstore the one about "the sweet, simple things in life" was everywhere, printed on bookmarks and plaques and pillows. I also thought of what Karen the Homeschooling Mom had said about how *content* the Ingallses had been in the Little House books.

Before she and her family left I talked to her one last time; I remembered I'd wanted to ask her how they had liked the Little House on the Prairie site the day before. "Oh, it was fine," she said. "It was definitely interesting. But here . . . *here* you can really sense, you know, what we all love about her . . . and the simple beauty of her life." She struggled to find the words for what she was talking about. Like four-year-old Laura back in Kansas, she seemed to want something but could not say what she meant.

Whatever it was, I was pretty sure I'd come here for it, too. Sometimes, Laura World wasn't a realm of log cabins or prairies, it was a way of being. Really, a way of being happy. I wasn't into the flowery sayings, but I was nonetheless in love with the idea of serene rooms full of endless quiet and time, of sky in the windows, of a life comfortably cluttered and yet in some kind of perfect feng shui equilibrium, where all the days were capacious enough to bake bread and write novels and perambulate the wooded hills deep in thought (though truthfully, I'd allow for the occasional Rose-style cocktail party as well). All of it was the stuff of my imaginary Laura lifestyle magazine, my own rendition of *sweet* and *simple*.

Probably most people who came to visit Mansfield had some version in mind, too. While we could all certainly appreciate the pioneer ordeals, the covered wagons, and the long winters, somehow Sweet and Simple had become our own dream frontier, our Oregon that we'd like to reach someday, always just beyond the horizon. We were looking for it wherever we could. Most of us had no use for someone like Rose, whose Bitter and Complicated life was at least as imperfect as our own.

❁

"People don't really come over to Rose's part of the museum, do they?" I asked the woman at the front desk, the one with the name tag that said PAM.

She paused before answering, as if to choose her words carefully. "Most people come here for Laura."

I pointed out it was sort of a shame, since Rose herself had led such a fascinating life. In fact, I'd just been reading about it, I told her.

"Oh?" she said. She smiled just a little. "And what books have you read?"

I sensed it was a loaded question. "Oh, just this one book I've been reading," I said. "Uh, I think it's called *The Ghost in the Little House?*" I said.

It occurred to me that maybe other people in the Mansfield area besides Mr. Dan L. White might have a problem with that book for the way it suggested Rose was the genius behind the Little House books. Pam shot off a look that said *Aha!* Oh, crap, I was busted.

"*That* book is not approved around here," she said. But then she laughed, and I felt better. "Rose went through some interesting times, there's no doubt about that." Pam actually knew a lot about Rose, about how she opposed the New Deal and started writing her political treatises. She even knew about Rose's somewhat kooky bent, when she refused Social Security benefits and tried to keep her income below taxable levels in order to avoid participating in what she called the government's Ponzi scheme. (She was able to pull this off in part by growing and putting up her own food; she once showed a reporter that she had eight hundred jars of canned goods in her cellar.) Had I known Rose personally I'm not sure if I would've gotten along with her, but I was glad that she had a fan here at the museum.

Pam talked a lot; I got the feeling she rarely had an opportunity to talk about Rose. She said she liked Rose's earlier books like *Old Home Town* and had been looking online for out-of-print copies. She'd even occasionally taken Rose's books out of the display cases and read them on slow shifts. She wanted to go see the archive of Rose's papers at the Hoover Presidential Library in Iowa someday. "One of these days, when I really retire, I'll go," she said.

I asked her why she thought Laura's books had endured more than Rose's. She thought about it for a moment. "Laura's stuff has a simplicity to it," she said finally. "That attracts people, I guess."

Pam said she'd grown up here in Mansfield; in school they'd all read the Little House books. "I can remember when Laura died," Pam said. She'd been just a kid. "The strange thing was that really everyone just thought of her as Mrs. Wilder who lived at the edge of town." For a moment I wondered what was so strange about it. Then I realized she meant that she could remember a time back before Laura was quite Laura, this figure we'd all come to feel closer to, this empty dress.

To see the Rock House you had to either drive about a mile down the road from the farmhouse and museum or else walk over, the way I did. I noticed the parking lot of this second house was vast but mostly empty; not as many visitors came over here. The Rock House tours ran only when enough people showed up.

There were just four other people in my group, and nobody

really seemed to know why the house was important. It was a pleasant but ordinary 1920s cottage with stone walls, hence the name. It looked remarkably suburban.

A woman next to me squinted up at it as we waited to go inside. "Is this where Rose lived or something?"

"I don't think so," I told her. "I think she just built it for her parents."

She didn't quite believe me, so she tried asking the teenage tour guide, who was just getting ready to give her introduction. "Okay, so *who* lived here?"

"LAURA AND ALMANZO LIVED HERE BETWEEN 1928 AND 1936," the girl replied, at a voice level calibrated for a somewhat larger group than ours. "SHE WROTE THE FIRST FOUR LITTLE HOUSE BOOKS HERE."

The tour didn't take long. The house was mostly empty inside—only draperies and a few bits of furniture. (Talk about simple!) The guide led us through three carpeted rooms and pointed out the nice tile in the bathroom and the custom-built shelves in the closets, as if our tiny group were prospective buyers at an open house.

At the end of the tour an older man raised his hand. "So Rose never lived here at all?" he asked the guide.

You really couldn't blame folks for being confused, because it was hard to make sense of the real story: Rose had it built to be a modern, comfortable place for her parents to live in their old age, and presented it to them as a gift on Christmas Day in 1928, when Laura was sixty-one. Except you couldn't quite imagine that Laura and Almanzo had really wanted such a gift, considering they had that gorgeous farmhouse up the road they'd spent half their lives building for themselves, complete with its customized tiny Laura-sized kitchen (and as for comfort and modernity, the tour guide told us that Almanzo eschewed indoor bathrooms all his life, preferring the outhouse). Moreover, the fact that they moved back to the farmhouse a few years later, once Rose had vacated it (because, remember, she moved in there *herself* after she'd relocated her folks to the new place), made you wonder what was the point of even building the Rock House in the first place.

The biographies I'd read didn't make things any less convoluted. Depending on which book you believed, either Rose was pushy about having the place built, or Laura was ungrateful; or else Laura had felt that she couldn't say no; or else Rose acted out of an overwhelming sense of obligation to her parents that hearkened back to her belief that as a toddler she'd somehow been responsible for the house fire on the Dakota homestead (not that any evidence of this exists outside Rose's own head, but *whoa!*), and in building the new house she was attempting to alleviate the primal guilt. Got all that?

The guide pointed to a short set of crumbling flagstone steps leading down from the driveway. "Almanzo built those steps," she told us, as if she was trying to convince us.

I could see why everyone kept trying to place Rose here. This house didn't quite fit in our Laura Ingalls Wilder imaginations, so it seemed an ideal residence for Rose, who didn't fit, either. Of course it wasn't like Rose really wanted a place in our Laura Worlds anyway. I didn't think so, at least.

I felt kind of sorry for the house, sitting out here all misunderstood: poor Little House in the Complicated Family Dynamic. But it really was pretty, the way it stood at the edge of a little bluff and faced the impossibly green valley all by itself.

❧

The way back to the museum was a path that ran behind all the buildings, up the hill and a mile or so through the farm property. When Laura had lived in the Rock House and Rose had lived in the farmhouse, this was supposed to be the path that Laura and Rose had taken to visit each other. You had to pay an extra three dollars at the museum to walk the path. I seemed to be the only person doing it that day. It had rained that morning and the grass was still wet.

On the walk over to the Rock House I had been the dutiful tourist, looking for things on the little map I'd been given, though really the only man-made attraction was a stumpy concrete thing, once a water cistern built by Almanzo. The rest of it was lush green country—little woods and neatly mowed clearings; a wild turkey had even appeared on the path in the distance ahead of me and scurried off as I approached. I'd expected the view to be nice; it was frankly gorgeous.

Now that I was heading back I found myself trying to take in as much as I could. I paid attention to *everything*—the plodding bird calls, the keening horn of a distant train. Since I was alone out here maybe I could really feel the spirit of the place, whatever that was. That was sort of the same question that invariably came up with Laura and Rose: not whether one of them had helped the other write the Little House books—because it's clear, from all the drafts and correspondence, that of course Rose had helped—but whose *soul* was in the books, who really inhabited them and made the girl in them come to life. But then what a stingy question it was, implying, sort of like that prayer in the TV movie, that it wasn't enough that they were good books; somehow they had to be the right kind of good. They had to be written by a woman who guilelessly wrote only the truth, or who loved the Good Lord, or who was a *real* writer, or a genius, or "progressive," or something. It was better to let go of all that.

Nothing happened while I walked, except that I knew I was seeing things that Laura saw, and that Rose saw, and I liked that. We were all sort of the same person out here, everyone who came to this place and looked and looked. The path was so hilly that the highway and the houses slipped away and for a while there wasn't anything else around, except for us.

7.

There Won't Be Horses

BACK AT HOME spring commenced. The rainy weather I'd seen in Missouri made its way up to Illinois and then turned mild. Seeing Laura's homey kitchen in Mansfield had made me excited to come home and continue my Little House lifestyle experiments. But after a couple weeks it was clear I was starting to run out of ways to live La Vida Laura.

I'd made a few more recipes from *The Little House Cookbook*, with mixed results. The two batches of vanity cakes tasted all right, though they lacked the exquisite, airy melt-in-the-mouth texture that Laura had described in *Plum Creek*, and which had always made me imagine them as the Krispy Kremes of the prairie. They were the ones that called for two pounds of lard for deep-fat frying, and for the rest of the day after I'd made them the whole apartment smelled like a state fair.

I'd also made a meal of fried salt pork and gravy, apples 'n' onions, and buttermilk biscuits one night for Chris and me. Since

I'd used the pork drippings to season everything, most of the meal was a raging success, save the salt pork itself, which was, well, *really* salty and much denser than we'd bargained for. After just a few bites, it was clear that a little salt pork went a long way. Chris pointed out that it was the sort of meal that was best eaten after a long day working in the fields, as opposed to migrating the contents of your in-box from the old version of Yahoo! Mail to the new one, which is what he'd been doing all afternoon.

I was getting tired of recipes, though, and both soap and candle making were just more recipes, when it came down to it. But I had only a vague sense of what else I wanted to do, just that it couldn't be anything too over the top, like build a log cabin. Ditto for anything that had an obvious component of drudgery (i.e., scrubbing laundry with a washboard) or viscera (as in animal butchering). By now I understood that there was a precarious balance to my Little House daydreams; it helped that the baser details had always been absent from the books so that one thought more about pretty butter molds than outhouses.

I briefly considered a weekend at some rustic destination, and friends sent me information on hippie resorts, backpacker waysides, remote spots deep in Montana and a five-hour drive from the airport. But I soon realized I wasn't interested in spending time off the grid for its own sake. I just wanted to be in Laura World, not a yurt. I didn't want to simplify my life or live in another era. I wanted the places I knew in the books to still be there and I wanted to see them.

Though I still didn't quite believe it was possible.

Years ago, maybe a decade, and long before I picked up the Little House books again, I came across a children's book called

Searching for Laura Ingalls while doing some work-related research at the Chicago public library. It was a nonfiction picture book by Kathryn Lasky, and it was about a girl traveling with her family to see the locations from the Little House books. The girl's name was Meribah and she was an avid Laura Ingalls Wilder fan, so the family set out in an RV to visit the homesites in Wisconsin and Minnesota and South Dakota. The color photos that illustrated the book gave it a casual quality that seemed part documentary and part vacation album. I remember flipping through the book and feeling a twinge of my old love for the books and even some jealousy. This girl had gone and had the Little House vacation *I'd* wanted as a kid.

But then on page after page in the book, the girl kept discovering that all the old things weren't quite what she expected. She was shown sadly regarding the log cabin that was smaller and emptier than she'd thought, and she warily eyed gift shop merchandise at one of the hometown museums. She stood on the asphalt in downtown De Smet, South Dakota, waiting for a Fourth of July parade that never happened. She squinted in the sunlight of an open field where the Big Woods had once stood. I remembered enough about the books—just barely—to know what she'd been searching for.

It figures, I'd thought, and put the book back on the shelf.

By May, I'd all but given up on finding ways to play Laura, when something, out of the blue, revived my interest: I discovered my dream farm. Okay, so it wasn't *my* farm, but still.

I was on a website I'd bookmarked back in the fall for its very good page on butter churning, complete with photos. The site had an extensive section of "homesteading lessons," which included instructions for making cheese, using a spinning wheel, and even rendering lard (which didn't look terribly gross at all), but until now I hadn't looked at the home page to see who was putting this stuff online. It turned out to be a couple named Samuel and Heidi Ackerson, who owned a small farm downstate. According to the website, Clover Meadow Farm sold homemade yarn and soap, raised heritage farm animals, and offered "a peek into the past."

"We continue the same farm practices that our ancestors used over a hundred years ago," the page read. *We* as in Samuel and Heidi, who lived in southern Illinois, only a short drive from Chicago.

The Ackersons, I discovered, worked their land with horse-drawn plows; they owned cows, pigs, and several heirloom breeds of turkeys, chickens, geese, and guinea fowl. They sold eggs from their front yard and took Thanksgiving orders for the turkeys. Heidi made soap, spun yarn, and made her own cheese and butter; Samuel had his own blacksmith's forge, which he used to make wrought-iron fixtures. It all sounded like the idyllically industrious Wilder farm in *Farmer Boy,* where Almanzo's mother worked at her loom and Father made roof shingles by hand, and the cellar was filled with bushels of homegrown apples and potatoes and jugs of maple syrup.

I was getting pretty smitten by this place, especially when I read that the Ackersons gave tours of the farm and hands-on classes in traditional skills. It was like a living history museum, except it was *real*. None of this earnest-volunteer-in-a-pinafore business like at the pioneer villages I'd visited as a kid! The Ackersons were like the Amish, I thought, except without all the bizarre rules and shunning.

I thought about contacting them, but would they understand that I didn't want to tan hides or raise chickens, that I just wanted to play Laura Ingalls Wilder every now and then?

I looked on the Ackersons' "About" page. Samuel's hobbies included historical reenactments, it said, and Heidi first fell in love with the past when she read *Little House in the Big Woods* as a little girl.

That was all I needed. I had to see this place.

I considered taking one of the tours that the Ackersons offered by appointment. But then I noticed on the site that they were hosting their annual "Homesteading Weekend" in June, a get-together for "like-minded people who would like to share their homesteading skills and learn from others." There was no set schedule, the description said, but the activities usually included demonstrations in blacksmithing, spinning, weaving, and cooking on an open fire with cast iron. It was just a few weeks away.

"Wait, so these people, you want to go to their house and learn how to make candles and stuff?" Chris said when I showed him the site.

"Not their house," I said. "Their *farm*." I knew it sounded a little weird, but these people were experts. Clover Meadow Farm had been featured on a History Channel series about rural American traditions. That sounded plenty trustworthy to me. "They're really serious," I told Chris. "They plow with horses and everything."

For me the greatest appeal of the homesteading weekend was that it seemed just Laura-esque enough. At last I'd found the next logical step beyond re-creating a few dishes in *The Little House Cookbook* and churning butter. Learning some of these "homesteading" skills, I figured, would be perfectly in the spirit of the Little House books and Laura's intentions. In *Little House, Long Shadow*, Anita Clair Fellman points out that by the late 1920s, when Laura was writing the pages that would eventually become *Little House in the Big Woods*, the highway near her home was being paved and "more than 50 percent of the population lived in urban areas and had ready access to canned goods and year-round fresh foods." No doubt this sense of a rapidly changing world must have motivated Laura to write down the domestic practices of her pioneer childhood with enough detail to ensure that Ma's ways were not completely forgotten.

The Ackersons seemed to have the same objective. For the most part.

I watched an online video of their History Channel segment, which showed lovely footage of the farm and the draft horses while the narrator called the farm "*Little House on the Prairie* come to life." The segment featured the Ackersons as they gave a tour to a Chicago suburban family who were thinking of taking up a similar lifestyle. The Ackersons were shown churning butter and spinning yarn while the children looked on.

Then Heidi gave an interview sound bite: "There might be a time in the future that these kids need to know this stuff," she said. "Our resources won't be around forever."

The meaning of that was not lost on me. Ever since I'd gotten the churn and started to build a small collection of "playing Laura" accoutrements, I'd occasionally think about how these things, along with my budding pioneer knowledge, might be of use. Wasn't it nice that I could make bread starter from scratch, and that I had a kerosene lamp that could come in handy in a blackout?

"You're so totally set for the apocalypse with all this stuff, you know," my friend Jami joked one night when I was telling her I was thinking about fermenting my own apple cider vinegar.

"Yeah, right," I said. But I felt a tiny swell of pride at the thought of being prepared for something. Even if I didn't see the point of thinking too much about that *something*, which of course could be anything: peak oil, global warming, terrorist attacks, zombies. Oh, I'd had a moment or two of Y2K panic back in the day, and in the months after 9/11 I'd collected a dozen cans of cheap soup and off-brand spaghetti and stashed them in a box under the sink, a gesture that in retrospect seemed more about managing anxiety than anything else.

Then there was the word *homesteading*. In the course of searching online for obscure butter-making utensils and other such things, I'd come across this word enough times to understand that it no longer meant proving up on a 160-acre land claim the way Pa Ingalls had done. It now stood for the pursuit of a self-sufficient lifestyle—living off the land, so to speak.

This appeared to mean different things to different people. Some of the homesteader talk I found on the Internet sounded pretty appealing to me—the emphasis on organic gardening and local food production was very much in tune with the Michael Pollan books I'd read. The stuff about one-world government conspiracies—well, not so much. Homesteading was definitely a mixed bag: from what I could tell, people in the online world used the term to describe anything from a home canning hobby to living in an off-the-grid Alaska compound.

So while I sensed that the Ackersons had some decidedly

non–Little House reasons for their homesteading lifestyle, I wasn't sure what they were. That was their business, not mine.

❈

Heidi Ackerson was extremely pleasant over the phone. She confirmed that, yes, anyone was welcome to come to the homesteading weekend, as long as they brought food for potluck. I told her why I was interested in coming, what with this Laura Ingalls Wilder hobby I'd developed lately. "I've churned butter," I said, as casually as I could manage.

"Maybe you can help show everyone how it's done," she suggested. She explained that at these weekends there were always more people coming to learn than to demonstrate.

"Really? Sure," I said. This churning business could get me places, I thought proudly. I liked the idea that I could trade on my butter skills in this homesteader economy. Didn't Ma Wilder trade her butter for tin? Or use it to pay the cobbler? Something like that.

Heidi said that weekenders could camp out at the farm, stay in a motel nearby, or even sleep on the floor of their living room, but I figured Chris and I could drive the two hours from Chicago.

"What time does everything start on Saturday morning?" I asked, thinking we could get there by nine a.m. if we had to.

"Well, we usually get started when we get up," she said. "Between five and seven."

"Sure!" I said, trying my best to sound unfazed. Well, it *was* a farm. We would have to come out Friday night and set up our tent if we didn't want to miss anything. And I did not want to miss anything.

We arrived early in the evening on Friday, when it was still daylight. It was a tiny place, with just a farmhouse, a low red barn, a couple of sheds, and two small fields. Heidi was coming out of the house as we drove up (I recognized her from online), and she waved at our car.

"You can park over by the tents," she called. She was in her late forties or early fifties, deeply tan, with shoulder-length brown hair she kept tucked behind her ears in a way that made her look younger.

As we slowly drove in, I could see that the farm had exactly the sort of barnyard one visualizes in children's books like *Charlotte's Web*—teeming with geese and chickens and turkeys. A border collie romped ahead of our car. I could see a large garden beyond the barnyard, and behind it, a meadow. It was even better than I'd hoped.

There were three tents set up already at the edge of the fields, and people had gathered in the yard next to the house, where there were picnic tables and a fire pit. Some were setting up food at the table; nearly a dozen others were sitting in lawn chairs around the fire. A few children were playing on a nearby tire swing. It all looked like a typical picnic except for the two women who were working at spinning wheels. Spinning wheels! All right!

We set up our tent and then joined the group around the fire pit. We introduced ourselves to Samuel, Heidi's husband, who was tending the fire, and then several others whose names I hadn't learned yet. Besides the spinning-wheel ladies, there was a woman in pigtail braids with a big book in her lap, two long-haired guys who were assembling a cooking tripod, two sweet-looking older women in pastel sweatshirts, and a tall, wiry guy with a baseball cap.

"This is our first time here," I confessed to the group as Chris and I set up our lawn chairs.

"Same here," said one of the pastel-sweatshirt women. The other nodded.

The guy with the baseball cap spoke up. "But we all came down together," he said. He motioned to the sweatshirt women and the men by the fire. "Us over here. And then Rebecca here, and Jim over there is her husband, and those are her kids, and then those guys over there by the tents are all with us, too. We came down from Wisconsin." His name was Ron and he pumped Chris's hand when he introduced himself.

The woman with the pigtail braids was Rebecca. "We're all from the same church," she told us. "We heard about this on the Internet."

"So did we," I said. "We came from Chicago."

"All the way from *Chicago*?" said Rebecca's husband, Jim.

"It's only about two hours," Chris explained.

I looked around. Except for Samuel and Heidi and a handful of others (including the spinning-wheel duo, whom I'd spoken with just enough to learn that they were local friends of Heidi's and liked to spin more than make small talk), most of the people were with the Wisconsin group. Like us, they were camping overnight here on the farm.

Heidi explained that more people would be coming on Saturday and Sunday—locals, mostly—but even she and Samuel seemed surprised at the Friday-night turnout. "These Wisconsin folks called me up to make sure we had room for them," she said. "I said, 'why not?'"

Some of the Wisconsinites kept to themselves, but the ones who sat near us were friendly. The book in Rebecca's lap was a guide to identifying edible wild plants, and she explained that she'd just been out picking a salad, which sounded impressive.

"So, you came out here from Chicago looking for something . . . different?" she asked me.

"I guess," I said. "I already know how to churn butter. I even have a churn." I told her about my fascination with the Little House books.

"That's great," she said. "That was an amazing family. They could make all their own food and they had everything they needed."

Well, not everything, I pointed out. "Pa would go out and bring back sugar, right?" I was trying to remember the various going-to-town scenes in the books. "And cornmeal. Oh, and salt pork." Those were always my favorite scenes, with Pa coming home with provisions wrapped in paper.

"Which book was that?" she said, but she didn't wait for me to answer. "They just had so much *wisdom*. How to raise the livestock, and harvest the honey, and all those things you'd have to know if supermarkets weren't available. It's just such good knowledge."

I nodded. Rebecca was interesting. Along with her braids she wore a short green sundress, little wire-rimmed glasses, and Birkenstock sandals. She had an even deeper tan than Heidi. She made the kind of eye contact that seemed to search your face as you talked.

We had come just in time for the dinner the Wisconsin group had prepared. Rebecca got up from her chair to serve everyone Styrofoam cups of hot, yellowish tea. It tasted a little like mint tea but with a slightly bitter note.

"It's homemade nettle tea," she told us. Chris kept blowing on the water of his cup as if to cool it.

"It's not that hot," I told him.

"I know," he whispered. He set it down by his chair.

The spread of food included beef stew, macaroni salad, and green beans that had been grown and canned by the church group. Rebecca had foraged the salad and the tea.

"Nettles are so good for your skin and your lungs and your stomach," she told the group. "They have so many healing properties. It's just amazing to think about how nature is full of all these things God made for us, and everything has a purpose that He wants us to discover. It's all for us to use."

"What about poison oak?" Samuel Ackerson said. He didn't say much, but I liked him. "What's it good for?"

For once Rebecca seemed stumped. "Well," she said. "You just never know."

❁

I'd gone to the car to get a sweater and Chris followed me.

"Is it just me, or are these people just a little Holy Roller?" he said, his voice low. Dinner had started with a lengthy, multi-speaker blessing thanking the Lord for providing food, revealing the path of righteousness, making His purpose known, and bringing like-minded people together.

"I think it's because so many of them are in that church group," I whispered, though Heidi had led part of the grace, and I was beginning to wonder if the term "like-minded" was perhaps code for something that we weren't, even with Chris being a nice Lutheran boy who'd gotten me to go to church with him. "Look, some of these people who are into homesteading are just kind of like this," I told Chris.

I was keeping an open mind. And I had gotten used to encountering people of a somewhat more evangelical bent in the Laura

Ingalls Wilder fan world—plenty of homeschooling moms blogged about the Little House books, for example, and I'd noticed more than a couple fish symbols on the cars in the museum parking lot in Mansfield, Missouri. They were all nice folks who shared my love of Laura but maybe not my support for legalizing gay marriage. Well, *c'est la vie*. I'd liked Karen and Keith and their family just fine.

We went back to the fire pit. It was dusk now, and the fireflies were out in greater numbers than I'd seen in years. The meadow behind us appeared to glow with the fading sunlight. The fact that it was one of the most gorgeous summer evenings I'd ever seen gave way to thinking about where I was, and I finally admitted to myself that it felt strange to be here.

I'd struck up a conversation with the younger of the two pastel-sweatshirt women, Linda, who had prematurely white hair and a kind, round face. She'd been to Chicago once, she said, or just outside it, really. I asked her what it was like in Morristown, Wisconsin.

"Oh, well, a lot of people aren't working right now," she said with a sort of half-laugh. She explained that the engine plant had been laying off employees by the hundreds. She hadn't worked there, but she was having a hard time finding full-time work after her divorce. She had a voice that made her sound like she was always on the verge of either a question or a sigh. "You just don't know what's going to happen next," she said. "I guess that's why we're here."

I nodded, though I didn't know quite what she meant.

"We were off the grid for four days back in December," she said.

"In Morristown?" I asked. "Wow, what happened?" I thought she was talking about an ice storm or something.

"No, this was at our church," she said. "It was sort of like a drill. We all stayed there to see what it would be like if something happened."

For a moment I was dumbstruck. If *what* happened? I thought, but I didn't want to ask. So instead I said, "What was it like?" I was trying to imagine. "Was it cold?"

"Yeah," she said, with that half-laugh again. "We had a generator that we ran a couple hours a day. It really wasn't fun. But I guess you've got to be ready, you know?"

Before long it was dark. Chris was sitting across the fire with Ron, the baseball-cap guy. Ron was hunched forward in his lawn chair intently. He seemed to really like Chris.

"I can tell you're a man of deep faith," I heard him saying.

I needed to get Chris alone and tell him that the Wisconsin church group was a kooky survivalist sect whose name (Linda had told me) was something like New Life Testimony Revelation Ministry.

But before I could, Rebecca called me. "Heidi's going to show us her loom," she said. "Come on." All the women were heading toward the house.

Oh, no, I thought. They're separating the men from the women! Just like in cults!

As it turned out, we really *were* just looking at the antique looms and spinning wheels that Heidi kept in an upstairs workroom. But I could only pay attention to conversations about yarn for so long, so I excused myself and went downstairs to the kitchen. The kitchen was huge, part of an expansion built on the house, and there was one long wall of painted wooden shelves holding dozens of Mason jars of canned goods.

It was a gorgeous arrangement, almost mesmerizing: jars of peaches, fruit preserves, green beans, pickles, corn, tomatoes, even meat, their metal lids neatly sealed. I looked closely: they were real, not just the comforting décor that I'd long become accustomed to seeing at places like Cracker Barrel. What did they signify beyond that? Ma Ingalls would have likely been thrilled by this kind of abundance. Almanzo Wilder, struggling with Laura through one of their many setbacks, might have recalled his *Farmer Boy* childhood and conjured up an image of shelves like these. In 1944, Rose Wilder Lane had an entire cellar full of these jars, those eight hundred jars she displayed to a reporter as a symbol of her protest against income tax and the government. Heidi Ackerson had a hobby that was perhaps something more than a hobby. All the same, the jars were so pretty.

Rebecca had come downstairs and now she stood gazing at the shelves, too. "Look at those. Isn't it amazing?" she said. "It really reminds you that there are ways to provide in a time when you can't go to the grocery store."

It was maybe the third time that she'd said something to this effect. By now, I knew, she wasn't talking about late nights when you have to pick up the milk at the 7-Eleven. I knew, *knew* that she wanted me to ask what she meant.

"You keep saying that," I said. "Could you, you know, elaborate a little? As to the kind of circumstances where that would happen?"

The tiniest smile flickered on Rebecca's face. Then the line of her mouth straightened and she was serene.

"Could you just, you know, clarify?" I asked.

"Well, with the economy failing and all that's happening," she said. (I heard that phrase "with all that's happening" mentioned a few times over the weekend: I suspected it referred to the recession, terrorism, and the belief that the recently elected Barack Obama was evil incarnate.) "We're getting into an emergency situation, and people are going to panic. We just don't know what's going to happen next. Don't you sense that? And it's on a worldwide scale."

I nodded, only because I wanted her to go on.

"And all the disasters, which are signs," Rebecca went on. "I believe that we *are* in the end times now. And the Lord will summon us to Heaven soon, but we don't know what will happen in *this* world before that happens, and we need to be ready. What do you think about that?" she asked. "Does that scare you?"

"Thanks," I said. "I was just curious."

I really *had* been curious to see if she would say something like "end times." Lucky me!

"If you're worried, we can talk about it," Rebecca said.

"Not right now," I said. "But thanks!"

I walked outside. *She'd said "end times"!*

From everything that I'd read, End Timers were waiting for the collapse of civilization the way fans of the *Twilight* series awaited the trailer for *Breaking Dawn*. They were bracing themselves to endure the myriad destructive ordeals that would wipe out infidels, atheists, unrepentant sinners, industrialists, government officials, and Salon.com readers, with the expectation that they, the prepared ones, would be among the worthy few who would be raptured to Heaven either before or after (this part was never clear) the massive worldwide crapfest. Compared to these folks, Keith and Karen seemed as secular as Brad and Angelina.

I was heading back to my chair by the fire, but Chris intercepted me and led me in the other direction, away from the group.

"If anyone asks," he whispered. "We've been married three years."

"What?" I whispered back.

"Ron thinks we are. I didn't want to tell him we weren't. That guy is freaking me out. He was practically speaking in tongues."

"These people do survival drills!" I hissed.

"I know! Ron said they hid out for two weeks in the woods. He's freaking me out," Chris said.

"What did he say to you?"

"Too many things. He's freaking me out. What did Rebecca say?"

"Rebecca said 'end times'!"

"We're leaving tomorrow," Chris said.

Later on in the tent I got out my notebook. The church group's tents were only a few feet from ours, close enough for us to see the glow of their flashlights as they got ready for bed. We didn't speak for fear of being overheard.

I'm so sorry I made us come to this thing, I wrote in the notebook. *I love you.* I handed it to Chris with the flashlight.

He wrote, *I love you too but these people are freaking me out.*

We passed the notebook back and forth, writing our conversation. We decided that we would take in a couple of the skill demonstrations and leave by midday, sooner if things got any creepier. We also decided that if the End Times ever happened we didn't want to be anywhere the hell near Rebecca and Ron and would take our chances with whatever postapocalyptic fate awaited us.

I lay in the dark in our sleeping bag while Chris slept. How had my quest for Little House—style experience led us here? I thought about Rebecca in her sundress and pigtail braids. I had been searching for Laura Ingalls Wilder and I'd gotten Hippie Half-Pint instead, half full of her crazy, crazy Kool-Aid made from foraged berries.

But that wasn't the only thing that was making me uneasy. Deep down, I was starting to wonder if the Little House books had more to do with this sort of worldview than I'd been willing to admit. Not the end-of-the-world stuff, of course, but that "simple life" mind-set and all that it rejected. I thought about Rose and her cellar again. I thought about the moms who bragged online that their homeschooled kids were not only reading the Little House books but were learning from reprinted editions of the same *McGuffey's Eclectic Readers* that Laura and Carrie used, as if all of twentieth-century pedagogy simply didn't exist.

I was also remembering the 2005 Disney version of *Little House on the Prairie* and how it starts, like the books, with Pa wanting to leave the Big Woods. Only this movie version gives the impression that what the Ingallses *really* wanted was a lifestyle makeover. The movie makes the Big Woods seem like a downright lousy neighborhood: young Laura narrowly misses a bullet fired by a careless hunter, and Pepin, with its incessant wagon-wheel-and-horse-whinny traffic noise, is as bustling as a strip mall. Pa hates doing carpentry work for an uppity wealthy man who browbeats him and withholds payments, and whereas in the books a trip to the general store was always a fun occasion, in this version Ma stresses over the prices and the family budget, and Laura and Mary grab at candy just like they were in a supermarket checkout. The subtext of these early scenes seems to be: *surely there's a better way to live, a way to opt out of the materialistic rat race and the hassles of 1870s modern life!*

I could see how certain aspects of the Little House books could help nurture a twenty-first-century homesteading dream. And while my default Little House fantasy always involved befriending Laura and exploring our respective worlds together, I knew that there was another extremely common daydream as well, one that Anita Clair Fellman mentions in her critique of Laura Ingalls Wilder fans in the book *Little House, Long Shadow:*

> One woman, who wore out her Little House books, linked her childhood covered-wagon play with a recurrent pleasurable fantasy that some unspecified catastrophe would prevent everyone from using modern conveniences.

Admit it: you've gone there, and so have I.

I considered this as I stared up at the ceiling of our tent. Who knew how many times those books made me idly wish for a *now* other than the one I was in, that the world would somehow crack open and reveal a simpler life?

Chris and I were glad for daylight, even though it was five a.m. Getting up at dawn was hardly a problem, with two roosters screeching away over the continuous garble-gackle of nearly a dozen geese and turkeys.

"I can sleep through car alarms in our neighborhood," Chris said, "but not this crap." We were the first ones up besides Samuel, who hurried out of the house to the barn for morning chores.

The homesteading activities did not start, as Heidi had stated, between five and seven a.m. But she did serve the whole group an incredible breakfast of eggs, potatoes, biscuits, and gravy in the big kitchen, and despite all our offers to help, she did much of the work herself. Even though they'd gone and invited an apocalypse cult to their farm, I was still impressed with Samuel and Heidi and the life they'd made for themselves. By now, though, I was pretty sure that at least Heidi believed in this End Times stuff. While we cleared the breakfast dishes, she was at the sink talking to Rebecca, who I heard say that "with all that's happening" phrase again.

"My mother is still pretty skeptical," Heidi said. "She says I shouldn't let people hear me talk about being prepared because they'll think I'm crazy. Well, let them think I'm crazy."

I already thought Heidi was crazy on account of the fact that she had a whole room full of yarn. I still liked her, though.

Rebecca came up to me again after breakfast.

"You don't have to be frightened," she said. "I feel joy for what's to come because my family and I will be with Jesus. But I wanted to let *you* know, too."

"Thanks!" I said again. "I'm fine." I had no idea what to say to Rebecca.

After a night of End Times revelations, the soap-making demonstration was a little anticlimactic. Most of the women were gathered in the kitchen watching Heidi make a batch of scented cream soap. Chris and the men were in a shed across the barnyard for Samuel's blacksmithing demonstration. By now more visitors were arriving for the day's activities. It occurred to me that if we'd driven out from Chicago first thing in the morning, the way I'd originally planned, we might not have had such a close encounter with the New Life Promise Revelationers, or whatever they were called. This all might have seemed like just a nice day at the farm, and we might not have had any idea that it was about the end of the world.

The soap-making demonstration was almost over when I saw Linda's head drop back against her chair. She was snoring softly.

"Oh my," Heidi whispered. She had just poured liquid soap into a molding rack. "Is she okay?"

Evelyn, the older pastel-sweatshirt lady, had scooted her chair over and put her arm around Linda. "She's fine," Evelyn said. She explained that Linda suffered from sleep apnea and tended to nod off. She gently nudged Linda awake.

"My sister-in-law has that, too," one of the newly arrived weekenders said. "She has one of those machines that help you breathe at night."

"So do I," said Linda sadly. "But I'm trying not to depend on it too much." She looked miserable. I liked her more than the others in the Wisconsin group. At the campfire she'd told me that she'd been a social worker, but the job pressures had gotten to her. It didn't seem like she had a lot of options in Morristown. Unlike Rebecca, I got the impression that she wasn't terribly excited about the future. More than once she'd mentioned "being prepared" with a sort of weary shrug, perhaps because she sensed how hard the Coming Days would be for someone with a condition like hers.

While the soap cooled, Heidi gave a quick lesson on skimming cream from milk, setting aside the separated cream in a glass jar to churn into butter later.

"Speaking of butter," Evelyn spoke up, "we have a guide how to can it. The information's on the Internet but we typed it up, too." In the interest of sharing homesteading skills, she passed out printouts of the butter-canning directions, which involved melting butter, pouring it into canning jars that had been sterilized in the oven, and waiting for the heat to seal the lids. I was trying to figure out what the point was.

"Well, it's not *technically* canning," Heidi said, "but I've heard of people who've done it. How long is the shelf life?"

"Up to five years," Evelyn said. "No refrigeration needed!" She went over to the table and picked up a little jelly jar that I'd seen both at breakfast and dinner the night before but hadn't touched on account of the rancid tang of its mysterious contents. Oh, no—that was *butter*? It was both oily and oddly granular, and I'd thought it was some kind of homemade mayonnaise. "This is from a batch we put up last fall," Evelyn said. "You can do the same thing with Velveeta, too."

I went outside and found Chris.

"I just got an *F* in blacksmithing," he said. Samuel had showed them how to make little iron hooks, and his had fallen into the fire. "That's how I roll." He made the heavy-metal sign. "Anything horrifying happen during Soap 101?"

I told him about how Linda was preparing for off-the-grid life by trying to go without her CPAP machine, and about Evelyn's dubious-sounding butter-storage methods. "Let's go soon," I said.

"Now," Chris said. "We're taking the tent down *now*."

"Too bad you won't be able to help with the butter churning," Heidi said, when I told her we were leaving.

"Yeah, something came up," I said, knowing full well how it sounded: Oh, you know how it is with our hectic Chicago lives! We city people, we never change!

I bought several bars of her soap, which smelled wonderful, and thanked her for hosting. In my heart I wished her and Samuel well. "You guys are really living the dream out here," I told her. Whatever their dream was, that is.

Most of the weekenders had gathered in the barnyard, and Samuel was showing everyone how to put a bridle on a horse and clean its hooves. But Ron and Linda and Evelyn were sitting by the picnic tables, so we went over to say good-bye to them.

"We don't know how long we're staying, either," Ron said. "This ain't really the stuff we're needing to learn. I mean"—he nodded toward the barnyard—"this is nice, but it's not really practical for what we're wanting to do."

Ron was a little creepy, but you couldn't help but feel a little sorry for him: clearly he was hoping this weekend would be more *Soldier of Fortune* magazine than *Country Living*. I wondered what kind of world he thought he was preparing for.

"I mean, there won't be horses," he said.

"Good luck," I said to Linda. *We have room in our car*, I wanted to tell her.

"Thanks." She waved weakly.

Rebecca approached us one last time. To my relief, it wasn't to proselytize but to ask about our future Laura Ingalls Wilder trips.

"So are you going to see Mankato, too?" she asked. "Mankato, Minnesota?"

"Mankato? What's there?" I was pretty sure the place had never been mentioned in any of the biographies, and yet it sounded familiar.

"The Ingalls family were always taking trips to Mankato," she said.

I stared at her for a moment before I realized what she was talking about. "Oh, you mean on the *TV show.*"

I remembered now—*Mankato,* the town that the show's writers had designated as the go-to place whenever the plot veered into situations that required the amenities of a considerably larger town than Walnut Grove. Characters frequently went to Mankato to visit medical specialists, buy fancy dresses, and get into bar brawls. From the way the TV Ingallses planned shopping trips to Mankato, you get the sense that the place was a sort of nineteenth-century Mall of America, but there's no indication whatsoever that the actual Mankato, about eighty miles from Walnut Grove (which back then would have been a three-day journey), ever served that purpose for Laura or anyone else.

Rebecca nodded. "But they must have gone there sometimes in real life."

"I don't think so," I said. "The show made that up." I explained that *most* of the stuff on that show was made up and didn't happen in the books.

"Oh," she said. "I only read the first book, and then I watched the show. It wasn't the same?" She looked a little disappointed.

"No," I told her. "So, no, we're not going to Mankato. Why do you ask?"

"It just always sounded like a great place," Rebecca said.

It took about an hour on the road before we could start to laugh at the whole experience.

"I can't believe that just happened," Chris said. "I can't believe those people."

"I can't believe Rebecca thinks the End Times *and* the TV show are for real," I added.

"There won't be horses," Chris said.

"But there *will* be butter," I pointed out.

We were so glad when we could see the Chicago skyline again, and when we merged onto the expressway that would take us back to our doomed and worldly life.

That business about canning butter really stuck with me—something about it seemed to epitomize our strange encounter at Clover Meadow Farm. So shortly after we got home, I looked it up online. The practice, said to have originated with Oregon Trail settlers, now appears to be a very popular emergency-preparedness home project. This despite warnings from food preservation experts that letting butter recongeal in jars doesn't really count as canning and that subsequently keeping the stuff around for a couple years perhaps isn't the best thing to do. Since plenty of other staples could be used in place of butter (unless your emergency food supply consisted mostly of muffins), butter canning hardly seems worth the effort and risk, but lots of people do it anyway.

I noticed that just about everyone who posted about canning butter on a blog or a bulletin board seemed to be preparing for the possibility of a Biblically sanctioned calamity more than any other kind of event. Or, at the very least, they were *thinking* about preparing. I suspected that was the appeal of butter canning: as preparedness methods go, it's cheap and easy, a much less complicated endeavor than, say, building a reverse-osmotic water purification system.

Most of all, it is homey—people often call canned butter "sunshine in a jar" and remark on how pretty it looks. Impractical though it is, I could see that canning butter was a way to play God's pioneer, imagining a better life on a new frontier of mankind. It lets you create a comforting narrative of security and resourcefulness, an impulse that is very human, and, I have to admit, very Little House as well.

❈

In the weeks after our trip to the farm, I had a made-up story of my own, a variation on my childhood imaginary friendship with young Laura Ingalls, where I'd lead her around and show her the marvels of my modern life. Only now instead of Laura, I was mentally ushering around Linda from the Wisconsin church group, who had seemed so lost and sad. The night we'd talked by the fire she'd asked me all kinds of questions about living in the city: Did we know our neighbors? (Most of them, I told her.) Where did we park our cars? Was it hard living on the third floor and having to walk up all those stairs every day? What kind of people ride the subway? What about crime? I'd wondered if she was curious about living another kind of life.

So for much of the summer I walked around the city with this Linda woman in my head, showing her the neighborhoods, imagining her walking with me down the tree-lined streets, greeting the people we passed, stopping in and talking to the owners of the grubby little grocery stores in Albany Park. *It's friendly here, see?* I'd tell Imaginary Linda. *It's a different world, but you could live here.*

❈

And then, for a while afterward, one question kept nagging me: what would Laura Ingalls Wilder think of all this—the homesteading movement, Samuel and Heidi Ackerson, the Wisconsin church group and their preparedness retreats? Like Rose, Laura disliked FDR and the public-works programs of the New Deal. They both valued self-reliance (so much so that in the Little House books they'd made the fictional Ingalls family more independent than the real one); they likely would have admired some of the modern homesteaders' efforts and been impressed by Heidi's kitchen. I already suspected that if the adult Laura were alive today, there'd be something of a cultural divide between us.

One night, though, I was rereading *Pioneer Girl*, Laura's unpublished memoir manuscript, and skimming a bit, since much of the last half is material also covered in the final books in the series. I came across a passage about one of the town jobs Laura worked at in her teenage years, the stint sewing shirts at Clancy's dry goods store. In *Little Town on the Prairie*, Laura has to listen to the constant quarreling of the merchant, his wife, and his mother-in-law.

But according to *Pioneer Girl*, what she had to endure instead, in real life, were the two women's rantings about "the Catholics," who they feared would take over the government and do terrible things to Protestant women and children:

> While we sewed, the daughter would work herself up . . . wringing her hands and declaring that they should never take her Bible from her, never, never! no matter what she suffered.
>
> Then a comet appeared in the sky and both women believed this meant the end of the world, so they were more frightened than ever.
>
> I sat sewing and did not say anything. I did not believe what they said about the Catholics or the comet, but it made me feel sick to hear them talk.

Chris heard me laugh out loud as I read this.

"What's so funny?" he asked.

I showed him the page. "Check out the good old days," I told him.

Maybe it was futile to think about what kind of ideology Laura Ingalls Wilder would have if she lived today. After all, the Laura of fifty years ago wrote *The Long Winter,* a story not just about survival, but about the survival of a family with a few too many mouths to feed and a tendency to rely on luck. And yet the story never for a moment becomes a cautionary tale about preparedness (though it's certainly true the Ingallses *weren't* prepared) or depending too much on the railroads for provisions (also true). It assigns no higher meaning to the relentless blizzards and terrible cold. In the end it's enough that everyone survives.

Chris and I had made it through our strange farm ordeal, but I was beginning to doubt that these excursions were getting me any closer to the world of the books. In less than a month we were going to see the places where the last five books took place—Minnesota and South Dakota, with a stop in Iowa, too, but I wasn't even sure what I was looking for anymore. Suddenly I wanted to talk to someone who had done what I was about to do. It wasn't just a trip I was going on—by setting out for the remaining homesites, I'd be excavating my childhood neverland once and for all.

Maybe the weirdest e-mail you've gotten all week, I wrote in the subject line of an e-mail to a person I knew only from a book.

I had found that *Searching for Laura Ingalls* book at the library again, that picture book with the photos of the kid traveling with her family in the RV on their Little House vacation. And then, because I can't leave well enough alone, I'd found the girl, Meribah Knight. I'd searched her name online just out of curiosity and because she had a distinctive first name, but when I found out she was living in Chicago, I knew I wanted to talk to her.

Meribah had been in grade school in 1993 when the book was published. Her mother, the children's book writer Kathryn Lasky, had cowritten the book with Meribah, and her father had taken the photos. Now she was a journalism grad student in her mid-twenties. I wondered what she'd think of the fact that someone else searching for Laura Ingalls was searching for her.

She wrote back right away. "This is so hilarious," she wrote. Well, yes, it was.

We met for coffee about a week later. In *Searching for Laura Ingalls*, when she was eight, she wore a pink prairie skirt and matching blouse to go wading in Plum Creek; now she had cute silver cat's-eye glasses and tattoos on her arms. I'd worried that she wouldn't want to discuss Laura Ingalls Wilder at all, that the trip had left her disillusioned. But she was more than happy to talk about it—the saga of her Cambridge, Massachusetts, family trying to navigate the world of the midwestern RV parks; her teenage brother listening to the Dead Kennedys on his headphones; eight-year-old Meribah insisting that her mom braid and pin up her hair every morning to simulate a nineteenth-century hairstyle.

Meribah said she thought one reason why she'd gotten into the books in the first place had something to do with her liberal Cambridge upbringing in a neighborhood with Harvard professors. When Meribah dressed up as Laura for her third-grade class's Biography Day, so did another kid—a boy. "That's so Cambridge." She laughed. "I grew up with all these progressive ideas, all these people who were pushing the boundaries of things. So what could I rebel against?" As a result, she became fascinated with "ordinary things," which of course the Little House books celebrate in spades. "I mean, Laura was an average girl," she said.

I could tell Meribah and I were the same kind of Little House fan: we'd both never bothered with the TV show, since it didn't in any way resemble our own impressions of the books, and like me, she'd had the giving-Laura-a-tour-of-the-twentieth-century fantasy, though her version involved treating Laura to a modern Christmas, where "she'd get way more than just an orange and a piece of candy." But most of all, she kept talking about the trip as a way to visit a *world.*

I asked her if she'd felt like that world had still been there.

"Well, there were a few jarring things, but sure," she said. It turned out the disappointments she'd experienced along the way—finding Silver Lake drained, discovering De Smet mostly deserted on the Fourth of July—hadn't diminished the experience for her. Sixteen years later, long after she'd moved on from the Little House books (in fact, she'd forgotten plenty of the specifics, to the extent that at one point she asked, "What was Laura's husband's name? Alfonso?"), she still thought of the trip as one of the best experiences of her life.

"So it's all real?" I asked her. "I mean, you can say this?" Even though I knew I would still have to find out for myself.

"Oh yeah," she said. "It's for real."

8.

Fragments of a Dream

ETIQUETTE DICTATES THAT you can't invite yourself to a wedding, you shouldn't drop in on friends unexpectedly, and you really can't talk someone into letting you stay in their sod house. I found that last one out while planning the next trip, which was to be my most ambitious excursion into Laura World, in which Chris and I would visit three states and three and a half Laura Ingalls Wilder–related destinations in a single road trip.

The main objective was to see Walnut Grove in Minnesota, the setting for *On the Banks of Plum Creek*, and De Smet, South Dakota, where the rest of the books about Laura and her family took place—*By the Shores of Silver Lake, The Long Winter, Little Town on the Prairie, These Happy Golden Years*, and *The First Four Years*. Both towns had summer pageants—outdoor stage productions based on the books—and since they were only a few hours' drive apart from each other, it was possible to see both pageants in a single weekend. Of course I had to see them; doing so seemed to be one of the pillars of advanced Laura fandom.

Our big trip was planned for July and would also include stops in Spring Valley, Minnesota (I counted that one as only the "half" destination, since there wasn't much there), and Burr Oak, Iowa, the one childhood home that Laura hadn't written about in the Little House books. We'd be driving from Chicago across Wisconsin to Minnesota in a fourteen-hundred-mile loop across the upper Midwest. If we hadn't already visited Pepin in the spring, we could have easily added it to our route. Plenty of families, including Meribah Knight's, made a point of hitting Pepin, Walnut Grove, and De Smet in a single epic trip, and the towns tended to coordinate their festival and pageant schedules accordingly.

I started to get more of a sense of the history of Little House–related travel as I planned the trip and researched the homesites. It seems Laura tourism began in earnest partly as a result of the *Little House on the Prairie* TV show. Several of the homesite foundations and memorial societies were formed in the mid-'70s to address the mass interest in the real-life places where the Ingalls family had lived; suddenly there was a need for more than historical markers.

But Little House pilgrims had been popping up for years before that, even during Laura's lifetime. In addition to her visitors at Mansfield, Laura had received an enthusiastic letter in 1948 from a family who'd passed through De Smet, where one of the local residents had shown them her parents' things and had even let them take buttons from Ma's sewing box. I'd read about this in the introduction to *The Little House Guidebook,* by William Anderson (the Little House expert who'd begun his career in his teens). There's no indication as to whether or not Laura found it creepy to learn that her old neighbors were letting strangers rifle through her mother's belongings. God knows what they planned on giving away when they ran out of buttons. Good thing the pageants were created, I thought, no doubt in part to give folks something else to do besides paw through the Ingallses' sock drawers.

One of the places I wanted to see the most—to the extent that I'd gotten a little obsessed with it—wasn't a Little House site at all. It was an attraction called Sod House on the Prairie, a short drive east of Walnut Grove in Minnesota. It's exactly what it sounds like: a sod house, built and furnished twenty years ago by a local family, the McCones, using authentic historical methods. The exhibit on the McCone farm includes a dugout house, a log cabin, and a patch of restored prairie.

Until a few years ago, Virginia McCone had also been running the place as a bed-and-breakfast, where guests could spend a night in the sod house without electricity or indoor plumbing, only oil lamps and an outhouse.

Somehow the website made this sound appealing. Actually, it made it sound *totally amazing*. It was full of photos of the sod house against sun-dappled prairie vistas. The page for the bed-and-breakfast was still up, and it featured a photo of a woman, presumably a guest, sitting at an antique desk in the soddy wearing a prairie dress and reading a book. The guest testimonial read: *I feel the magic of Laura Ingalls surrounding me when I snuggle under the quilts, when I read by the oil lamp, and when I wash my hands and face using the pitcher and the basin.* Clearly this Virginia McCone lady understood the stuff of Laura World.

I was pretty let down when I realized the bed-and-breakfast option was no longer available. I'd even written Virginia an effusive e-mail to say how excited I was to be coming out to see the

Sod House on the Prairie on my Laura Ingalls Wilder journey and how *wonderful* it would have been to stay the night there, but *I understood* that it wasn't possible to do so anymore. Though of course by "I understood" I really meant "please make an exception for me, the hugest, sincerest, specialest Laura fan with my great big heart made of calico and sunflowers."

She wasn't buying it. She wrote back a nice e-mail that politely ignored my veiled groveling, telling me she'd love me to stop by and say hello when I came to Minnesota—if she was around, that is. "Now that I am retired from my Bed & Breakfast, I come and go more freely," she wrote. How dare she thwart my prairie dreams *by having a life*! I thought. But of course we could still see Sod House on the Prairie during the day.

I got over my disappointment, though, once I'd figured out that we could stay in a covered wagon in South Dakota. It turns out that the land claim that Pa Ingalls had filed on in *By the Shores of Silver Lake* had been turned into a living history park and campground, with space for tents, RVs, and a few "covered wagons," which rented for about fifty dollars a night. They weren't exactly the covered wagons of the books: from the pictures on the website they appeared to be sort of rustic hard-top campers with sleeping bunks, but it was enough for me. I'd called in April to make sure we could get one in July, and we were just lucky enough to get a small one for a single night. The lady who'd taken my reservation mailed me my credit card slip to confirm the transaction; it arrived, a week later, in a tiny hand-stamped envelope with "Ingalls Homestead" in De Smet, SD, printed on the return address.

Yes, *that* Ingalls Homestead: it hadn't really sunk in until I saw the envelope. For a moment I was mystified that it had come from that place. To give you an idea of how far gone I could get with my Laura World obsessive moonie-ness, remember that by now I'd been to Mansfield and seen Laura's house, her clothes, her bathroom, and yet I was still totally enchanted with the thought that the De Smet homestead land, this physical space where Laura had lived, actually still existed and *that mail came from there*. It was like getting a letter from the North Pole, only better.

As the week of the trip approached, I didn't want to leave anything to chance, so I ordered tickets online for the Walnut Grove pageant. The website for the De Smet pageant instructed me to call a phone number to order tickets in advance, but when I called, a young and slightly bored–sounding guy said, "Uh, the thing is? We've never run out of tickets. In like all the years we've been doing the pageant. I mean, you can just buy them when you're here."

Walnut Grove, Minnesota, was our first destination, a full day's drive from Chicago. The place has dual significance in the greater Little House universe. First, it's where the Ingallses lived on and off between 1874 and 1879, when they weren't recovering from crop failures or trying to run a hotel in Iowa. *On the Banks of Plum Creek* recounts the family's first stint living near Walnut Grove, first in the dugout near the creek, and then in the "wonderful house" that Pa built. In the book, Walnut Grove is simply "the town," the realm of all things store-boughten and nonprairie: the school, the church with its expensive bell, Beadle's and Oleson's rival mercantile businesses, and, of course, Nellie Oleson with her petticoats and parties and sugar-white cakes.

In the NBC show, Walnut Grove is all that and then some: Walnut Grove is *Walnut Grove*, the legendary TV town that took most of the "prairie" out of *Little House on the Prairie* and instead gave viewers a community of folks in old-timey clothing who bravely endure blizzards, droughts, epidemics, racism, drug abuse, gang violence, and franchise restaurant encroachment.

Late in her life Laura Ingalls Wilder wrote to the Walnut Grove newspaper and said that she was sorry she never mentioned the town by name in her novel. In light of that, it's a little ironic that now the words *Walnut Grove* tend to invoke the world of the TV show rather than the actual town and its role in Little House lore. Then again, maybe name checking the town in the books wouldn't have made much of a difference. After all, how could the Walnut Grove with a few intermittent years of Ingalls family history associated with it possibly compete for public attention with the Walnut Grove of ten television seasons plus twenty-five years of constant syndication?

I'm pretty sure the TV town was a little more populated than its historical counterpart, too: census statistics for 1880 state that the real-life Walnut Grove, Minnesota, had only 153 people living there, whereas the Internet Movie Database entry for *Little House on the Prairie* shows a sprawling cast list 234 names long. At any rate, it's not hard to tell the Walnut Groves apart. From what I've gathered from various *Little House on the Prairie* fan sites, the TV Walnut Grove even has its own separate history: founded in 1840 by that jolly Norwegian guy who ran the lumber mill; destroyed by dynamite some forty or fifty years later by its own citizens.

I know, right? You know, when I decided to try and catch up on watching *Little House on the Prairie* decades after the fact, there were a lot of things I hadn't counted on, like the crush I developed on Doc Baker (it's got to be those sideburns, I think) or the way I wept when some kid died of typhus, but I *really* hadn't counted on seeing the town get all blown up at the end of the series. No, seriously, *they blow it all up*, supposedly to foil a crooked real-estate developer who suddenly owns the town somehow, and honestly, I don't remember any of the other details beyond THEY BLOW IT ALL UP.

By that point, the plot of the show sort of didn't matter; by then, the story was really about the cast and crew who were saying good-bye. Among other things. According to Melissa Gilbert in her memoir, *Prairie Tale*, Michael Landon's decision to blow up the sets was a deliberate gesture, since no one at NBC had bothered to officially notify him that the show had been canned despite the fact that he'd been working for them for over twenty years. When Gilbert quotes him saying, "I'm going to blow the whole fucking thing up," my brain reflexively responds in Ma's voice: *Charles, no!* But of course blowing the *effing* thing up was very much in the spirit of the TV *Little House on the Prairie*, where there was no grievance that Michael Landon-as-Pa couldn't settle with a good swift punch. (But only if he *had* to, which was approximately every other episode.)

But in a way, the whole cancellation situation was also a little reminiscent of the original Little House books, with their moments of failure and disappointment. Here were these people who'd worked hard for ten years to cultivate their own little settlement on the prime-time frontier—because when you think about it, isn't every TV season a wilderness to be braved? What show doesn't want to stick it out through the long winters of sweeps months long enough to prove up on its time-slot claim?—only to find out that they'd lost it, that it was time to move on. Melissa Gilbert says that the cast didn't want to see the sets used in other productions, "to have other people tromping through places where many of us had grown up." There's something decidedly Little House-ish about that, too, though it's probably not the sort of thing the real-life Ingallses would have concerned themselves with, in all the times they had to move and leave everything they'd built behind. No, being homesick for all those little houses has long been left up to us, the readers.

And the TV viewers, too. Because lest you underestimate the deep connection some people feel to the NBC Walnut Grove, I submit these verbatim excerpts of a Tripod.com webpage that I found one night, written in 2004 by a man known only as "Lorenzo." It seems that the remaining *Little House on the Prairie* exterior sets in Simi Valley, California—the titular Little House, the church, the school for the blind, and a few more structures that hadn't been "blowed up" in the finale—had burned down in 2003 during the destructive wildfires that year. Apparently this news left Lorenzo so bereft that he put up a single webpage to announce an ambitious endeavor:

> What I am looking forward to doing, is rebuilding the Little
> House and the rest of the Town as well as planting Trees because
> the sets burned down, I will need to get the blue prints of all the
> sets and I would like to locate all locations of where each house in
> the town were located. . . . hopefully we could find trees the same
> size and put them in the same locations if possible—it would be
> great to have this Scenery again. It must be sad for Melissa Gil-
> bert to see no trees or grass no town, since she grow up there.

Lorenzo (whose only available e-mail address bounced, to my dismay) hadn't quite worked out the particulars of his plan—"I will still need to get permission to rebuild the whole town of Walnut Grove, so please check back soon," he wrote—but he was hoping that with the help of volunteers, donated materials, and proceeds from selling *Little House* memorabilia, T-shirts, and other merchandise that he had yet to procure, he could make it happen. He believed the rebuilt set could not only function as a tourist attraction for fans but also open up the possibility for new *Little House on the Prairie* episodes and TV movies to be filmed. He also seemed to just want to experience a little of the community spirit that the TV Walnut Grove embodied—that sense of hey-we'll-all-come-together-and-build-this-thing that characterized so many episodes. It would all start, he said, with a fund-raising rally in the parking lot of the Simi Valley set location.

"And I would like to have a Dance party there," he wrote at the very end of his missive. "So bring your dancing Shoes, to dance to the 80's."

(That part makes me especially wish that Lorenzo's vision had come to pass.)

And who could blame him for wanting a place like Walnut Grove, this place he knew so well in his mind, to still exist? It was the same reason why Chris and I were driving over five hundred miles in a single day, across the dullest part of Minnesota ever.

It was late afternoon when we started seeing the wind turbines, dozens of them. They filled the horizon and kept emerging from every direction ahead of us. Sometimes they loomed close to the road, great big spindly things with huge pinwheel heads turning slowly. We'd never seen so many of them before and had never seen a landscape so transformed by them. The sight was like something Laura would have seen—the open land one day changed by the seam of railroad tracks and the swooping lines of telegraph wires; the whole main street of De Smet emerging above the prairie in just two weeks.

We drove through the turbines for nearly an hour. The last ones we passed stayed visible for a long time behind us, lit up by the low sun in the rearview mirrors. I could still see them by the time we turned onto Route 14, the Laura Ingalls Wilder Memorial Highway.

Like a lot of the towns we passed, the first thing you see of Walnut Grove is its grain elevator. The business district lies behind it, beyond a gas station. The railroad tracks that run through town—parallel to the highway—look to be the same line that was still being built west at the time of the Little House books.

There's plenty of indication, official and otherwise, that the town is a Laura Ingalls Wilder destination, from the signs by the road to the faded but elaborate mural that depicts Laura in front of Plum Creek, looking a little grim-faced as she carries two giant buckets.

This Walnut Grove, the real one, had its first settlers in 1870; they were the Nelsons, the same Norwegian family who were neighbors to the Ingalls family in *On the Banks of Plum Creek*. When the railroad came through in 1873, the town began to establish itself; it was still a new town when the Ingalls family moved to nearby Plum Creek a year later.

The history on the town's website doesn't go much beyond that—you'd almost think the town just ceased to exist sometime in the late 1800s the way the TV town did (albeit with less of a bang). What happened instead was that Walnut Grove simply stayed a small town. You can guess that some of what's not written about Walnut Grove's past 120 years is also the history of thousands of small towns in the rural Midwest: the decline of family farms and job opportunities.

For the last thirty years, the connection to Laura Ingalls Wilder has influenced the town's fortunes in ways both typical—i.e., Little House tourism—and unexpected. Minnesota has one of the largest Hmong immigrant populations in the United States, and some accounts say that Walnut Grove's first Hmong residents were attracted to the town by the TV show. According to a 2004 Minnesota Public Radio segment, Harry Yang, the proprietor of an Asian grocery store in Walnut Grove, settled there on the advice of his daughter, who was a fan of the show and who thought it would be a good place to live because the people on the show seemed nice. The subsequent Hmong who moved there increased Walnut Grove's population (to nearly nine hundred, by some estimates), and now make up a quarter of the community. An essay by David Griffith in the book *New Faces in New Places: The Changing Geography of American Immigration* reports that the Hmong families in Walnut Grove helped the housing market, kept a school from closing, and have been admired by many of the longtime residents for their traditional family values.

Indeed, we saw Harry Yang's grocery store on Main Street. It was closed for the evening, along with the handful of gift stores, the museum, and Nellie's, a diner that faced Route 14 and appeared considerably more unassuming than its namesake restaurant on the TV show. The business district was only about two blocks, and there weren't any motels in town. We had reservations at the Wilder Inn in Tracy, a town just to the west, so we headed back out on Route 14.

"Wait a minute," Chris said, after we'd been driving for a few minutes. "*How* far is Tracy?" He was reading *By the Shores of Silver Lake,* which meant he'd just read the part where Laura, Mary, Carrie, and Ma had taken their first train ride, to the end of the line in Tracy, an experience that merited its very own chapter, "Riding in the Cars," one of my favorites.

"Seven miles, but that doesn't sound right, does it?" I'd seen how close it was on the map, but I didn't quite believe it myself. I'd always had the idea that the train ride described in *Silver Lake* took hours. Well, maybe not *hours* but certainly long enough for Laura to give Mary a highly detailed inventory of the train's interior, the passengers, the view outside, and the fascinating water fountain (and didn't it sound like the best fountain in the world?); take a drink from aforementioned fascinating water fountain; buy candy from vendor; distribute candy among siblings; and finally, consume the candy in that protracted trademark Ingalls one-restrained-lick-at-a-time fashion, yes?

Now, though, the trip by car on Route 14 was just long enough for the oldies radio station to play "Oye Como Va" and part of "Bette Davis Eyes."

On our drive back to Walnut Grove for dinner, we tried to figure out the puzzle. Maybe, back in Laura's day, distances were measured in special prairie miles, or else the whole town of Tracy had simply been picked up by a tornado at some point and moved about thirty miles closer, or else there was a wormhole, or something. It wasn't until we remembered that the train in the book went only *twenty miles an hour* at its fastest that it started to make sense, in a wretched math-word-problem kind of way. A train nudging along the prairie at the same rate as the #81 bus in Chicago rush-hour traffic would be a long trip indeed, long enough for a rich, epic swath of Little House description.

We had dinner at the Walnut Grove Bar and Grill, which sported a Miller Lite banner reading *GREAT FOOD/COLD BEER/SMOKE-FREE ROOM/HOME OF LAURA INGALLS WILDER*. The waitress told us how to get to the pageant grounds, and so just past dusk we drove out, over the creek, up a hill, and into a little valley where the amphitheater lay. The final rehearsal was in progress—we could see just a glimpse of the stage, cast members dancing in a pool of light beyond the parking field. We turned the car around to head back. It was a warm night and we had the windows down as we drove down the hill. Even though the stage was a quarter of a mile away, voices from the rehearsal still carried; we could hear a girl's excited shriek on the wind.

We Invite You to Experience the Lifestyle of Laura Ingalls, read the sign along the side of the road just outside the McCone farm, home of the Sod House on the Prairie attraction. We'd come out here just after breakfast at Nellie's, driving east on 14. We parked in the driveway of the farmhouse and Virginia came out to say hello and collect our admission fee. She was in her fifties, and with her quiet good-naturedness she reminded me of one of my favorite grade-school teachers. She pointed out the gate that led out back to the exhibit.

"Enjoy it," she told us. "Feel free to look around as much as you want."

We walked along a narrow path through the prairie; the grass was tall enough and the sod house so low-slung that we could only see the roof, which had a thin layer of grass growing on top.

From the signs along the path we learned that the main sod house was "a rich man's soddy." As sod buildings went, the dugout where the Ingalls had lived in *On the Banks of Plum Creek* had been a pretty basic model, but the place the McCones had built was the extra-fancy kind, really the Cadillac Escalade of sod houses—big, with glass windows and wood floors and plaster walls. It looked a little crusty on the outside, but inside was one big, bright room, with two beds made up with patchwork quilts, an iron cookstove, a wooden table and chairs, a cradle, two rocking chairs, a wardrobe, and a washbasin and pitcher on a stand. The wooden ceiling beams were just a few inches over our heads and the door and windows were low on the walls. It all looked exactly like the place where an old woman would live in a fairy tale.

In fact, I'd forgotten for a moment that I'd come here to feel like I was in Laura World, but from looking at the guestbook on the table, it was clear that other visitors had had strong associations.

"I really do feel like I am in the time of Little House on the Prairie," one visitor had written.

"This place is so real," wrote a girl who said she was visiting with her grandparents. "It is just like Laura Ingalls used to live in. I read the books, too. I am from Connor, Minnesota."

Others had felt compelled to write poetic-sounding things: "I only wish today had the beautiful hearts of days gone by." Next to the guestbook was a binder filled with clippings about the exhibit, testimonial letters, and various journal entries and bits of creative writing composed by bed-and-breakfast guests. Flipping through the pages it occurred to me that Sod House on the Prairie was not so much a history museum as it was a sort of inspirational retreat, where people came to commune with the past and tap into its muselike powers.

There was a lot of misguided nostalgia, to be sure, but as someone who had once decided that her writing could only improve if she wrote first drafts in the same kind of orange-covered notebooks Laura used, and thus spent an hour and a half searching online to see if some stationery company somewhere still made them, I understood.

A few things in the sod house had *Do Not Touch* signs on them—a china cabinet, a little glass display case—but Virginia had encouraged everything else to be hands-on.

There were at least half a dozen sunbonnets on the beds, all different sizes and styles. The brochure had mentioned "prairie clothes to dress in" and I remembered the photo of the woman in the calico dress on the website. While I still wasn't sure how I personally felt about dressing up, I liked the notion of prairie clothes as amenities, courtesy items just like mints or hand lotion. Just like the marijuana bars in Amsterdam, you could experiment without judgment.

We went out and looked at the tiny log cabin, and then the dugout, which had the bare gray sod walls on the inside and a dirt floor that was packed so hard it shone. Over the bed there was a sagging clothesline with a couple of stiff cotton things hanging from it, as if the hypothetical tenants were too depressed to even go outside to dry their laundry. The brochure had promised the dugout would have an "eerie feeling of hardship," and there certainly was one, along with the musty smell and the shower of dust I got down my back when I stepped into one of the crumblier corners. Chris brushed off the back of my shirt for me.

"Okay, that was enough hardship," I said. "Let's go."

We tried going farther along one of the little paths through the prairie grass. It was gorgeous, but after the morning rain the heat felt unusually thick and prickly, enough to wilt my impulse to explore and stroll around like Holly Hobbie.

By now there were other visitors. Three of them, a pair of women with a grade-school-aged girl in tow, practically settled in at the big sod house. One of them rifled through an armoire and tossed antique books on the bed.

"Gina, what are you *doing*?" her friend said. She was trying out the rocking chair while the girl flipped through the scrapbook binders.

"They said we could explore," said Gina, as she opened a wardrobe. "What are these, nightgowns?" she asked, grabbing one of the things that hung from wooden pegs.

"They're *prairie dresses*, Gina," her friend called. "They're for putting on."

"What, like for taking pictures?" Gina asked.

"For whatever," the woman in the rocking chair said. "You know, for fun."

⚘

On our way out we stopped at the farmhouse to talk to Virginia. She pointed out her husband, Stan, who'd waved at us and the other visitors but appeared to be busy working on something farmy and important over by the big sheds across the yard. The sun was hot on the porch so Virginia invited us inside to her kitchen and talked to us while she tended a pot of beets on the stove.

She told us a little bit about the history of the sod house. Stan had gotten the idea to build one after he'd found an old sod cutter, a special kind of plow. "He used a tractor instead of horses to pull the cutter," she admitted. Apparently Virginia's husband was "one of those people who should have lived in another era"—she said that he'd built the sod house as a personal challenge and because he'd wanted to preserve something of the local history. There had once been plenty of sod houses in the area, but none had survived.

I was surprised that Virginia hadn't read the Little House books as a kid. She'd gotten so much about the Laura World fantasy *right* in the sod house exhibit that I'd sort of assumed she was building on a long-standing dream from childhood. "No, I grew up on a farm," she explained, "and my family were not readers." In high school, though, she was drawn toward English and for a while she was a teacher, she told us.

"Are you sure the beet smell isn't getting to you?" she asked us. She went over to the stove and checked the boiling pot. There was a slight earthy smell, but we weren't bothered. She sighed and shook her head. "You know, I can barely stand it," she said. "Beets are great, except when they're cooking."

Back to the subject of Laura: Virginia said she hadn't ever watched the TV *Little House on the Prairie*, either. In fact, she hadn't really discovered the books at all "until we were doing *this*," she said, nodding in the direction of the sod house.

"But now, she's an inspiration to me—Laura, I mean," she said. "Because I felt like I should write my mom's story." Virginia had written a book about her late mother's experience with Alzheimer's and published it on her own in 2002. It was called *Butterscotch Sundaes*, and there was a page about it on the Sod House on the Prairie website, with an article reprinted from a newspaper in Tracy.

In the book Virginia had written about how her mother had

gotten into wandering moods on the prairie; she'd tried to give her the freedom to roam around. She'd had to learn to understand her mother "wherever she was at," even if it was somewhere other than the present moment. Watching an aging parent for signs of illness, Virginia said, was like scanning the prairie horizon for storm clouds. (Yes, it was, I thought.)

Virginia said she'd been terrified to write the book, but she'd thought, well, Laura could do it. She'd started out writing for the local papers the way, she noted, Laura had written for the *Missouri Ruralist*. "Just writing those kind of human-interest columns, you know?" she said. For all the sunbonnet dress-up she endorsed, she seemed to know the real-person version of Laura Ingalls Wilder better than most people.

And as for the prairie dress-up stuff, "That was something I soon caught on to," she said, not too long after she and Stan opened the bed-and-breakfast in the completed sod house. The B&B had been his idea at first. "I thought, 'Who in the world would want to do this? And why would people want to pay us money?' I was totally out of touch about that." But of course the visitors started coming, and eventually Virginia figured out that they were coming for Laura.

"People would ask, 'Is this where she really lived? And how long did *she* live here? And when did *she* move?'" At first Virginia wondered who this "she" was. But once she understood, she put a few bonnets and aprons in the armoire of the sod house, just for ambience. "And then people would ask, very gently, if they could put them on," she said.

Now that the sod house was no longer a bed-and-breakfast, the place officially opened at sunrise. Visitors stopping by on their

way to Walnut Grove could drop their admission fee in a pay box
if the McCones weren't up yet.

"Do people really show up that early?" I asked her.

"All the time," Virginia said. "You should have been here."

By the time we were back in Walnut Grove, there was a line of
parked cars and RVs along the grass by the railroad tracks outside the museum, which was housed in a relocated railroad depot
building. The museum is a monument to the two Walnut Groves.
The first room is dedicated to the usual Ingalls family history stuff
and exhibits about some of the real-life locals who'd been the basis
for characters in *On the Banks of Plum Creek.* You can see a photo
of Nellie Owens, one of the three girls on whom the character of
Nellie Oleson was based, and who, like her fictional counterpart,
had a brother named Willie and a father who owned a mercantile
store in Walnut Grove. She looked ordinary, ordinary and bru-
nette; I would read later that the golden ringlet curls were a trait of
one of the other two girls on whom Nellie Oleson was modeled.
You had to feel a little sorry for Nellie Owens, that so much of her
life was appropriated and yet she didn't even get to have the hair.

I must admit to you now that we spent far more time in the
second room of the museum. Yes, the *TV show* room. After the
gently lit glass cases, didactic placards, and careful foam-board
displays of the real Walnut Grove history, the museum room dedicated to the NBC *Little House on the Prairie* was lit with fluorescent lights and full of fabulous crap. A TV on a stand in the corner
of the room played episodes with the sound at low volume, and
the walls were lined with framed stills and commemorative plates.

Chris stopped in front of a promotional still for a 1983 episode titled "For the Love of Blanche," in which Mr. Edwards inherits a baby orangutan. In the photo Victor French is holding an ape. The ape is wearing a sunbonnet.

"Why have I not seen this episode?" Chris demanded. "WHERE HAS THIS BEEN ALL MY LIFE?"

"We'll try to TiVo it when we get home," I told him.

At the far end of the room was the front of the actual fireplace mantelpiece salvaged from the set of the Ingalls family kitchen. It had been installed in the wall, with the hearth painted black. Nobody seemed to pay it much attention, though I'd read in Melissa Gilbert's memoir that when she'd visited here she'd sniffed it to see if it still smelled like her old memories of the set. (She said it hadn't.)

The real appeal of the TV show room seemed to be all the vintage merchandise from the '70s on display—lunch boxes, dolls, buttons, paperbacks, posters, even a board game with spaces that proclaimed "Good Harvest" and "All's Well That Ends Well." It was a little stunning to see relics from the era of my own childhood, wonderfully cruddy stuff. We could have stayed there all day, flipping through the binders that held clippings, photos of cast member visits, and even a *Mad Magazine* parody (which was titled "Little House, Oh So Dreary," and Chris could barely contain his joy when we found it).

The museum continued in the lot behind the depot, in a series of scaled-down replica buildings: a tiny chapel, a schoolhouse, and a little frame house that was reportedly similar to the "wonderful house" that Pa had built. Inside, a sign encouraged us to "notice the fresh pine smell from the sawed lumber." (It was a nice scent, but such an utterly familiar one that I found myself wishing that the mantelpiece back in the TV show room really *did* still smell like Melissa Gilbert's childhood, because how many people can say they've smelled *that*?)

Despite all these sensory prompts, there was so much about the Ingallses' real life that I couldn't quite grasp. The museum had its own replica dugout (the second one we'd seen that day), a little hutlike dwelling that was built to actual-size specifications. Supposedly it was as big as the place where the Ingalls family lived. It was also smaller than a freight elevator.

"Well, the Ingallses were *small* people," I pointed out to Chris at first when we looked inside. I would find myself saying that a lot whenever we came across the tiny living spaces where Laura and her family had lived. I realize now what I meant was that the size of these places seemed right and wrong all at once. The real Ingallses, I knew, were somewhat on the wee side, and they lived in a time and place where fuel for heat was scarce. Yes, I'd admit to myself, they could certainly live in little rooms like these with their relatively few possessions and their cultural acclimation to living in close quarters. Yes, of course, the Ingallses were small people, living in their cramped, chilly history.

But as for the Ma and Pa and Laura and Mary of the books, the Ingalls family of *my mind*—no way was *their* dugout this small, I kept thinking. Once again, the actual past and the Little House world had different properties. Later that night we would go back to the motel and I would flip through *Plum Creek* to see how much weirder things were with these new dimensions. I'd seen how the room was so small that you could see everything in a single glance, and yet, in chapter 2, when the Ingallses move into the dugout, the book says Ma *found* a broom in the corner of the room. Which sort of implies that she had to go *looking* for it.

"Well, you said Ma was small," Chris pointed out.

"Small like a person. Not *Tinkerbell* small," I said.

And then there was that part when Laura and Mary made the button-string for little Carrie at Christmas; they'd had to keep it a secret from Carrie by hiding it and only working on it when she was napping. Now, when I imagined how it all took place in that tiny room, the whole thing was absurd. What had once seemed like a cozy scene was now practically a Beckett play, with everyone having to turn their backs to everyone else for privacy. All the cooking and fiddling and ironing and living that the Ingalls family did in that room seemed nearly impossible. Except in Laura World it wasn't. I had to keep remembering that.

❧

I'd had a crazy notion to walk out and see where the family had lived near Plum Creek. After all, it was only about two miles from town—Laura and Mary had walked the distance to school on a daily basis, in bare feet no less; surely in my flip-flops I could get a sense of what it was like, yes? I asked the woman at the museum gift store who'd been giving us directions.

"I *guess* some people walk out there," she said. "But you really should drive. Because, I mean, you walk out there, and then you gotta walk *back*." So we drove. Good thing, because the barefoot prairie jaunt I'd imagined would've amounted to trudging two miles of shadeless cornfield at one p.m. in July.

The Ingallses' preemption land claim is now private farmland, still owned by the same family that was visited by Garth Williams on his research trip in 1947; until then, nobody in Walnut Grove had really been aware of the connection between their town and the Little House books. By the time Williams showed up, the house that Pa had built in *On the Banks of Plum Creek* was gone, with only a few guesses as to its location or fate, but Williams found what was left of the sod dugout on the creek. The site began to get regular tourists in the 1970s when the TV show became popular.

I'd heard that until the museum was built in town, the family who owned the property had had to contend with confused visitors who often descended on their house believing it had once belonged to the Ingallses. Now things were considerably more organized, and for a small fee they allowed a steady stream of cars and tour buses to wind through their front yard on their way to the creek area. We pushed a few bucks into the self-serve pay box by the barn and then drove until we came to a clearing and parked. The creek was ahead, somewhere in the trees; we could see a medium-sized footbridge that led across to the dugout site.

"This is perhaps the most unchanged of all the book locales," *The Little House Guidebook* proclaims of this area. I was skeptical at first, until I saw the creek. Which really *is* just a creek, and at first glance you can easily forget that it is in fact a famous creek until you really look at it and recognize it. And I did: I *knew* it, and my mind shrieked *Plum Creek!* It was clear and shallow and flowing healthily along. I made Chris stop on the footbridge so I could look.

"Here it is," I told him, as if I'd found it myself.

We went on over to the high bank on the other side, where the dugout house—the real one—had been. It was now a hollow spot marked by a large wooden sign; the ground was marked off with ropes in a rough square, either to show where the walls had been or to keep people off. Locals believe the dugout had caved in at least twenty years before Garth Williams had found it, and it was clear something had broken there under that particular patch of ground.

People kept coming up the path to the dugout; we all hovered around and stood at the ropes, peering over. "Anybody could walk over this house and never know it's here," Ma had said in *On the Banks of Plum Creek*, but now anyone could see where the house had ceased to exist. More than any of the other sites, the dugout ruin was simply evidence. Unlike the log cabins I'd visited or the two replica dugouts I'd seen today, there was no pretense at trying to capture what it felt like to live here, no invoking those proverbial Eerie Feelings of Hardship. Somehow it was enough to see the surroundings, the shady creek bank, and the prairie that began at the edge of the crumbled roof. None of it was different from anything I'd seen before (it really *was* just a creek), but something about that little pit in the ground changed everything. It felt as if the dugout hadn't so much collapsed as it had simply turned inside out, so that the immediate world around it felt intimate and removed, as secret as a cave.

I was going to wade in the creek. Others were doing it—both adults and kids were seeking out clear spots along the bank where it was easy to step into the water. I found a place where the dirt was smooth from the feet of other visitors. I took off my flip-flops and stepped awkwardly down the slope of the bank. The water felt nice. A little cloud of silt rose up with each step, just like *On the Banks of Plum Creek* had described. Or it was just like each step I'd taken in the creek at the campground where my family spent weekends when I was a kid. I don't know which had come first, my own experience or the book, but either way, that smokelike swirl that wavered in the water was how I knew the book was true.

I stopped wading and stood still. I had to forgive the awkwardness, the feetfirst unwieldiness of trying to enter the world of the book this way, standing in the water with my shoulder bag and my cameras. It helped a bit to listen to the water and all the summer noises, birds and things rasping away and making clattering calls to each other; somehow it was quiet enough to hear them.

I looked up. A little girl about seven years old was standing on the bank. She'd stopped short when she saw me, and I could tell she was trying to reconcile her sense of Laura World with the strangely crowded reality: here was Plum Creek, but here was this *lady*, too. Over the course of the trip there'd be other little encounters like this, usually with kids but sometimes with adults, too, where everyone's reveries bumped up against one another. Chris told me later that the girl at the creek looked at him as if to say, *Is she going to stay in there all day?* But I knew it was time to get out. I climbed up the bank and picked up my shoes.

As we walked back to the car, I could see other people trying to have their private creek moments, children and adults alike, everyone standing in their little rings in the water.

We had time to kill before the historic bus tour and decided to wait it out over lunch at the Walnut Grove Bar and Grill. We sat in the bar room, at a table next to the only other people there, two guys nursing a pitcher of beer. They both wore baseball caps. The older guy was big, with a shaggy gray beard and overalls; the younger guy had a sunburned face and he kept getting up to throw darts at the electric dartboard.

"You in town for the Wilder festival?" the big guy with the

beard asked us. Yes, we told him, and I asked him if he lived nearby. He shook his head. "We're here for fishing," he said.

"From Iowa," the younger guy added as he poured more beer into his glass.

"We were at that lake around here yesterday. Lake Shetek," Big Beard said. "And then we heard about that Laura contest, so I brought my grandkids down so they could enter."

It was then that I noticed the two girls at the pool table in the corner. They looked to be about nine or ten. They appeared almost identical at first, both sweetly chubby and with their fine brown hair French-braided into pigtails. They were taking turns trying to hit the pool balls, the huge pool cues teetering in their hands.

"The Laura contest? Wow," I said.

The girls sensed our attention and wandered back over toward the table where their grandfather sat; they seemed happy to not have to entertain themselves. One of the girls wore glasses and appeared to be slightly older; the younger one grabbed a handful of popcorn from a basket on their table. She had a black T-shirt with something spelled out on it in rhinestone letters.

"So you're here with your grandpa?" I asked them.

"Our uncle, too," the younger girl said. Neither girl seemed particularly shy. They both had a deadpan matter-of-factness about them that I loved. They didn't tell me their names, but I didn't ask, either.

Grandpa Big Beard told us about how they hadn't been quite sure when the Laura contest was; he and his son had been coming up to fish for a couple of weekends hoping they'd catch it. Finally they'd figured out the right weekend. Only the contest wasn't until tomorrow.

"Grandpa thought it was *today*," the older girl said.

"But we're going to do it tomorrow," her sister said.

"Are you going to get all dressed up in your prairie clothes?" I asked them. The girls exchanged a look with each other.

"Well, we already are," the older girl said.

"Oh," I said. Now that I looked more closely I could see both girls were wearing longish skirts. The older girl had one with a handkerchief hem, a brief trend from a couple of years ago, and she wore it with a slightly crumpled white button-down shirt. To my eyes it looked more parochial school than prairie, but I tried hard to see what kind of elements might have appeared right to her—a certain flounce in the skirt, perhaps, and with the tucked-in blouse, a sort of Sunday-morning sense of propriety as reassuring as the ribbons Ma tied in Laura's braids. "Oh yes . . . you are dressed up, aren't you?"

"See my skirt?" the younger girl said. Her tiered brown prairie skirt went almost to her ankles and was a little too big in the waist; I wondered if it was borrowed from an older sister, maybe. I could tell that her shirt had once said *Farmer's Girl*, but the rhinestone letters spelling *Girl* had worn off completely.

These little girls here in the bar, I watched them as they drank Mountain Dew and ran over to the self-serve popcorn machine and filled their baskets. I wondered how it would go for them the next day when they'd line up with all these other little Lauras—lucky kids in pristine color-coordinated prairie dresses that their mothers had bought (or perhaps even sewn for them in between homeschooling sessions). I didn't want to think about it. The older girl was wearing a scruffy pair of women's shoes, chunky old platform loafers with buckles. Clearly she understood the essential grimness of nineteenth-century footwear and had tried to find something similarly dreary. How did she know there's nothing bleaker than dress shoes from 1998? In her own way, she'd nailed it, I thought. I admired her.

While we waited for our food, I'd taken out my laptop so I could upload some pictures to it from my camera. The younger girl came over to watch the screen. Meanwhile, Grandpa Big Beard talked to us about the TV show, which he said he watched every day. He said he liked it better when the Hallmark Channel aired the episodes in the morning instead of the afternoon. Recently they'd put the show on hiatus for a month and put *Golden Girls* in that time slot and he'd had to "get on the computer" so he could protest. He noted that he'd gone to the network website just two days after the show had stopped airing and he was the 127th person to post a complaint.

"Who wants to hear about the sex life of that woman, you know, what's her name, Bea Arthur?" he said.

"Not many people," Chris guessed.

The older girl stopped in front of our table on her way back from the popcorn machine.

"I'm going to be a singer when I grow up," she said to us. "My favorite singer is Taylor Swift."

Whatever her prairie fantasies consisted of, they existed right alongside dreams of superstardom. I'm sure it had been the same way with me and every other girl who'd ever been nine years old and loved the Little House books. I wondered whether wanting to be both a pop star *and* Laura meant that you understood, on some level, that you probably couldn't be either. Then again, who was I to second-guess these girls? They played with the touch screen on the Internet jukebox, gazing at one screen after another, sharing the space the way the Ingalls girls might have shared Pa's big green book of animals.

I noticed their grandfather was wearing a Laura Ingalls Wilder Museum T-shirt and I asked him about it. He said he'd gotten it last year when he visited. "Carrie and her twin sister came up here to the festival last year," he told us. I knew he was talking about Lindsay and Sidney Greenbush, the twins who'd played Carrie Ingalls on the TV show. They must have made a guest appearance in Walnut Grove, the way some of the *LHOP* cast members did. "So I was going to try to see them, but they was gone by the time I got here," he said. I liked how he seemed to do things at his own pace.

Chris checked his watch. We had about fifteen minutes before the bus tour started. Then again, it was only a block away. Everything in Walnut Grove proper seemed to be only a block away from everything else.

"So which one of you is going to win the Laura contest?" I asked the girls, who had pushed their chairs over so far they were practically sitting at our table by now. "Or are you both going to win?" It was a dumb question, exactly the sort of thing a grown-up would ask.

"I don't know," the older girl said, shrugging at her sister, who shrugged back.

"Ummm . . ." said the younger girl, picking at the rhinestones on her shirt. Finally she pointed to the older girl. "She'll win."

"Yeah, I'm going to win a million dollars!" the older girl said. She paused and thought for a moment. "Wait, so what do you win, anyway?" She looked at me, but I didn't know.

"I'm going to win a million *dolls*," the younger girl said. "That sounds good."

"It does," I agreed.

"And you could be Ma," she said. The older girl nodded in agreement.

"You think so?" My heart leapt at the suggestion, even though I didn't know what it meant, although it could mean lots of things. Over the last hour the girls had gravitated to Chris and me as if to say, *Take us with you maybe*.

"Sure," the older girl said. "If there was a contest."

"I wish there was a contest," I told them. It was true. The idea of dressing up in prairie clothes as an adult had been a slightly foreign notion that I was willing to entertain, but suddenly I wished, right then, that the Walnut Grove Annual Laura-Nellie Look Alike Contest had a grown-up division that I could enter; and that I had a green delaine dress and a straw bonnet that I could wear. I wished that these girls had calico dresses with matching pinafores and sunbonnets and that we could sit around all day together eating popcorn. I would teach them how to cross-stitch and resist the negative messages in fashion magazines. We could make button-strings, braid rag rugs, and wash and dry dishes carefully. I wanted to be their Prairie Ma, sort of like a fairy godmother but more earthbound, making sure, to paraphrase Caroline Ingalls, that all was well and that they ended up well.

We boarded the school bus for our tour and waited as the cramped seats filled up with people. From the front window of the bus I could see down the block to the restaurant, and I watched for the two girls, hoping that their uncle and grandfather hadn't forgotten about the tour. I was relieved when at last they all came up the street. They were almost the last people on the bus.

On the tour we saw where a lot of things had once stood: the schoolhouse, the church, the house where Laura's teacher had lived. "That's probably not the original house," the young woman guide kept saying of the places we passed. The irony of Walnut Grove as a pilgrimage destination is that for a place that so strongly evoked "town" in *On the Banks of Plum Creek*, almost nothing of the town that Laura knew has survived, and the only physical trace left is the dugout, the countriest of country things, which had been left behind in the wake of progress.

We *did* see the church bell that Pa had helped pay for, though the Congregational church that Reverend Alden had built was long gone. The bell now hung in the belfry of a squat, modern brick Lutheran church, and the bus stopped in front while the guide ran inside to ring it. We all bent forward in our seats to try and peer up at the belfry as the bell clanged away, at least a dozen medium-bodied peals.

It turned out the tour also stopped at Plum Creek, so we wound up there a second time. It was late afternoon, and now the place was more crowded; everyone paced up and down the paths and milled around the dugout site.

We saw a large family where more than half the members were in prairie garb—two women, a couple little girls, and a boy in a white shirt and suspenders. A teenage girl in jeans and a tank top slouched alongside them. I was hoping that I could just walk up to one of these sunbonneted women and talk to them, that when they responded they would be speaking back from the place they were trying to get to by dressing like that and I would learn something along the way. But all I could manage when two of the women passed close to me on the path along the creek was "Hello."

"Hello!" the two women called back. One woman's eyes met mine for a moment. A little too long of a moment, it seemed; too long for either of us to begin a conversation naturally. I nodded at the women and let them go.

There were even more people in the creek—whole families gathered at the banks in organized wading expeditions. Parents shouted directions: *Roll your pants up more, Tyler. Now get your shoes back on. We're heading back to the car.*

As we walked along the creek again, we saw the older of the two girls we'd just met. "Did you get to go in the creek?" I asked her.

"Yeah," she said. She smiled shyly. She seemed more self-conscious out here in the sunlight and grass, and her big clunky shoes looked uncomfortable now. She must have hated to put them on again. She shrugged at me and hurried off to catch up with her family.

At the pageant that night we found our seats in the rows of folding chairs. The stage set was a replica of everything we'd seen that day: a row of mock storefronts simulating Walnut Grove; a dugout on the stage-right side, complete with a soft halo of prairie grass hovering above it; and even an artificial garden pond to represent Plum Creek.

The Walnut Grove Wilder Pageant is titled "Fragments of a Dream," and according to the program guide it was first performed in the auditorium of the Walnut Grove school in 1978. The original script had been from Ma's point of view, but over the years it had been revised with more of an emphasis on the town and the founding residents. There were nearly fifty roles in the pageant, including more than a dozen walk-on roles for kids, and nearly half the cast list was comprised of Bedals, Kennedys, and Nelsons, families the Ingallses had known. (The Owens were still called the Olesons, though, most likely because their fictionalized counterparts were so well known from the TV show.)

The really great thing about the program booklet was that instead of running cast member bios it included brief histories of these founding families, some of whom had had their own share of pioneer misery: "Lafayette Bedal was killed in a sawmill accident in Aiken, Minnesota," read one of them. Another described how Amassa Tower, a church deacon, was killed by lightning on the prairie; his wife, who'd been Laura's Sunday school teacher, drowned in a well during an attack of insanity. I pointed that part out to Chris.

"Is that going to be in the pageant?" he asked in amazement. Probably not, I told him.

The rows were filling up and people were setting up lawn chairs on the grassy hill behind us. We had come a little too early, and after the long day the folding chairs were already uncomfortable. I began to wish we were back at the motel watching TV. I remembered Meribah Knight telling me she hadn't much liked the pageants on the trip she'd taken. "I already had a version of the book in my head and it wasn't anything like the stuff onstage," she said. "Everyone was just sort of shouting their lines." I could definitely understand how it might be that way. I began to wonder why anyone even went to these things.

The lights on the stage changed and the music started. A row or two in front of me, two teenage girls pulled their sunbonnets up on their heads in a gesture that seemed silly and cute and reverent all at once.

The stage was empty, but then just beyond the set, on the hill that rose gently behind the row of mock storefronts, was a covered wagon. You could just see the top of it as it went along down the hill, but its shape was unmistakable. There was a slight stir in the crowd as we watched it make its way slowly. Somehow the sight of it seized me and my eyes welled up. I'm not sure if I can completely recall what I was thinking, but it was something like, *Oh my God, the lonely little wagon.* Whatever: it was beautiful and then it disappeared behind the set.

The rest of the pageant was impressive, with live animals, pyrotechnics, and other special effects. The covered wagon and other horse-drawn vehicles crossed the stage several times, and huge, elaborate sections of the set pulled out on rails and unfolded with remarkable efficiency. Meribah was right in that the action on the stage didn't much resemble the books: the cast was so vast that I could barely pick out Laura among the girls in calico dresses. Clearly the outdoor stage was better suited for a role like Nellie Oleson, and the girl who played her flounced and screeched with nearly professional skill.

And of course, there was spectacle. One of the high points was the church-building scene, where the men of Walnut Grove pulled on ropes until the clapboard tower and belfry of Reverend Alden's church stood upright; then one of them scaled the tower to place a cross on the very top. The church in the real Walnut Grove had been torn down more than fifty years ago, but for six nights every summer the pageant cast valiantly brought a version of it back to life.

In fact, the pageant itself felt a bit like church—in a good way, full of ritual and stories. The fact that it was called "Fragments of a Dream" had sounded a little goofy at first, but perhaps it wasn't, not when you thought about the kind of dream it could have been: more than a century ago people came out here imagining a better future, only to see their prospects fall to pieces as a result of grasshoppers and fires, blizzards and depression; sometimes they got struck by lightning, mangled in sawmills, drowned in wells. The early history of the town was a dream that found its way into snippets of fiction, and then a TV show further rearranged all the bits and blew them into oblivion. In a way—in lots of symbolic ways, really—the town had been dismantled over and over again. This production, with its intricate sets that folded out, one little house turning into another, was a fervent affirmation of survival. The show was for everyone who had come to Walnut Grove wondering what was left. It was something like Lorenzo's dance party, only more fully realized, of course: it was faith that whatever was lost could simply be called back or restored or resurrected.

The amphitheater lights came up. By then it was nearly midnight. We joined the line of cars that crawled up the hill to the road, and we followed taillights in the dark all the way back to Tracy.

After my funny delusions back in Pepin, it was a kick to be in a town where the people really *were* talking about Laura Ingalls Wilder. Well, at least the families eating in Nellie's diner on the Saturday morning of a pageant weekend probably were—families with little girls, including one girl whose blond biracial hair allowed her to sport a pretty stunning crop of Nellie Oleson–style ringlets.

While Chris went up and paid the bill, I noticed how quiet a lot of the girls were. They seemed to slump a bit under the load of expectations a place like Walnut Grove carried, where everything was supposed to be fun and important at the same time. This wasn't like going to American Girl Place, an experience meticulously engineered by retail experts. In a place like this you saw everything, the things that hadn't changed and the things that had, the prairie grass and the gas station. And even as you tried to sense the spiritual presence of young Laura Ingalls at Plum Creek, you could see her image everywhere: on the town mural and various hand-painted signs, the bobblehead dolls and coloring books in the museum store, depictions that ranged from attractive to awkward to unrecognizably lumpy.

If I were one of these little girls, would I willfully ignore any of it, or would I take it all in and tell the Laura in my mind about it? *That's a Sinclair station, Laura, and it's for cars. Do you know what cars are?* What were they seeing?

Watching the girls with their families made me think about something else, too. I knew my decision to make this trip was in some small way informed by the fact that Chris and I had decided not to have kids. In other words, I knew if I wanted to see these places, I'd have to go for myself; I wouldn't ever be sharing the experience with a daughter, the way Little House fans often do. A friend of mine who similarly lacks the childbearing instinct once said, "I don't want kids because I don't want kids," and it's always made perfect sense to me. I've never really regretted being childless, but it started to feel different after my mother died, in a way I couldn't describe.

But here in Walnut Grove I knew what it was: *I* felt invisible sometimes. Not ignored, but anomalous and ghostly. I wasn't the girl anymore, and I wasn't the ma.

I was grateful Chris had come along. I'd worried that he would be bored, like those TV boyfriends who sit outside department-store dressing rooms, and that it would dampen my prairie-wandering spirit. But he was my anchor. If it wasn't for him, I was sure, I'd still be back at Plum Creek, or in one of the sod houses taking inventory. I'd kept picking up those stupid flatirons (both the sod house and the museum had signs that encouraged visitors to do so, to *try it* or *feel it*) and I never knew what to make of the foreign heaviness in my hand. Sometimes it almost felt like there was a trick to it, that if I held this thing long enough I'd somehow be more human than I was now, here with my head full of someone else's life.

⚛

The pace in town had suddenly picked up now that the pageant weekend was well under way. The covered wagon outside the museum, permanently bolted to the ground, was constantly crawling with kids, whose feet thumped up and down the length of the wagon bed so much it sounded like it had been hitched to a team of panicked Clydesdales.

Already the Walnut Grove city park was starting to fill up with young Lauras. The Laura-Nellie Look Alike competitions wouldn't take place until the afternoon—by then we'd be on the road to De Smet—but the contest registration table had just been set up, and a line of girls and parents had formed. According to the sign near the table, it cost five dollars to enter the contest, and contestants had to be between eight and twelve. (It did not specify girls, a loophole that Meribah's third-grade classmate probably could have exploited if he'd wished.)

Today was the Walnut Grove family festival, where the park, a green and shady square block just west of the center of town, hosted a rummage sale, food tents, and live music. The Hmong Cultural Center had its own table, as did a woman who ran a makeshift salon offering French-braided Laura pigtails. I bought yet another sunbonnet, and at the rummage sale picked up a commemorative plate depicting Doc Baker from the TV show. Now I was watching the contest registration.

I looked around for the two girls we'd met yesterday, the ones who'd improvised their costumes, but I didn't see them. All the girls waiting in line so far were in full Laura drag.

"I think the competition is going to be stiff," I told Chris. But maybe winning the contest was only a secondary objective. More than anything, the contest gave girls an excuse to dress up like Laura Ingalls or Nellie Oleson for a day. They'd be judged in part on their knowledge of the characters, but what's a little trivia when there were long pretty dresses to be donned?

The essential Laura look, of course, consists only of pigtail braids, a sunbonnet—preferably hanging down the back—and some sort of prairie dress. Everything else is extra credit: pinafores or aprons, hair ribbons (personally, I would award bonus points to any Laura whose braids sported blue ribbons in homage to that scene when Ma gets her tedious Laura/pink, Mary/blue color coding all mixed up for once), lunch pails or other accessories, and shoes.

Ah yes, the shoes. It was one thing to sew or buy a reasonably convincing prairie dress, quite another to get the footwear right. Most girls weren't doing much better than my clunky-shoed friend from the day before: only a couple girls had the high-buttoned boots; perhaps they were the more competitive Laura contenders. A few wore Mary Janes, which had a certain quaintness that sort of worked. But most of the girls just wore sandals or gym shoes under their dresses.

"I'm already judging the contest based on feet," I said. "Look, that kid has Birkenstocks."

"How do you know some of the girls aren't going to take off their shoes and go barefoot when they go onstage?" Chris asked.

"Oh, good strategy." Barefoot would be the most authentic Laura touch of all. And the most ironic, I pointed out, since Laura had felt so ill-equipped when she showed up on her first day of school and saw that the other Walnut Grove schoolgirls had decent shoes and dresses.

"You're really thinking about this too much," Chris said.

We'd spotted only a couple of entrants for the Nellie contest around the park. They appeared to be very good Nellies, though, with their hair done up in blond curls and wearing ruffled dresses: one girl in pink, the other yellow. I couldn't tell if the dresses were historically accurate, but then again, I suspect the only thing that has to be authentic about impersonating Nellie Oleson is the attitude. I asked the woman at the registration table if she thought there'd be more Nellies showing up later—there still were a few hours before the contest, after all, and it would be rather Nellie-ish to show up at the last minute and upstage everyone.

"You know, there just aren't a lot of Nellies," the woman told me. She said the Laura contestants always outnumbered the Nellie ones, sometimes by as much as six to one. "Most girls just want to be Laura." I supposed any kid who read and loved the Little House books enough to come to Walnut Grove would most likely feel an affinity for Laura. I could see how perhaps it took a special kind of girl to want to be a Nellie, someone who was willing to cross over to the dark and frilly side.

I had given up hope that *my* girls would show up, the two we'd met the day before. Maybe they'd lost their nerve, and you couldn't count on Grandpa Big Beard to get the time right.

We were crossing the park for the last time on our way to the car when I finally saw them—the girls, their uncle, and Grandpa Big Beard, waiting in line to sign up for the Laura contest. They wore the same clothes they'd been wearing the day before—the older girl in the crooked skirt and white blouse, the younger with her brown-tiered skirt and black rhinestone T-shirt. Now, though, they both had brand-new sunbonnets, in red and pink. I pointed the girls out to Chris.

"We could stay another couple of hours to see the contest," Chris said. "You could tell them to take off their shoes."

"That's okay," I said. I didn't want to see who'd win or not win. The girls had new sunbonnets and that was enough for me. The older girl had the pink one and she wore it hanging down her back. It was bright enough that I could still see it from the car across the street as we turned the corner to get back to Route 14.

9.

Anywhere East or South

HOW DO YOU DESCRIBE a place like Ingalls Homestead? I hesitate to call it a Laura Ingalls Wilder theme park, but that's a pretty good approximation of what it is. It's situated on the open prairie just a couple of miles from the town of De Smet, just like the original Ingalls homestead shanty is in the books. *Just like*—but of course I had to keep reminding myself that Ingalls Homestead *was* on the original land the Ingalls family had bought. Now the 160-acre plot has nearly a dozen buildings and exhibits, including an 1880s schoolhouse, a real 1870s shanty, a replica dugout (the fourth we'd see on this trip), a lookout tower, a welcome center with a gift shop, and a camping area. It has its own *slough*. And a horse barn with miniature ponies. And covered wagon rides! When you're at Ingalls Homestead, you can be simply walking around, admiring the prairie view, and a friendly fellow with a straw hat and suspenders will just come up to you and say, "Have you taken a covered wagon ride yet? Would you like one?" Of course you would! And, of course, we did.

⚛

It was early afternoon by the time we'd arrived in De Smet after driving the two hours from Walnut Grove. The land in South Dakota was flat, as we'd expected, but also the sky had grown or seemed to press down more. We couldn't tell at what point along the two-lane highway this change had taken place.

"Laura couldn't say how, but this prairie was different," it says in *By the Shores of Silver Lake*, as she rides with her family in an open wagon toward the place where the town of De Smet would eventually be built. Pa senses it, too, but is similarly unable to put his finger on what it is. The book finally describes it as "an enormous stillness that made you feel still," a strange sentence but a true one, as we found. Somehow all the usual noise sounded distant: the car radio and the air-conditioning and the engine on cruise control, all of it oddly faint under that sky.

"Who are you messaging?" Chris asked me. He'd looked over from the driver's seat and seen that I'd taken my phone out and was looking at the blank screen for sending text messages.

"I don't know," I said. I had simply acted on an impulse. "Maybe Jami?" I thought about it. "I just want to send a message to some-one." It felt like we could disappear out here. You could drive ten miles per hour faster once you crossed the state line and entered South Dakota, but despite the increased speed limit, I could feel, yes, the stillness. We pushed through it all afternoon.

De Smet was a bigger town than Walnut Grove, with a modern business strip along Highway 14 that had a couple of motels and convenience stores. But even on a pageant day, the quiet persisted.

We stopped the car and parked along Calumet Avenue, the original main street that had risen from the prairie mud in 1880.

The wooden buildings from that time had been replaced just a few years later by brick buildings, the kind with the tall Victorian windows. At one point there'd been an opera house along this street, and later, an auditorium where dances were held and Lawrence Welk's orchestra had played. These days, what drew visitors to Calumet Avenue was the Loftus' store, the general store that had been mentioned in the books, still on the very same site. It had become a gift shop that sold merchandise labeled LITTLE TOWN ON THE PRAIRIE and little burlap sacks of seed wheat to commemorate *The Long Winter*. (You'll remember in the book that Mr. Loftus had put up the money for Almanzo and Cap Garland to buy a remote homesteader's wheat supply and then caused an uproar by trying to sell it to hungry townspeople at a profit. If the price of the souvenir wheat was any indication, clearly the days of markup outrage were long over.)

You could also see the corner where Pa's building had stood: a brick building with a law office was there now. Much of the block was given over to businesses that were closed on a Saturday. The street had the same stoic calm as its old photos.

Just across Second Street was a coffeehouse, also closed for the afternoon, but a sign that boasted *Wireless Internet* hung outside, and there was a bench by the door.

"Hang on," I told Chris. My twenty-first-century twitches were getting the better of me. I sat down and pulled out my laptop. "I don't know why I'm even checking right now," I said sheepishly. But sure enough, the coffeehouse had an open network. "The Wi-Fi at the motel was pretty weak this morning," I said to Chris, by way of an excuse. But here I was, just across the street from the very place where the Ingalls family had endured the hard winter and twisted hay into sticks, checking my e-mail. Right over there, Pa had shaken his cold-stiffened clenched fist and raged at the keening wind! He had shaken it, in fact, to the northwest, in the very direction where I was sitting with my white MacBook. This is so not right, I thought.

I was less conflicted by the time we got to the visitor's center at Ingalls Homestead, where we sent Chris's mom a virtual postcard from a little kiosk across from the front desk. The center is like a well-built barn, spacious and rustic yet air-conditioned. Ingalls Homestead has been open since 1997, but it still has all the exuberance of a new enterprise; it feels like what I imagine being in De Smet in its early years was like. Even the bathroom stalls at Ingalls Homestead were built with planks of golden lumber that looked fresh and sturdy.

The woman at the front desk gave us the key to the "covered wagon" where we were staying for our first night and explained that our camping fee included admission to all the exhibits for the duration of our stay. She handed us a brochure with a map and marked the visitor's center with an *X*. I read the building description: "Enter the prairie through the back door," it said. So we did.

There are few, if any, sidewalks or walkways at Ingalls Homestead. People simply walk across the expanse of mown prairie, wandering in all directions. We moved dutifully through a row of buildings at first, the small museum and the dugout and the shanty, but before long we gave in to the urge to just drift across the open field. There was a little hay-roof barn that sat all by itself against a gentle slope, and when we went inside, a brown-and-white cow peered up at us from her pen. She lounged in the straw with her calf, and her hide looked so silky that I wanted to climb into the pen and spoon against her side.

Beyond the hay-roof barn was the place called "Ma's Little House," the reconstruction of the claim shanty that Pa had built in 1880—which, in the books, is at the end of *By the Shores of Silver Lake*. The replica had been built on the very location and to the same dimensions as the original shanty (which had disappeared sometime after Pa sold the land in 1892): a little board-and-batten house, handsomely weathered gray and determinedly cheery, with a tiny front porch.

The door was wide open, and inside it was surprisingly airy and light. Most of the other dugouts and houses we'd seen on this trip had been pretty musty, but here there was a breeze through the kitchen, which had a stove, a table, and a nice woman in a prairie dress who said, "Welcome to Ma's Little House! Would you like to know more about homesteading in the 1880s?"

I'd already read most of what she had to tell me, but how could we refuse?

There was a room just past the kitchen that I recognized instantly as the part of the house Pa had built for Mary's parlor organ, which stood by the back door. Or rather, the battered antique organ that stood in for the real thing. Although nothing here had ever belonged to the Ingallses, it hardly mattered. We were free to touch anything: to play the parlor organ, try the sewing machine, scrub laundry on a washboard in a tin tub that stood just outside the back door, then hang it to dry on the clothesline by the vegetable garden. You could pet the gray kittens curled up on the patchwork quilts in the bedrooms (I'd spotted another one darting around the front porch) or pump water from the well.

"Is there anything you want to try?" Chris asked.

"I don't know," I said. "I'm not sure." Somehow I was wary of doing the hands-on things, though I'd churned butter and ground seed wheat at home. I felt superstitious and weird at the thought of doing anything beyond just looking. It would be like touching a spinning wheel in a fairy tale. I'd either break a spell or invoke a new one.

All the same, we found ourselves on a wagon ride, which traveled along wheel ruts in the grass. It was full of visitors like ourselves, and the sides were open so that we could see the prairie all around. Our driver was the kind of young man you might call "strapping," and when a girl sitting near the front of the wagon asked if the horses had names, he said they were called Skip and Barnum.

"They're named after Almanzo's horses," I whispered to Chris.

The wagon took us to a genuine one-room schoolhouse that stood at the far corner of the homestead, and once inside we sat in wooden desks while a genuine retired local schoolteacher told us about the history of rural schools like this one. She pointed out how the legs of some of the desks had little messages of encouragement in molded letters in the metalwork. *TRY AGAIN*, said the desk next to mine. Then she let us pull the rope to ring the bell in the little belfry as we filed back out into the sunlight.

I was quickly becoming a model student here at Ingalls Homestead. On the wagon ride back, the driver quizzed our group about the requirements of the Homestead Act. "Anyone know how long you had to live on a claim to own it?" he asked.

"Five years!" I piped up.

At the activity center near the horse barn, a teenage staff member showed me how to feed dried corncobs into a hand-cranked corn sheller and wrap a scrap of calico around the stripped cob to make a little doll.

"And do you know what the name of Laura's corncob doll was?" she asked.

"Susan," I said proudly.

The wheels of our covered wagon were partly buried in the ground, as if the imaginary settlers who drove it had simply decided to stay in the place where they'd gotten stuck. Beneath the wagon bed, in the spot where Jack the bulldog would've walked, there was an electrical hookup, and in back a short set of steps led up to a padlocked door. We opened it with our key. Inside was an efficient little compartment with benches and a bunk tucked in the back; the roof was fiberglass over a wood frame. The four sleeping wagons at Ingalls Homestead were modeled after the hard-topped sheepherders' wagons used in Montana and Idaho: as far as luxury went, they were considerably less posh than the pop-up trailer my family had owned when I was a kid, but probably a heck of a lot cushier than the Ingallses' covered wagon.

We carried our sleeping bags and pillows from the car and stowed them in the bunk, then sat at the picnic table outside. Around us was the camping area, a gentle slope dotted with the wagons and a few tents. Up by the parking lot was a hookup area for camping trailers and RVs. Our camping neighbors were mostly families with children.

"There's a kid in a prairie dress at that campsite," I pointed out to Chris. "And I saw another one over by that blue tent."

"And did you see the folks at that bunkhouse?" Chris asked. The bunkhouse was uphill from us and it was the fanciest lodging available at Ingalls Homestead, a tiny clapboard house with air-conditioning and a microwave. It was hard to imagine that the family staying there was much attracted to the modern amenities, though, since all four of the girls were wearing long calico dresses, and so was their mother. They'd come out of the little house one by one and we watched them head over to the visitor's center. Their faces were glowing, as if they'd been rolling barrel hoops with sticks all day. But it hardly seemed strange anymore to see people in period dress. Over at one of the tent sites, a woman wore a long dress and a flower-trimmed porkpie hat as she stood tending a grill—looking, I thought, very much like Laura might have looked when she and Almanzo and Rose camped along their journey to Missouri in 1894.

There was even wildlife in our midst: slinky ground squirrels that scurried over the grass; their holes were everywhere. The stillness we'd felt before had given way somehow, and now the whole landscape seemed impossibly animated, with all the scurrying and the rippling of the fields in the breeze.

Chris wanted to sleep for a little bit, so I took a walk by myself.

It was late afternoon, and the high July sun had only just ceased to be relentless. It would still be a few hours until sundown and the De Smet pageant. I walked until I reached a large swath of thin green stalks that grew dense and tall; the top of it rippled in the wind, and the rest of it teemed with the noise of birds and crickets and locusts and countless other rural creatures whom I only knew by name—chiggers, peepers, creepers, whatever they were. This had to be the slough, that mysterious natural expanse whose nature I couldn't quite understand when I first read the Little House books—was it a lake, a field, a bog? If you were lost in it, would you drown? Of course I knew now that a slough was a kind of wetland. As I peered into the green depths, I marveled at how much this resembled the slough of my childhood imagination.

I walked along the edge of it for a while until I reached a sign that stood in front of it. That's when I learned that this whole time I'd been gazing at an oat field.

Oh. Never mind. I supposed that just because I was in Prairie Storybook Land it didn't mean I could instantly recognize everything. The oats grew alongside fields of wheat and corn—thirty acres all together, to show visitors how much cropland was required on homestead claims. (I had better luck identifying the corn and wheat.)

The afternoon shadows were growing longer. The visitors were beginning to thin out, and the brown cow and its calf were being led across the field to the livestock barn for the night. I wandered over to the corner of the homestead land where a grove of cottonwood trees had grown from the seedlings Pa had planted. They were huge now. I couldn't believe this place.

Even though we were making several stops on this trip, and had two more places yet to visit, I'd been thinking of this place as the true destination of our travel. After all, it was the place of fulfilled destiny, the place that I'd hoped Laura and her family would find from the moment they abandoned their lonely cabin in Kansas, which opened in me a deep need to see them find another little house on another prairie. More than anything, that's what stayed with me about the books, that they made it out here. Never mind the Long Winter or anything else that followed: they were here, the *here* of completion, the embodiment of Laura's Now.

Everything I'd been doing for the past year, all the reading and cooking and traveling, I realized, was really about getting here, out to the farthest reaches of the big long dream that was the Little House series.

Back at the wagon, Chris was at the picnic table reading *By the Shores of Silver Lake*. I sat down beside him.

"Look at this," he said, showing me the book. He had just begun chapter 8, and we looked at the illustration on the facing page: it showed Laura standing on a little rise of ground looking out over the railroad camp and the land beyond it, all the gentle swells of treeless prairie that reached back into the horizon under the banner of sky. Then he lowered the book. From the hill we were on we had the same vantage point.

"I just looked up," Chris said, "and there it was."

It looked like the same place. It *was* the same place.

While Chris read I watched the covered wagons, tiny in the distance, travel steadily back and forth in their tracks across the prairie. There were two of them making the trip to the schoolhouse and back. They'd wait by the little white school building, and a few times every hour, the bell of the schoolhouse would ring, its wispy peals punctuating the calm. Somehow it never got old. Then the wagon would make its way back while another one headed slowly toward the schoolhouse to repeat the pattern. I could've watched all day.

For the De Smet pageant, a performance of *The Long Winter*, we brought our camping chairs and sat near the back of the crowd. We didn't feel the need to be up close, since it was our second pageant in as many nights. It was being held in an open field just across the road from Ingalls Homestead; its set was a cluster of low-slung little buildings, almost like boxcars. We were far enough from the stage to see how the prairie dwarfed it. But of course this was the kind of country where you really had to take a step back to see everything: everything lent itself to these distances. The sun was setting to our right, the sky epic, the darkness deepening as the crowd settled in.

"I get the feeling that the De Smet pageant doesn't have as much to prove as the Walnut Grove one," Chris would say after the show.

"I know what you mean," I said. It was a simpler production, with its faithful, straightforward rendition of the book. Maybe it seemed a little odd to stage *The Long Winter* in the middle of July, but the lack of snow was explained by a cute little note in the program about "the fickle prairie weather." I'd read later that the pageant tradition had actually started with *The Long Winter*, which had been adapted for a Hallmark Playhouse radio production in 1950; a few years later the town had gotten permission to perform the script on its own. Now every few summers the De Smet pageant switches to *These Happy Golden Years* or one of the other books set in town, but keeps returning to *The Long Winter*—which, after all, is as much about the town's survival as the Ingalls family's—and lets the story speak for itself.

The prairie grew chilly as we watched the familiar scenes: the family enduring the October blizzard, Ma grinding wheat for bread, the Wilder brothers in their feed store making pancakes, with Almanzo's brother Royal tilting his chair back just like in the Garth Williams illustration. From our far-off spot the little lit-up rooms of the set looked like pictures, or rooms in a dollhouse. Sometimes I'd look over in the distance beyond the set to Ingalls Homestead; I could almost see where the little replica shanty stood in the dark. I tried to imagine what it would be like in winter, with snow up to the eaves of all the houses, and wondered what that would be like from the inside.

❀

The sky had been starless for most of the show, but we hadn't thought of rain until we felt a few scattered drops as we walked back to our car.

There were no lights in our sleeping wagon. We had our flashlights and a fluorescent camping lantern that I'd set on the little table that slid out from beneath our bunk, but it was too low to cast much light in the cavelike space. Chris nodded up at the curved top of the wagon.

"It's like being in a giant mailbox," he said.

"Or a barrel," I pointed out. "Or, I don't know, a churn?" I was trying to think of appropriately nineteenth-century things that being in this covered wagon could be like, if it wasn't quite like being in a covered wagon. Not that I wasn't excited.

"It's better than a tent," Chris said, as a smattering of rain hit the roof. It had yet to rain in earnest, but the little bursts of precipitation came regularly enough that there was no use building a campfire outside. We tried reading by the light of the lantern for a few minutes. Finally we decided to go to bed early.

"I think this is what people did in the old days anyway," I said.

"Slept in giant barrels?" he said.

"No! Went to bed early." I laughed. "Because there wasn't enough light to do anything else."

Our bunk felt a little cramped, but then again it didn't seem right for the bed to be *too* comfortable, either. There was a tiny louvered window above our bunk at the front end of the wagon. It faced the parking lot and the road, but it was too dark to see anything. Across the road, a ways off in a neighboring field, was some kind of utility tower; the little red light at its top blinked gently.

I wondered if the sheepherders who slept in wagons like these ever felt claustrophobic. I turned over to sleep and fought the canned-in feeling by thinking about the world that lay outside— the wide-open prairie, the fields and their eddying surfaces, the enormous sky.

❀

A burst of rain against the roof woke me up. It was louder than it had been earlier. And it had another sound to it, a more acute clamor. Hail? I thought of the hailstorm that had ruined Laura and Almanzo's wheat crops in *The First Four Years*. Oh, no, I thought.

I sat up in bed to try to see out the window. Chris woke up just then.

"I think it might be a hailstorm," I told him.

"Whoa," he said. "What about the crops?"

I loved him for saying that.

I couldn't see anything through the bunk window; it was too dark. I wondered if it really was hail, and if so, how big were the hailstones.

"In *The First Four Years* it said the hailstones were as big as hen's eggs," I told Chris.

"So *that's* how people described hail size before golf became popular," he said. "I guess I always wondered."

"Now you know," I said. I had climbed down from our bunk and was trying to see out the window panel in the wagon's door.

I thought better about stepping outside to look, since Ole Larson, Laura and Almanzo's neighbor, had done that in the book and been promptly conked out by a hailstone to the head. From the sound of the hail outside, that wasn't too likely to happen, but this would be a hell of a time to tempt irony, wouldn't it?

I opened the door just for a moment; I could make out tiny bits of hail on the wooden steps. Just when I wished it wasn't so dark, the sky lit up and a jag of lightning shot out over the horizon.

"Whoa!" I shut the door. "Never mind." I climbed back into the bunk and listened to the rain until I dozed off again.

Sometime later the lightning flicked me awake again. I opened my eyes and the windows flashed.

"Are you awake?" Chris said.

I opened my mouth to answer and a thunderclap split everything open. It sounded like a gigantic shiny axe that would kill us all.

"Oh, shit!" I gasped.

It was raining even harder now, slapping against the sides and roof of the wagon with the rhythm of the wind. We both sat up in the bunk. We peered out the window and could see headlights in the parking lot. "Someone's leaving," Chris said. "I wouldn't stay out in a tent in this weather, either." We could just barely hear the engine start up over the rain, and we watched the lights disappear through the downpour.

I thought about all of these kids out here, who knows how many little girls with their families braving the lightning and rain in their tents and RVs and wagons like ours. My God, how were *they* faring? They had to be either frightened out of their minds or having the time of their lives. Or both, I thought, since when you're a kid, it's possible to be both. I remembered that much.

"What time is it?"

Chris checked his watch. "About one thirty."

We were glad we weren't in a tent in all this wind and lightning, but was it that much better to be *here*, in what was essentially a wooden box stuck in an open field above an electrical outlet? We couldn't think about that.

"We went through some thunderstorms like this when my family went camping as a kid," I told Chris. We were trying to distract ourselves with conversation.

"Me, too," Chris said, though I could tell he was staring up at the roof at the thick metal bolts that were screwed into the wooden frame. Up here in the bunk, our feet were almost always touching one. I knew he was thinking, like I was, that if lightning hit the wagon those things would turn into little joy buzzers of death.

Another clap of thunder set off a car alarm in the parking lot. (Nothing in *The First Four Years* prepared us for that.)

"On the map it said the campground shower building is also a storm shelter," I said, remembering.

"Do you think we're supposed to go there?" Chris asked.

Just then the lightning and thunder hit together. *CRAACCCK!* Out the window, a molten crack of light seared down the sky. Down to something somewhere across the road.

"Oh my God, I *saw* that!" I was trembling. "It hit somewhere right nearby. Did you see that?"

"We're going to die," Chris said. "Just like Amassa Tower and his wife." He was remembering the story of the Walnut Grove church deacon who was struck by lightning on the prairie.

"His wife went insane," I reminded him.

"We're going to die *and* go insane," Chris said.

It was one of the worst thunderstorms either one of us had ever experienced, we'd decided. "Except for that one last year," Chris said. Once, a late-night storm back home had produced a thunderclap so massive and sudden that it caused us both to wake up shrieking and grabbing at each other like crazy folk. We'd been so shaken that we turned on the bedroom TV and spent the next two hours drinking scotch and watching infomercials in the wee hours of the morning. But when you've decided to take a Laura Ingalls Wilder journey out into the middle of the Dakota prairie, you'd rather not admit that you miss infomercials, even when there are times (such as two a.m., in a covered wagon, with no scotch to be had) that you do.

We looked out again, but outside there was nothing: no headlights, no alarms. I couldn't see the little red light on the tower in the distance. Everything was just storm.

At dawn when I woke up it was gray outside; there was soft thunder but no rain. I walked through the wet grass to the bathroom building, keeping my eye on the mass of dark storm clouds that hung in the sky beyond the visitor's center. So much for the glowing prairie dawn I'd hoped to experience. It was around five in the morning, but I wasn't the only one up: some people were breaking camp, or hanging things to dry along the rail fence by the parking lot. I encountered a woman in the bathroom who confirmed that lightning had struck nearby during the storm. She also seemed pretty unfazed that her family's tent had partially collapsed in the night.

"Oh, we were fine in our sleeping bags," she said, as she brushed her wet hair. "They were only really wet on the outside."

I was a little jealous that Chris and I had stayed so safe and dry and that our own tale of Dakota gumption wouldn't be nearly as impressive as hers. And it occurred to me that ever since the first burst of hail last night, I'd been forming the story of the storm in my mind, what we would tell people when we got home, how we *totally* thought we were going to die just like the hapless pioneers we read about in pageant programs. I wouldn't mention how, deep down, we knew we wouldn't die but thought it anyway because we're wimps.

On my walk back to the wagon, I saw a family striking camp: a mom and her three kids were working desperately to shake out the water from their tent and fold it at the same time.

"Do you see the sky?" I heard the mom snap. "Let's get a move on. *Now.*"

I was sure that for these kids this disastrous camping episode had only enhanced their Laura World experience, the way I'd heard back at Walnut Grove that sometimes children aspired to get their own leeches in Plum Creek.

Had it been that way for us last night? I could see ourselves telling friends about how we'd lived life to the fullest on our Little House vacation, where we'd paid fifty bucks to sleep in a covered wagon and gotten our very own prairie calamity for free. And after all, the whole point of going on a Little House Big Adventure was that the simple life, the exposure to the elements, and the inspiring example of the Ingalls family would make you realize what was important to you, right? Except that maybe we discovered that what was really important was having a TV where we could watch the ShamWow! guy. We could claim to have felt the trepidation and awe that the Ingallses and the Wilders must have felt in their little houses, but all I knew was that last night we'd been too rattled to feel like anyone but ourselves.

❀

The first thing Chris said when he woke up was, "We have to go check on the wheat!"

"I know!" I said. We got dressed and hurried out across the grass. Worrying about the wheat had been our one true Little House thought during the whole storm.

To our relief the field was completely intact: still golden, the stalks swaying just as beautifully as they had the day before. "I guess the hailstones weren't big enough to flatten it," Chris said.

"It's nice to see that someone can actually grow some wheat out here," I pointed out. To read the Little House books, you wondered if anyone ever managed to harvest a successful crop, since it seemed the minute the wheat grew ripe enough, something horrible always happened.

The Ingalls Homestead attractions had just opened up for the day. The activities building was still empty except for the two high school kids who worked there.

"Would you like to make a corncob doll?" a girl standing by the shelling machine called over to me.

"Actually, could you show us how to twist a haystick?" I asked her. There wasn't anyone over at the hay station, and making my own haystick—the little improvised bundles that Pa and other prairie settlers burned for fuel during the Long Winter when the coal and firewood ran out—was one of the few hands-on things I wanted to try.

She shrugged. "Sure." She came over and grabbed a long shock of hay from a big bin, twisted it until it doubled in on itself, and then tucked the ends in. She handed a bundle to me to try. I'd wanted to do it ever since the winter, when my Internet searches started picking up news items about various Laura Ingalls Wilder–related educational talks: they were at public libraries, park districts, community colleges, always somewhere in another state where I couldn't attend, and almost invariably, they involved haystick-twisting demonstrations. There was something deeply appealing about it. After all, we'd all just watched the economy's strange, sickening lurch that past fall—we'd seen the news, stared in shock at our own 401k statements with their freakish, dismal numbers, and while we knew what they meant, we couldn't touch them, could barely comprehend them. So I couldn't help but think that twisting haysticks must be damned good therapy, that it would let you *feel* the hardship, knowing that this *thing* that you held in your chapped hands made a difference, even as it was destined to burn away and vanish, just like a chunk of retirement savings! Hay twisting was literally a productive wringing of hands.

So I tried to twist my hay, wanted to twist it as tight as I could. I'd seen haysticks hung on the walls at the Oxbow, the one family restaurant in town, and they'd been twisted tight and shiny as pigtail braids; the one the girl made frankly looked more like a tidy tumbleweed. But then, I couldn't get mine to look any better: the hay crumbled if you twisted it too hard. "It's awfully loose," I said. "Shouldn't it be denser so it can last while it burns?" I asked the girl. The thunderstorm had eroded what little pioneer credibility I'd imagined for myself, but it still seemed important that I understand haystick thermodynamics as much as possible.

She shrugged again. "That's just how the hay is this time of year, I guess. But you can take this one and try burning it on your campfire and see what happens." She handed the one she'd made to me. (It was still better than mine.)

"Thank you," I said, taking it reverently. It was almost big enough to cradle like an infant. It was a scraggly bundle of dried grass, but like dried grass, it also smelled clean and barnlike and nice. I held it gently.

"You're not really going to burn your prairie baby, are you?" Chris whispered as we walked back to our wagon.

"No way," I told him.

Chris was letting the car idle down Second Street.

"Why are you slowing down?" I asked him. We'd picked up a paper map of De Smet that showed sixteen different historical points of interest. I looked over at an old frame house. "Is that where the schoolhouse used to be? What are you looking at?"

"Nothing," Chris said. "I'm driving this slow because the speed limit in this town is fifteen miles per hour. I can't believe it."

"Maybe it's so we can get a feel for what it was like to ride around in a buggy," I said.

We'd just turned in our wagon key at Ingalls Homestead, since we'd had the wagon for only one night. We decided to set up our tent later, after we'd seen the attractions in town. Now we were approaching the Laura Ingalls Wilder Memorial Society, which operated a gift shop and tour operation out of a Victorian house on a side street in De Smet. Next to it stood a completely unassuming little white clapboard house, though I'd seen it in photos and knew exactly what it was.

"There's the surveyors' house!" I said as Chris parked the car.

"*That's* the surveyors' house?" Chris said incredulously, since like everything else from the Little House books, it was smaller than we'd thought.

I was glad Chris was reading *By the Shores of Silver Lake*, because it's really hard to explain to people who don't know the books why the surveyors' house is such a big deal. It shows up in *Silver Lake* a few chapters in, when Laura and her family, having recently arrived in Dakota Territory, are staying at the railroad camp in a cramped shanty with a dirt floor. One day Laura looks out and notices, among the assemblage of temporary shanties and bunkhouses, a lone house—a *real* house on the shore of Silver Lake. "I wonder what that house can be and who lives there," Laura says to herself.

I remember having to wait two whole chapters to find out that the big fancy house was for the railroad surveyors and all their tools, which of course was a letdown, since nothing's more boring than surveying tools. But then, just as the Ingallses are considering the depressing prospect of going back east for the winter, Pa announces that the family can spend it *living in the surveyors' house*. Which has to be the best house-sitting gig ever, and all Pa has to do is make sure nobody steals the surveying tools (like *that's* hard); the place is stocked to the gills with provisions, and later the family even makes extra money by running the place as an impromptu hotel during the spring land rush.

One of my favorite scenes in the whole series was when Laura enters the house at last: she gets to run ahead of the wagon and be the first to go inside and see the house in all its glass-windowed, multiroom glory. She opens all the doors (so many doors!), discovers the six-lidded stove, and steps into the pantry storeroom filled with heretofore unheard-of delights like canned peaches, soda crackers, and a whole barrel full of salt pork. *Silver Lake* made the house sound like a yawningly huge place, the largest house Laura had ever lived in. From what I could tell as a kid, living in the surveyors' house was like getting to live in the house from *The Brady Bunch:* certainly not an extravagantly wealthy existence but a hell of an improvement on the everyday one.

Silver Lake had been mostly drained in the 1920s, and eventually the surveyors' house was moved from its original spot by the lake into town, where the Memorial Society now runs it as a museum. By modern standards the house is about the size of a three-car garage, albeit one with an attic. But that hardly mattered to me—what mattered more was that it's the only Ingalls home mentioned in the Little House books still standing.

It's sort of bittersweet that of all the places where the Ingalls family lived over the course of the entire Little House saga, the only one to survive wasn't one of the little houses that Pa built, but a place where they'd had a borrowed bit of comfort, lived a life that wasn't quite their own. But I still wanted to see it, to see the dream that they'd lived briefly. I thought again about the little perception game I'd play when I was younger, when I'd come home from school on latchkey afternoons and imagine that I was Laura going to the surveyors' house alone for the first time, walking into each empty room and seeing a version of my life that was somehow better.

Now inside the surveyors' house for real, we knew where all the doors led. I think everyone in our tour group did: the bedroom, the stairs, the pantry, the lean-to. There was even a whatnot like the one the family had made in *Silver Lake*, the fancy-trimmed knickknack shelf that had brought a touch of Victorian fussiness to Dakota life. The time we spent in the house felt too short, but what was there to look at besides the stove, the few bits of furniture, the whiteboard walls? It was the paradox of all the little houses I'd visited, but especially of this one. You could see at a glance that the pantry was nearly empty, but one by one we all still went to the doorway and peered in.

Wait, there *was* one place that Pa had built that was still standing, and it was the house on Third Street. It was the last stop on the Memorial Society tour, after we'd gone through two schoolhouses, including one where Laura and Carrie had attended school. The Third Street house was built by Pa in 1887, and it was where the Ingalls family had lived after they'd moved off the homestead. Pa had won his bet with the government and fulfilled the homesteading requirements, but he'd given up on farming and eventually sold the homestead land, turning instead to work in town as a carpenter, a storekeeper, and even an insurance salesman.

The De Smet house wasn't in the Little House books, though in *On the Way Home* Rose had mentioned it as her grandparents' house. It was bigger than the surveyors' house, an ordinary but genteel two-story frame house with tall windows. It was the best house Pa had built, and his last one. The street it was on was shady with tall old trees. The house had sort of a stunted air around it in comparison with the signs of life in all the other houses on the block, with their lawn ornaments and garage driveways.

The guide, a college-aged girl in a prairie dress, led us into the wallpapered front parlor and told us about how Carrie and Mary and Grace had all lived in the house at various times in their adulthood. We saw cloudy photos of Carrie and Grace with their husbands; they'd moved elsewhere in South Dakota and hadn't had children. If you didn't already know that the Charles Ingalls family hadn't any descendants other than Rose Wilder Lane, you'd find out here.

As a kid, I would have loved seeing the Victorian parlor furniture and knowing that Ma and the girls were at last living in the kind of civilized comfort that her china shepherdess implied, but now it felt more poignant, knowing that much of the family quietly faded away here. We learned that after Pa died in 1902, Ma had rented out the rooms upstairs, and in the front hallway was an old wall telephone that Ma hadn't much liked to use but Mary had taken to well. Hearing about these later chapters in the Ingalls family chronicle, the marriages and quiet dotages and deaths, made them all seem like distant elderly relatives. We went upstairs and looked into their dim bedrooms, carefully arranged with combs and trinkets that had belonged to them.

"So now you know what happened to everyone else," I told Chris when the tour ended. "They all died."

"Well, of course people die," he said. "It's history, right?"

"I guess," I said. "Maybe I like Ingalls Homestead a little better. To hell with history!" I was joking, but it was also true: I had to admit that I liked Ingalls Homestead because nobody got old and died there, and wheat survived hailstorms, and land claims weren't abandoned after years of drought. Pa may have given up the homestead, but the spirit of free-land perseverance lived on at Ingalls Homestead: you could always *TRY AGAIN* there, or at least pretend to. I felt guilty. I knew that just like in the books, my Laura World thrived on the true stuff as much as the fiction, but here I was, a sucker for the awesome prairie fairy tale that was Ingalls Homestead.

Chris checked his watch. It was early afternoon. "So you're ready to head back there and play Laura, then?"

"Not yet," I said. Because that was true, too.

❀

We drove a few miles south of town to see the twin lakes where Laura and Almanzo went on buggy rides during their courtship. Then we drove a mile north of town to see the field where they'd had their doomed homestead claim in *The First Four Years*. We'd bought sandwiches at the Subway on the highway strip and were looking for a place to have a picnic, but I was feeling restless and found myself telling Chris to just keep driving.

First we went slowly along the narrow road that divided Lake Henry and Lake Thompson. More than once, in *These Happy Golden Years*, the couple travels this same road, and in one scene Laura looks out at the lakes and imagines how they must have been in the days when the prairie was wilder, teeming with antelope and buffalo and wolves and herons and swans. The lakes' surfaces picked up the perfect blue of the sky and rippled as serenely as the water on the book's cover.

After turning back north, we finally pulled off the road by the historical marker that designated the low empty hill behind it as Rose Wilder Lane's birthplace, the site where the Wilder claim shanty had stood. We sat in the car and ate our sandwiches, staring west at the scrubby cow pasture where Laura and Almanzo had lived their luckless existence. But it was also beautiful. There were no trees here. It looked the way the country must have looked when the railroad first came through. Ever since yesterday, when we'd watched the pageant, I had the feeling that there were two worlds here, one layered upon the other, and that everyone who came here was always trying to see through one prairie to the other.

There's a moment like this in the books, for me at least: In *By the Shores of Silver Lake*, the Ingalls family is outside the shanty watching Pa plant some cottonwood seedlings that he brought from Lake Henry. The happy occasion turns terrifying when they realize that Grace, who is just a toddler, has wandered out of sight, and a panicked search ensues. Pa and Ma rush to the treacherous Big Slough to look for her in the tall grass, and Laura runs to the south on the flat, shadowless prairie, trying to think where Grace could have gone.

It's one of the most dramatic scenes in the series, and the point of view, as always, is in the third-person limited: "Laura felt cold and sick," it says. "If she were little and playing all by herself, Laura thought, she wouldn't go into the dark Big Slough." It's a thought-space that Little House readers know well, where we are both in and out of Laura's head. But then, for just a few lines, as Laura runs and calls out for her sister, there's a strange shift when her thoughts come out as they never have before in the series—in the *first* person, a little flash of interior narrative:

She ran on and on. Grace must have gone this way. Maybe she chased a butterfly. She didn't go into Big Slough! She didn't climb the hill, she wasn't there. Oh baby sister, I couldn't see you anywhere east or south on this hateful prairie. "Grace!"

I never fail to be disoriented whenever I come across this little passage: I lose track of who the *she* is and can't discern if this new *I* is speaking out of urgency or memory. It seems both accidental—an error in style—and purposeful, a meaningful blip. Briefly, it always seems to me, the worlds overlap in this spot, a place as strange and anomalous as the deep, violet-filled hollow where Laura finds her sister a few moments later. I wanted the world to be like that, for all its layers to be visible.

From the parked car we stared out at this little hill where nothing was and where someone was born. Then we got out and stood along the wire fence because I couldn't get close enough and I couldn't quite be still.

It was still too hot and bright out to set up our tent for our second night at Ingalls Homestead. We would do it when the afternoon sun got a little lower in the sky, I decided, when we could sit in our lawn chairs and look out over the prairie again. In the meantime we went by the cemetery where Ma and Pa and Mary and Carrie and Grace were buried; we saw the train depot; we looked at nearly everything on the map we were given. I wanted to see everything we could, then go back to Ingalls Homestead for the night, sleep in contentment, wake up to a brilliant prairie dawn.

I kept checking the weather. When we drove, I searched the car radio tuner for the local forecast.

"It looks a lot less cloudy now," Chris said. "Like it's clearing up."

"I don't want to take any chances," I told him. "Let's just make sure there won't be any more storms like last night."

When we stopped for coffee at the Oxbow, I took out my laptop and started looking up De Smet on various weather websites. "If there's any chance of rain, I don't know if we should stay," I said. "I mean, if we had to, we could get on the road this afternoon and just find a motel in Minnesota or something." It was true that we had an arduous drive scheduled the next day. Hours and hours, along that stifling stretch of I-90, to our last two stops in Minnesota and Iowa. "If we had to go this afternoon, we could break up that long drive."

Chris nodded. "Whatever you want to do," he said.

"Well, it's not what I *want*," I said. "It would be only if the weather was going to be bad again tonight."

Weather.com said only "partly cloudy." So did the webpage for the Sioux Falls news station. "Chance of precipitation: less than 10 percent," read the forecast on a third page, with a peaceful-looking icon of a moon and a handful of little clouds. It would be a fine night: no rain, temperatures in the low seventies. I let out a deep breath and looked up at Chris.

"So what's the verdict?" he asked.

"I don't know," I said, even though, suddenly, I did. "I think we have to go," I said. "It's not going to rain. But still. Maybe we should go."

"You mean, leave today?" He looked confused.

"Yes," I said, though I was feeling an odd weight slink down my spine. Something like dread but also like relief. I had to say it again. "Let's just go."

※

Yes, we left De Smet a day early.

Maybe I was set on leaving before I fully realized it. All we had to do was put up the tent (more than once Chris had reminded me), and all day I'd kept putting it off, kept waiting for it all to feel *right*. It had, at first: those first few hours at Ingalls Homestead the day before, the way the world of the books was so wonderfully wrought that for a little while I could imagine it was my own.

And then it all started to feel less certain. Nothing had changed; there hadn't been any disappointments. And yet behind all my expectations there was a restlessness that I hadn't accounted for at all. It kept insisting that something wasn't right. What was wrong? And just then I knew exactly what it was: what was wrong was that *I was not Laura.*

I actually laughed out loud a little bit in the restaurant when I had that thought. I was not Laura Ingalls Wilder! And this was not my town, with its fifteen-miles-per-hour speed limit, and its highway display of memorial crosses for the unborn babies of South Dakota. I did not like the heat or the stillness. I did not really like the Oxbow restaurant, which for lack of other options in town we'd visited three times already, and two of those times something had gone so profoundly wrong with their regular service that they'd steered us to their sad, sad buffet instead. And I'd wanted so badly to love the place, with its décor of beribboned haysticks and old town photos, that I did not like my feelings, which were beginning to extend to other things, radiating outward like rings on the surface of Silver Lake. Which somehow I did not even want to see, even though I'd been told that if you drove behind the cement plant you could, since all the rain this summer had filled it up again.

Reader, I did not mention all this before now because what kind of asshole would have bad thoughts about the Little Town on the Prairie? Would not want to see Silver Lake, even though it had magically reappeared like some watery Brigadoon? I was that kind of asshole, apparently. In the moment I decided to go, though, I had suddenly realized that I did not *have* to like it here:

this was not where I had been born; my childhood was not here, even though I'd felt I'd gotten glimpses of the Laura World I remembered.

I knew, too, that what I felt wasn't really the fault of the place itself: the people were not unkind, and truthfully all of it—the town, Ingalls Homestead, everything—was as beautiful and compelling as I'd hoped. But for much of the time I'd been here I'd had a sort of manic fatigue, the feeling of someone who had to stay up all night watching guard over something, knowing that with a moment's rest or inattention it would vanish. I was exhausted. I wanted to feel like myself again more than I wanted to experience a breathtaking prairie dawn, and I was just now becoming reconciled to the fact that the two things were not the same. The Laura in me had seen everything she wanted. But I hadn't let myself believe that what *I* wanted could be anything different, and it was. I wanted to go.

"Are you sure?" Chris asked.

I was sure.

I wanted to see a few last things. One was the Big Slough, which was between the town and the homestead land. There was an overlook off the highway where you could park by the edge and look in. The grass was much taller than the oat field I'd seen the day before. And vaster. I could see how people could disappear in it. To the northeast of it somewhere was what was left of Silver Lake.

"We could still try to go see it," Chris said. I'd said before that I hadn't wanted to, but he knew I changed my mind a lot. Case in point: we were skipping town.

"No, it's okay," I said. It was almost starting to feel okay.

Then we went back to Ingalls Homestead for a final look. "I just want to walk around a little, one last time," I told Chris.

Walking across the giant green pathless sprawl of this place was an uncanny sensation; I'd felt it when we'd come here yesterday and I felt it again: like walking into a painting, the sense of being there and never quite arriving at the same time. Every direction I turned it would happen.

I looked for a place to go. There was a little building over on the eastern edge of the homestead, just a resting area for the walking trail, the map said, and I'd meant to go and see it, whatever it was, because then I would have seen everything. "Let's go that way, I guess," I said, but after a couple minutes of walking I could feel my eyes filling up and I had a catch in my throat, a sob, and Chris heard me and we stopped and I pressed my face into his shoulder.

"We can stay," he said. "Do you want to stay?"

"No," I said. I was giving up. I couldn't see you anywhere east or south, I thought. It's okay, I thought.

We went back to the car. The haystick, the messy, half-assed haystick, was in the backseat. I stuffed it in a plastic supermarket bag and tucked it in next to our luggage.

"So we're really taking that with us?" Chris asked.

I laughed. "I think so."

The lump in my throat began to unclench itself as we drove east to Brookings and then south to Sioux Falls. It was nearly gone by the time we were back on I-90 in Minnesota. We listened to an improbably wonderful oldies station that played things like "Dancing in the Moonlight" and "Ain't No Woman (Like the

One I've Got)." We were driving away from the sunset and into the dark and I did not mind.

We didn't want to stop, or maybe I didn't. Finally, we did near Albert Lea, Minnesota, where we found a Holiday Inn that cost too much. We hadn't had dinner and the only place we could find that was open after nine p.m. on a Sunday was the Applebee's across the street, which was shiny and horrible inside, with music we hated. The lead singer of Nickelback bellowed over the speakers while we ordered monstrous burgers and slumped in the booth. *Fine,* I thought; I was fine. If I'd been under some kind of prairie spell, it was good and broken now.

10.

The Road Back

THE SKY HAD SHRUNK and was simply the size of the Holiday Inn window now. Here in eastern Minnesota things had reverted back to normal, and nothing was too flat or still anymore. But I felt better: we looked at the maps and the travel directions and realized that if we'd stuck with our original plans and left De Smet this morning, the drive wouldn't have left us time for both our other stops. Today we'd gotten to sleep late and eat muffins from the hotel lobby; we were on vacation, after all.

Months after all this I would talk to Sandra Hume, who'd been to most of the Little House sites two or three times, about the way I'd felt about leaving De Smet, how everything had seemed wonderful until suddenly I couldn't wait to get the hell out of there. Was that weird?

Sandra didn't seem to think so. "There really is a point where it gets to be too much," she said over the phone. "You can't keep pretending it's not the real world or else you'll just go crazy. But here's the real question: do you want to go back there?"

Well, it's really out of the way, I told her. I mean, I'd always figured that seeing it would be a once-in-a-lifetime thing, and as such I couldn't imagine that I'd *get* to travel all that way and go there again if I wanted to.

"But do you want to?" she repeated. "Forget whether or not you can. Logistics aside, *do you ever want to go there again?*"

I didn't even have to think. "Yes," I said. "Despite everything." I didn't know why. I just did. I knew it would always still be there and I would still want to go.

"That's how it goes," she said. "And you always know it'll never be perfect, but you go anyway."

⚘

Back at the Holiday Inn in Minnesota I had yet to forgive myself, but a few hours of overpriced hotel life had done us good. I felt like a regular person, one you'd never suspect had a bundle of slough hay in the hatchback of her car.

But something still nagged at me, and when we were back on the road I realized what it was. I was at that confounding place again, the point where the books left off and I didn't really know what happened next. I mean, I knew that she went to Missouri, traveled to San Francisco, wrote things in notebooks, but I'd hated that there wasn't a story to live in anymore. I thought I could find the way past it, but I'd gone all this way, and the prairie hadn't led anywhere, and here I was again.

But Chris said, "You look happy about something."

"Just that it's our last day," I said.

⚘

"So what are we seeing here again?" he asked as we drove into Spring Valley.

"A church," I said. "And maybe a barn."

"That's it?" he said.

I looked at one of the guides I'd printed up. "Uh, you can see an 1874 fire wagon?" I shrugged. "It won't take long."

Only the completist in me had insisted that we stop in Spring Valley, Minnesota, where Laura and Almanzo had lived briefly. It was billed as one of the five towns on the Laura Ingalls Wilder Memorial Highway; we'd already seen three of them, and this place was en route to the final one in Burr Oak, Iowa. It was also the biggest town, with a population of about 2,500. At this point it seemed practically a city.

Spring Valley was where the Wilders—Almanzo's family—had lived. While Almanzo's boyhood in the book *Farmer Boy* had taken place in upstate New York, the family had moved west a few years later in the 1870s. "They quickly established a farm just as successful as the one they had left behind," says William Anderson in *The Little House Guidebook*.

Of course they did! I have to admit I found the Wilders a little boring in *Farmer Boy*, with their hardworking prosperity and Father always knowing best. I've always gotten the sense that the Wilders would be the kind of family who poses for their Christmas card photo in tasteful matching sweaters in their showplace living room. Nice folks and all, but, you know. Obviously, circumstances were different for poor Almanzo and Laura (*see:* multiple crop failures, house fire, diphtheria, etc.), and thus the main reason why

Spring Valley can be considered a Historic Laura Ingalls Wilder Destination is because the couple, along with Rose, moved in with the Wilders in 1890 for a year and a half to recover from the multiple-tragedy pileup they'd suffered during the events of *The First Four Years.*

There are few details about this couch-surfing-at-the-in-laws juncture in Laura's life; it's hard to imagine what else she and Almanzo did besides attend Sunday services at the Methodist church that now serves as the town historical society. The Wilder family farm was long gone, but the guidebook mentioned that you could get a peek at the old barn, now in someone's yard, from a side street.

To be honest, if it hadn't been right on the way to Burr Oak, I probably wouldn't have bothered stopping here. Wilder family lore was for the history nerds who really cared about things like where the cousins mentioned once in chapter 3 of whatever wound up. Even the student tour guide who led us through the Wilder exhibit in the old church sanctuary sounded a little apologetic in her narration, as if she was sorry there wasn't more to see than a display of old photographs. I did like finding out more about Almanzo's sister Eliza Jane, whom, despite her unfavorable portrayal as the incompetent schoolteacher in *Little Town on the Prairie,* I'd always considered to be the coolest Wilder, a sort of proto-feminist who'd homesteaded as a single woman and had a government job in Washington, D.C. In 1890!

But the real kick was the rest of the museum, in the church basement, which housed, in addition to the 1874 fire wagon, a stunningly demented inventory of antique curiosities. Spring Valley, and I mean this in the best way, could be on that show *Hoarders.* There were old movie theater projectors, nineteenth-century coffins, local high school cheerleader outfits from the 1980s, a vintage stapler exhibit (no, really), a taxidermied wolf. Our guide was an octogenarian named Lucinda who ushered us through the aisles of insane relics with a tiny-stepped but unstoppable gait and a very deliberate course. Once, we reached the end of an aisle where Chris saw a display case of old cameras. "Wow," he said, stepping closer to look. "I remember those Kodak Disc thingies—"

"Sir, we are going *this* way," she said as she turned down another aisle. There was no messing with Lucinda. She did not much go for questions, either. But Lucinda could deliver. She showed us a terrifying 1930s hair permanent machine, the kind with roller clamps attached to a Medusa-like array of cables. "You used to get your hair done with one of these," she said. "Burn your head that way. I do not recommend it." We saw a case full of native rock samples, an Inuit sled someone had brought back from Alaska, and a torturous-looking electrical contraption with an array of knobs, once used, Lucinda said, for treating arthritis. "I do not recommend it," she said. She showed us a hand-pumped antique vacuum cleaner and said she did not recommend that, either. It was all such a trip that when Lucinda finished, we asked her if we could stay a bit and look around. I wanted to see more of the room full of old kitchen items, including a Dazey hand-cranked butter churn, which Lucinda had said was like one she used to use, and did not recommend.

"You have to turn out the lights when you're done," Lucinda said. We thanked her and she headed slowly back to the stairwell, where she forgot about us and turned out the lights herself.

Our verdict: despite the rather low Laura quotient, Spring Valley ruled.

"I give it three and a half sunbonnets," Chris said.

"Definitely," I said. "Though I guess we forgot to see the historic house." On our way out of town, after we'd peeked at the Wilder barn (which was, yes, a barn), I realized that for an extra five bucks we could have seen an authentically furnished nineteenth-century house across the street that *The Little House Guidebook* said "offers a glimpse of the farming life the Wilders knew in Spring Valley."

"We should have seen that," I sighed. But then, maybe I wasn't so interested in seeing 1890s Minnesota farming life. It wasn't really Laura and Almanzo's life, after all, which from this point on had been pretty bonkers for a while, a series of false starts and bleak transitions. After their stay in Spring Valley, they'd boarded a train and spent an uncomfortable year in the piney woods of southern Florida. Rose's semiautobiographical short story about this time, "Innocence," makes the whole place sound like the swamp in *Deliverance*. Laura hated the climate and felt like an outsider. (You could say she did not recommend Florida.) Following that, they moved back to De Smet, where farming conditions had become even worse. Their last bit of farmland had been taken by the bank and they turned to odd jobs instead. It was here that Laura told young Rose they were "camping" in their house with barely any furniture. Reportedly they even considered moving to New Zealand. Finally, they got in a wagon and traveled for three months and wound up in a crappy cabin in the Ozarks. It was impossible, of course, to fully see the Almanzo Wilder family's failures and eccentric history, but we'd seen an entire church basement full of abandoned crap, and in a way, that felt right. Never mind glimpsing life; we'd glimpsed the crazy.

❁

When I'd planned this trip, I almost made Burr Oak, Iowa, the first stop; it was the closest site to Chicago and only a half day's drive. And since it wasn't really a Little House site—just another transitional place, really, where the Ingallses had spent a couple of years that hadn't been part of the books—I thought perhaps we ought to stop there before hitting the places I "knew." After all, the Burr Oak years had been left out of the Little House story altogether, possibly because they weren't very good times. If Laura wanted to forget Burr Oak, I reasoned, maybe it was better to see it first and forget it, too.

But now I was glad we'd saved it for last. I had to admit that I wasn't in Laura World anymore. I'd been outside the story ever since we'd left De Smet. I wanted to see what else was outside.

Most of what's known about the Ingalls family's "lost" years in Burr Oak comes from some of Laura's letters and her unpub-lished *Pioneer Girl* memoir. Ma had given birth to a son, Freddie, in Walnut Grove, Minnesota, but when the grasshopper plagues and crop troubles continued, Pa wanted to leave what he called the "blasted country" and accepted a business proposition to run a hotel in Iowa with another Walnut Grove family. But by the time the Ingallses had relocated a few hundred miles east to Burr Oak, baby Freddie had taken ill and died. For about a year, when Laura was nine going on ten, the family lived in less-than-ideal circum-stances as they worked among strangers at the hotel. Eventually Pa gave up his share of the business (the partnership may have gone sour) and found other work. Another child, Grace, was born, and in the face of mounting debts Pa decided to pack up and leave in the middle of the night (oh, yes, he did!) and move the family back to Walnut Grove. There they lived in town, Pa worked various jobs, and Mary had the fever or stroke that left her blind.

The long-held belief is that Laura Ingalls Wilder skipped over these years in the Little House books because they were too painful, though some biographers think that's too simple an explanation. Laura told readers that "it would bring in too many characters," meaning perhaps she felt the story would have become too complicated. In *Laura Ingalls Wilder: A Writer's Life,* Pamela Smith Hill points out that in a letter to Rose, Laura explained that the Burr Oak era "does not belong in the picture I am making of the family." In other words, a family that always moved west, endured noble, spirit-galvanizing tragedies instead of senseless private ones, and always, no matter what, had happy Christmases. Whereas in *Pioneer Girl,* Laura reported that "Christmas was disappointing" when they lived in the hotel in Burr Oak. "Ma was always tired, Pa was busy," she wrote. "Then Mary and Carrie and I had the measles, all at the same time. The hotel was a noisy place to be sick in, people were coming and going all the time, and doors slamming." *Not a single piece of candy* is mentioned. "It was not a happy time."

Not even Burr Oak itself fit the hopeful Little House ethos. It had been established around 1851 during a settlement rush in northern Iowa, and it had been on a major westward route. In the 1850s more than two hundred covered wagons passed through the town every day, but by the time the Ingallses moved there it was past its prime. Laura wrote in *Pioneer Girl* that Burr Oak "was an old town, and always seemed to me old and dark and dirty. I liked a new town better." There was no railroad nearby, and while the two hotels in town still drew plenty of business from people passing through, the place itself was a dead end.

Now Burr Oak barely exists: it's an unincorporated part of Decorah, Iowa, that still bears its old name on some maps. When planning the trip, I'd discovered, almost at the last minute, that I'd printed up erroneous driving directions and made a motel reservation an hour's drive away from where we were supposed to be, because the online map I was using couldn't locate Burr Oak. Or rather, it insisted it was in the middle of a cornfield near Osage, Iowa. For once my habit of peering down at the homesites via satellite photos, which had always made me feel like some kind of historical stalker, had saved us from being lost.

But the two-lane highway we were on now was the right one, and it was so quiet as it wound and dipped over little puffs of hills in the bright sunlight that it felt like we were floating, that maybe we really were off the map. We drifted over the border between Minnesota and Iowa; the town was only three miles from there.

The present-day Burr Oak is a sort of rural subdivision: a loose cluster of houses, a church or two, and the remnants of the main street where the Masters Hotel, now the Laura Ingalls Wilder museum, still stands, a big white house built in 1850. The office and gift store where we bought our tour tickets were in a tiny brick building across the street; we learned it had once been a bank where a locally famous robbery had taken place in 1931, in which two gunmen had ordered the bank employees into the vault while they made their escape. It's the sort of story that endures mostly to prove that things once happened here.

The whole street block was terrifically ghostly: only a few buildings left, one an empty building where a café had been. Next to the museum was the only other establishment, a bar called Barney's.

If you think it's a little unwholesome to have a watering hole smack next to a Laura Ingalls Wilder museum, you don't know Burr Oak. "A certain grittiness, even seediness, characterized the episodes Wilder remembered from her life in Burr Oak," says Pamela Smith Hill in her book. There had been a barroom in the hotel and a saloon next door (though not in the same place as the current bar), which the elder Ingallses had found so dismaying that after it caught fire one night, Pa admitted that if it could've burned to the ground without taking the rest of the town with it, he wouldn't have helped out with the bucket brigade. In *Pioneer Girl* Laura reported that there were bullet holes in the door of the hotel barroom where the previous owner had shot at his wife in a drunken fit, and that in the saloon the hired girl's boyfriend went on a drinking binge so severe that when he lit a cigar the fumes on his breath ignited and he was killed instantly. (Who knew that was even *possible*?) Even though the incident was over 130 years ago, I liked to think that maybe they were still talking about it at Barney's.

From the tour you could tell this was a different Laura World. There wasn't quite the same prairie-dress-clad seriousness that had characterized the attractions we'd seen elsewhere. If her T-shirt was any indication, our teenage tour guide was named Monica and she'd just attended volleyball camp. She knew her tour speech well, reciting the history of the Ingalls family's years in Iowa, and was most enthusiastic at the end of it: "And then Pa skipped town in the middle of the night!"

Monica led the two of us around the rooms of the hotel, bounding up and down the stairs with a summer-job insouciance, which didn't seem out of place, considering that the whole museum was dedicated to a girl who'd had to work there over a hundred years ago. She pointed out the chamber pots that Laura would have had to empty in the bedrooms, the dining room where she and Mary would have waited on guests eating breakfast, and the kitchen where the girls washed dishes. Nothing in the Little House books ever indicated that the family would have been familiar with a place like this. In *By the Shores of Silver Lake*, Ma and the girls have dinner at a hotel by the train station in Tracy, and Laura drinks in the details as if she were visiting Mars. And in *Little Town on the Prairie*, when the question of Laura working in town comes up, Ma really clutches her pearls over the thought of her daughter taking a hotel job.

The irony of the Masters Hotel is that it *looks* awfully nice, much bigger than the surveyors' house, and more refined, with wallpapered rooms and "boughten" furniture. The upstairs bedrooms had cozy sloping eaves, patchwork quilts on the beds, and dressers adorned with doilies and porcelain pitchers and washbasins. Aside from the cramped rooms, the place looked to me like it could be a pretty cute bed-and-breakfast. It was only when Chris and I listened to the tour narrative that we realized how grim things had been. Monica told us that twenty-five to thirty people stayed at the hotel every night.

"All at the same time?" I asked. There were four tiny bedrooms, each with one bed. I'd neglected to remember reading that if you were a nineteenth-century hotel customer (and not a rich one), your twenty-five cents a night (the equivalent of sixty dollars, Monica told us) paid not for a room but for the privilege of sleeping crosswise on a bed, or whatever cot or floor space was available, plus meals. I noticed the rooms didn't have doors, because why bother? With sleeping people piled everywhere, a typical night here must have looked like the aftermath of a frat house kegger. I realized that the social prohibitions against women traveling alone weren't just an uptight custom. Oh, the beautiful heart of days gone by, how crudely it could palpitate.

We saw the tiny room on the lowest floor where the entire Ingalls family lived for a time. "All of them?" I asked, even though it was about the same size as the dugout in Walnut Grove. But I wasn't having to reconcile a room in my mind from the books with the ones here. There were no cozy scenes of Little House comfort to contend with. But all the same I kept conjuring up sweet images of Ma cooking in the kitchen, even though she'd had to do it for up to twenty people, three meals a day, every day.

The museum also seemed a tad confused about how visitors ought to visualize the Ingalls family. Because when we went into the parlor, there they were, in life-sized doll form, seated on the high-backed chairs and divan.

"What the . . ." Chris said under his breath.

"These are soft sculptures of the Ingalls family," Monica told us. She explained they'd been made by a local artist and dressed in historically accurate clothing. Their heads were stuffed fabric, with the features scrunched and stitched into place, and their hair appeared to be real, or wigs, or something. Monica introduced a couple of them. "This is Pa," she said, stepping over to the bearded one limply holding a fiddle. Ma had Grace (a sort of baby-shaped pillow) on her lap, and Mary was the blond one in the rocking chair. Monica motioned to the last two dolls, who both wore prairie dresses and were propped sort of awkwardly on the divan. "You know which one is Laura?" she asked us.

No, I thought, because they're freaking soft sculptures. I pointed to the one with the sunbonnet and pigtails.

"No, that's Carrie," she said. "Laura is holding her rag doll, Charlotte. See?"

My brain protested: *Do not look directly at Soft Sculpture Laura!*

From what I let myself see, though, I could tell that in their demented way they really did look a bit like the Ingallses, inasmuch as one could look at an old photo and render it in pillow form. And who was I to take issue with how someone else imagined the Ingalls family? They were propped up in their seats, their heads tilted back a little as if they were daydreaming.

The tour ended in back of the house, where Monica pointed out a little herb garden by the kitchen door like one Ma would have kept. The house was built into a little hill that sloped down to a grassy yard with a tiny creek, the same one that had flowed in Laura's time, looking very much like the kind of place where I would've played Laura as a kid. Things felt familiar here, but not at all the way the other places we'd seen had been familiar.

We had lunch in the dim bar coolness of Barney's, with the sounds of the TV behind us and the bright ghost-town street out the window in front of us. There was a slowness now instead of a stillness, and for the first time in days I felt sure of where I was, in the sense that it was real, and also in the sense that it was just where I wanted to be. I pointed this out to Chris.

"Well," he said. "We *are* in a bar in Iowa that serves pork tenderloin sandwiches."

He was right. Who wouldn't want to be here?

❈

One more place to look: the Burr Oak cemetery. It was just a few blocks from the museum, next to a small abandoned church, and with well over a hundred headstones, dozens of them old and weathered.

Nobody related to the Ingallses was buried here, but it was a place that Laura associated with some of her better memories of Burr Oak. In *Pioneer Girl* she writes of walking there with a school friend on Saturday afternoons. She thought "the old grave-yard" was a beautiful place and not at all sad; she described it as a place with tall dark evergreens. Of course, I'd loved the idea that Laura Ingalls Wilder had a little bit of a goth streak, but it was also her description of the place that made me want to see it.

The big evergreens were gone: it was bright and open, and Chris and I went around in the sun looking at all the old gravestones, the ones that were white and rain-softened, their embellishments slowly melting away. There was a big stone for a man who had been killed at Little Big Horn, and a great many headstones for children. I noticed how many of the inscriptions measured life-times not just in years but in months and days. All these people and all their days. At first I looked for graves with dates earlier than 1877, so that I could see the same stones that Laura had. But after a while I just wandered. It was nice not to be looking for anyone anymore.

❈

The Super 8 motel had a sign that said *VELKOMMEN TIL DECORAH*. After Burr Oak we'd driven another twelve miles to Decorah, Iowa, a small city born from the same land rush that had put Burr Oak on the map, and largely settled by Norwegians. Somehow, on this final afternoon of our trip, things had slowly grown enchanted again, starting with the cemetery and continuing as we found the motel with its charming sign and drove around Decorah. It was almost dusk, and with the shade from the steep hillsides everything was half in deep shadow and half dazzling, the windows on the streets blazing with reflected light.

At the edge of the business district we saw a bookstore in an old brick house and we stopped and went inside. The store was a warren of little rooms with armchairs; the place served coffee and played soothing music. Invariably in places like this I stumble around feeling happy, but with my mind mostly blank. Thus I found myself staring at a shelf marked *Local Interest*, and then at the spine of a book called *A Little House Traveler*.

I don't know why I bought the book; I didn't need it. It was billed as a compilation of "writings from Laura Ingalls Wilder's journey across America," and it contained books I already owned, *On the Way Home* and *West from Home*. Those two books had been the uneven road beyond the Little House books that as a child I'd tried to follow, only to find myself lost amidst those dry diary entries about Nebraska agriculture and letters that spoke in a voice I didn't know. In the last year I'd reread both books and found them more interesting this time but still unsatisfying. So I bought *A Little House Traveler* out of a faint sense of obligation, of wanting to buy a book in this nice store, and of thinking it was pretty cute that this book about Laura Ingalls Wilder traveling should appear to me on the last night of my Laura Ingalls Wilder travels.

Our motel room smelled smoky, and from my Burr Oak reckonings it cost something like five hundred frontier dollars, but we opened the windows wide and let the cool air in. Chris opened his laptop and I lounged on the wonderfully awful bedspread and flipped through *A Little House Traveler.*

It turned out there was a third section in the book I hadn't known about. It was called *The Road Back*, and it was another travel diary of Laura's, which she had written in 1931 on a visit back to South Dakota from Missouri. She'd traveled with Almanzo and their dog, Nero, in a 1923 Buick nicknamed Isabelle, on a summer trip to see Grace and Carrie, now her only living sisters. Laura was sixty-four; she had recently worked with her daughter, Rose, to write what would become *Little House in the Big Woods*, and in the next year it would be published. Since the move to Missouri, she'd only been back to De Smet once, nearly thirty years earlier, when her father had died. Like her *On the Way Home* diary, this one was mostly for practical purposes: she recorded expenses and miles driven and described meals and the roadside cabins where they spent the night. But these pages felt more familiar, even though I'd never read them before.

"So here we are in South Dakota," she wrote, as they crossed the border, and a line or two down added, "So far we don't like South Dakota."

A day later they reached Manchester, the little town just past De Smet where Grace lived with her husband, Nate. And then a day after that Laura wrote, "Grace seems like a stranger, only now and then something familiar about her face. I suppose it is the same with me."

Something clicked open in me when I read that, and I read on. That same day she'd gone into De Smet and visited places that I knew had been on Calumet Avenue. Her account is often cranky: "Ran around town awhile then sat at music store waiting for Manly and Nate to show up. Stupid, tiresome, hot. I got tired of it and went by myself up the street." She writes of driving out to the place where Pa's homestead used to be, the road "nearly in the place where Carrie and I walked to school and Manly used to drive Barnum and Skip," and then back through town out to the land she and Almanzo had owned, which, she noted, was simply fields now, all the buildings on it gone. They must have sat in their car and looked out at the empty hill just as we had the day before.

The diary was simple and the events it described were unexciting, but I found it strangely uplifting because it reminded me so much of what I'd just experienced. Throughout her visit she complains of the hot winds, of feeling ill; she is disappointed and joyful and irritated and wistful. "It all makes me miss those who are gone," she writes. "Pa and Ma and Mary and the Boasts."

I know, I thought. I'd always been a little at odds with this woman, this Bessie or Mrs. Wilder or whatever she was really called, who was not quite Laura and not quite *not* her, but I felt like I finally knew the story that continued, that I'd been where it had gone.

Now it was almost dark and we went to dinner, some place that was tucked into the hill behind the motel, close enough that we could walk. As we went we counted out loud, doing an inventory of all that we'd seen: six parlor organs, five dugouts (including replica, ruins of, and stage set), eight covered wagons, including the one where we'd stayed; countless girls in sunbonnets, at least fifty people in nineteenth-century dress onstage and almost as many offstage, Chris pointed out, if you counted the girls at the Laura and Nellie contests. Five chamber pots, three washboards.

Three times we'd read or heard about the origin for the phrase "sleep tight," two of them erroneously attributing it to tightening the ropes on a bed frame. Three cows, two china shepherdesses, six RVs. Ten to twelve disturbing artistic renderings of various members of the Ingalls family, not counting the Laura dolls, of which we'd seen about six, including the bobblehead figure I'd bought in Walnut Grove. Seven flatirons, three whatnots, eight decorative haysticks, five teenage tour guides. Maybe a dozen iron cookstoves. Two signs that advertised both Laura Ingalls Wilder and Miller beer. At least six horses. Two girls who weren't really dressed like Laura at all. We could go on.

By one of the back doors of the Super 8, back where the owner or manager must have lived, there was a small garden like the one we'd seen earlier that day, with carefully tended sage and basil plants. It made me think of an Elizabeth Bishop poem, the one about the filling station with the improbable doily and plant in its waiting room. *Somebody lives here*, the line went, and it was true, true and in the present tense.

It didn't feel like the last night of anything anymore, just that the world went on and would follow us home.

11.

Be It Enacted

LESS THAN TWO WEEKS LATER I was in New York City, seeing friends. More than once I thought about this as I'd go up the stairs from the subway into the sunlight, not quite believing that I'd just been out on the prairie and now I was here. I've visited New York at least once a year for a while now, but this time the city's age, all its great, worn, beautiful, burnished parts, was more visible to me in a way it hadn't been since my first trip here. I liked being somewhere so vast and old.

One night when I met a friend for dinner in Greenwich Village I got off the subway a stop early so I could walk by a building on Jones Street where, according to *The Little House Guidebook*, Rose Wilder Lane had once lived in 1919. (She was a working writer in her thirties by this point, close to my age but still adventurous enough to spend a winter living so profoundly on the cheap that she'd slept under newspapers on a set of bedsprings on the floor.

The place had been unheated and she warmed her hands under her arms as she sat at her typewriter during the day. She'd written about the experience years afterward in a letter to a friend and made it all sound like a blast.) Later I rode a battered elevator in an old factory in Brooklyn up to my friend Jami's apartment, where we pulled chairs along the concrete floor over to the great big windows and gazed out over the East River and the skyline at night.

Ever since I'd come back from the trip west, I'd been having moments where I'd tell myself to look around, to *look at this*, as if I'd needed to be apprised of my own life. It reminded me of what I used to do when I was little, when Laura was in my head. Now, though, it was just me, and that was all right.

"You're not seeing the *Farmer Boy* house?" Sandra Hume had said back when I'd talked to her in the spring. It was hard to tell over the phone, but I think she'd actually said it in *horror*. I didn't think it was a big deal whether or not I saw the place where the book was set and where Almanzo Wilder had been a boy. Like all the other book locales, there was an official homesite museum there now, but since it was of miles east from all the other Little House destinations—as far upstate in New York as you could get, really, up near the border of Quebec—visiting it would require a trip all its own, a trip I'd kept leaving out of my plans.

Because, and I'll confess right now, I wasn't a big fan of *Farmer Boy*. That was really the reason why I hadn't made it to upstate New York.

I mean I liked *Farmer Boy* just fine, but I'd never read it as many times as the Laura books. Often I forgot about it. It hadn't captured my imagination the way the rest of the series had. As far as I was concerned, *Farmer Boy* wasn't really in Laura World. I didn't identify with young Almanzo the way I did with Laura, perhaps in part because he was a boy, and also because I thought his family was a little too perfect. While I'd enjoyed the book, it felt secondary, like (forgive my nine-year-old mind) a spin-off of one of my favorite TV shows. I know some Little House fans will be extremely dismayed by this comparison to *Joanie Loves Chachi*, because *Farmer Boy* is one of the most beloved books in the series. It's also the most schismatic book, since plenty of people, myself included, consider it the one book in the series that you could skip if you had to.

I've always felt that the book starts off well enough, with that terrific early scene where the mild-mannered schoolteacher defeats the bully with a borrowed whip. After that, though, things get a bit dull, and the book plods along with its hardworking values, and character-building chores, and Father's two-page-long speeches about the value of a half-dollar.

But at least there are pancakes. Because, yes, *Farmer Boy* is not without its supreme pleasures, some of the best moments in the series. There's a coveted colt, a visit from the tinsmith, ice blocks, a pet suckling pig, and spreads of food so fabulous they eclipse even the sugaring-dance feast in *Little House in the Big Woods*. Honestly, without *Farmer Boy* in the series, *The Little House Cookbook* would be a much grimmer compendium, consisting only of Ingalls family frontier fare like bean broth and johnnycake instead of Mother Wilder's stuffed goose and pumpkin pie. So I will not begrudge anyone their love for young Almanzo and his virtuous but cushy life. I just wasn't sure if I wanted to experience *Farmer*

Boy beyond the apples 'n' onions recipe. (Which, by the way, is *incredible*.)

So when I told Sandra that I didn't think I'd be going out to see the *Farmer Boy* house, I could tell she was on the other side of the schism, a real Almanzonian. But then she pointed out that the Wilder farmhouse was the *only* house mentioned in the Little House books that was *still on its original foundation*, which sounded pretty impressive. Would it be more full of ghosts, for instance, if there really was such a thing as ghosts?

"Trust me, the place is really SPECIAL," Sandra told me over the phone, with something of a don't-say-I-didn't-warn-you emphasis on the word *special*. And then I knew that if I didn't go I'd always wonder.

Fine, then, I would go to see the dadblanged *Farmer Boy* house. I decided as long as I was in New York I'd make a detour upstate. Chris couldn't go with me this time, so I asked one of my oldest friends, Michael, whom I'd be seeing in New York City, to come along. We'd taken road trips together before: in college we'd gone to Washington, D.C., for a Pride march; more recently we'd gone to Iowa City together, spending the whole drive from Chicago comparing our worst ex-boyfriends. Now he was willing to fly from LaGuardia airport to Burlington, Vermont, with me, and drive two hours through the Adirondacks in a rented car just to see some place where a kid with a funny name once picked potatoes.

Michael had never read the Little House books, so he had only a vague sense of our destination.

"So this is the house of the guy that Melissa Gilbert marries on the TV show?" Michael asked. "Almanzo, right?" He pronounced it "Al-MON-zo," the way most people do, since that's how they said it on the NBC show.

Yes, I told him. "But actually, it's pronounced 'Al-MAN-zo.'"

"How do you know?"

"Because that's how *Laura* said it." I was so excited to get to tell someone about this. "There's this one recording of her speaking voice, and she says *Almanzo* with the flat *a*, but when she says *Iowa* she pronounces it 'Ioway.'"

"Oh my God, you know so much about this now," Michael said.

"I know!" Over the course of the drive, I let all the Laura knowledge I'd collected over the past year unspool while he listened. I told him about the real Ingalls family who'd kept moving to the wrong places and the fictional family who'd always just followed the sunset and their destiny, and the traces where they'd both been, all these hollows in the ground and these remade little houses. I explained who Rose had been and how she was both a part of the Little House books and a world unto herself. I talked about the storm in Kansas and the lightning in South Dakota and the frozen lake in Wisconsin, and how for weeks after our visit I'd look up the local news around Pepin to see if the ice had finally broken.

Michael was a good listener. You could do a lot worse than drive through the Vermont countryside near the end of summer with your best friend of twenty years, telling him about these people, these places that you were starting to know by heart.

Back at home Chris was reading *Farmer Boy*. (It's officially the third book in the series, but I tend to think you can read it out of order, since it's a stand-alone story.) He said he wanted to have some idea of what I'd be seeing on my trip. One night when I was still in New York City I called home to Chicago.

"I don't get why you don't like *Farmer Boy*," he said on the phone. "This book rules. This kid has the best life ever. There's *a doughnut jar* in the kitchen."

"The doughnut jar really is cool," I admitted.

"'In his right hand he held a doughnut, and in his left hand two cookies,'" Chris said. I knew he was reading from the book. "'He took a bite of doughnut AND THEN a bite of cookie.'" He was quoting the birthday scene, where Almanzo gets to stay home from school and go sledding and wander through the kitchen double-fisting baked goods. "That is some bad-ass action right there," Chris said.

"Whatever," I said. "You haven't gotten to the part where it says he can't wait until the Fourth of July celebration when there will be speeches. What nine-year-old boy looks forward to SPEECHES?"

The day after that Chris had finished the book. "I think I know why you don't like this book," he said on our next phone call. "It's because everything always works out for these people, Almanzo and his family."

"Maybe," I said. But, I pointed out, there was always a sense in the other books that the Ingalls family, the storybook one at least, ends up okay.

"No, no. In *Farmer Boy* they *always* win. Their horses are *the best* horses in the state. The mother makes *the best* butter anywhere. Everything they do is the most amazing successful thing ever in the history of anything." He was right: the Wilders excelled at bully defeating and pumpkin growing; they always escaped every peril, whether it was frost in the cornfield or robbers who lurked outside the farmhouse (who were chased away by a stray dog that *of course* knew to side with the Wilders). Even when things went wrong they somehow wound up turning miraculously right, like when Almanzo threw the brush of stove-blacking at his sister and it hit the parlor wall and left a big blotch, and his sister just came up with some brilliant solution to fix it so he never got in trouble. Full of win, that Almanzo kid.

Sure, the book constantly espoused life virtues and diligent chore doing, as if to imply that the Wilder family's charmed life was purely a matter of hard work and perseverance. I was never convinced, especially after seeing the fortunes of perfectly decent folk like the Ingallses repeatedly go up in smoke and clouds of grasshoppers.

"Yeah, everything just sort of happens magically for them in *Farmer Boy*," I said. "So annoying."

The Wilder farm was the most impressively historical-looking place of all the Little House sites I'd seen: a circa 1850s farmhouse painted a deep red with white trim; it stood in a shady grove with an array of barns and stables alongside it. It looked like just the kind of place you'd visit on a fourth-grade field trip, where you'd learn how a spinning wheel worked and get a little handful of carded sheep's wool to take home.

It also looked very much like the place described in the book, which is pretty remarkable considering Laura's knowledge was secondhand. She had never been there; in fact, no one in the Wilder family had returned after they'd moved to Minnesota. Only Rose had visited here once, in 1932, when her mother was working on the manuscript for *Farmer Boy*. The book was Laura's second children's book effort (though it's now listed third in the series order); she had started writing it a few months after that trip to De Smet in the Buick. She hadn't fully conceived of the Little House series at this point; certain territories of her life and family history had yet to be visited.

By all accounts she'd intended *Farmer Boy* to be a companion to *Little House in the Big Woods*: another detail-rich account of an earlier time, another *now* for Depression-era readers. This time she'd based it on her husband's recollections, which must have been vivid, even though he was reportedly a man of few words. There's evidence that Rose considered writing a biography of Almanzo, to be titled *A Son of the Soil*, but it's believed that he was so reticent in interviews she abandoned the project. Or perhaps it was because he lacked the optimism that Rose had likely hoped to convey. "My life has been mostly disappointments," he wrote in a letter to her in 1937. But Laura would go back to the beginning in *Farmer Boy*, just as she had when writing about the house in the Big Woods that was so cozy you wanted them to stay there forever.

Inside the Wilder farmhouse we could see what a comfortable life young Almanzo and his family had lived. The place was smallish by twentieth-century standards, but in the 1800s it would have been practically a McMansion, with its big, bright rooms with woolen carpets and stately furniture. All at once I remembered the thrill I used to get whenever I rediscovered this book and read it again, because while the book is never explicit about the Wilders' economic status, it's nonetheless clear: *they were rich!* They had a parlor *and* a dining room and, be still my beating heart, *three* barns. They'd been faithfully reconstructed here and I pointed them out to Michael.

"I know one barn's for the horses," I said, remembering. "And then they had oxen. And sheep. And pigs. Or at least Almanzo had one, and he fed it candy." The more I remembered of the book, the more useless I became in regard to actual facts. "They had, like, *hundreds* of animals."

"Really?" Michael asked.

"Well, I don't know. It seems like it, though."

We saw it all: the parlor with its fancy wallpaper, the kitchen, the upstairs bedrooms, then out to the barn complex where we learned more about nineteenth-century farm technology than we ever thought possible. I had to admit that it was one of the best house tours I'd been on throughout all my Little House travels, with the world of the past faithfully reconstructed and nary a soft sculpture doll to break the illusion.

Except that when we were in the kitchen, I'd whispered to Michael, "There's no *doughnut jar!*" No sugar barrel, either, to represent the one the Wilder children had consumed while their parents were on a trip (according to the book, the four kids had emptied that sucker out *in less than a week*).

"That was nice, but I wish there'd been pancakes," I told Michael when the tour was over.

"Um, it's a museum," he said. "What do you mean?"

I meant *pancakes,* ten—TEN—stacks of them on a platter on the stove, just like in chapter 8! I meant a gigantic spread of chicken pie and roast pork that Almanzo, according to the book, could "taste in every corner of his mouth." (Next time you eat something, try to simulate this effect. IT IS NOT EASY.) I meant that this was a lovely house, but it

couldn't really, truly be the *Farmer Boy* house unless all that insane food was there in some way, and I told Michael this.

"You mean they should serve pancakes here?" he said.

"No," I said, because of course that was ridiculous. But what, then? I racked my brain. "I guess I mean they should make us *think* of pancakes." That was what was important: not the pancakes themselves but the idea of pancakes. Like a Wallace Stevens poem but in reverse, *and with pancakes*.

And just then I remembered something I'd read in the introduction of *The Little House Cookbook*. There Barbara Walker pointed out that Laura, after a childhood filled with near-starvation experiences like the one in *The Long Winter*, wrote *Farmer Boy* not just as her husband's story, but as, Walker writes, "her own fantasy of blissful youth, surrounded on all sides by food." In other words, a whole book of wishful thinking.

With all its over-the-top dinner scenes and constant allusions to the Wilder family's good fortune, literal and otherwise, *Farmer Boy* wasn't really the smug when-I-was-your-age sermon I'd originally made it out to be, but more a wistful dream conjured up by a woman who'd spent much of her life enduring deprivation. It was a love letter to the original promise of success and prosperity that had so eluded her husband in his adulthood, when, like countless other settlers, he'd found out the hard way that the farming methods from back East were no match for the dry land of Dakota Territory.

Suddenly it all made sense—*Farmer Boy* was Laura Ingalls Wilder's *own* Laura World, an ideal realm she'd imagined, a homesickness for this place she'd never been or seen. On my trip west I'd been trying to get to the furthest reaches of a world

I thought I knew. Without even expecting it, I'd found the most secret and remote part of it here. I knew it wasn't the house itself, here in this almost impossibly green and lush countryside; it was more that this house marked the spot in the other world, designated the place where this amazing Farmer Boy, the Child Who Always Had Enough, lived in Laura's head and maybe all of ours, too.

At the gift shop I bought a little flask of local maple syrup, just to have something to represent the Idea of Pancakes.

Michael couldn't quite believe that I was ready to drive back to Burlington. "Are you sure?" he asked. "The guide said we could walk down to see the river if you wanted to see more."

"No, it's fine," I told him. *Farmer Boy* and I had come to an understanding, or maybe Laura and I had. I didn't need to see every last thing anymore. I stood on the grass outside the gift shop and watched as the next tour group made its way from the red farmhouse to the barns. A woman hung behind the group and stopped to sit on a little bench under the grove of apple trees. She looked to be in her sixties, dressed in crisp summer clothes. She simply walked up to the bench and stayed there as long as I stood and watched, as if she'd paid her ticket admission just to sit in that one place. She was still sitting there when we left.

There are other destinations I could visit. In central Missouri, near a town called Rothville, there is now a sign to commemorate the place where the Ingallses may have built a log cabin and lived for a year or less before setting out for Kansas. Laura would have been only a year old, and in the biography *Laura*, Donald Zochert refers to the place as "this little unremembered house on the Missouri prairie," a phrase so forlorn that it sometimes makes me want to drive out there just to stand at the edge of the field.

I could drive a considerably shorter distance to a place in Elgin, Illinois, where Charles Ingalls, Laura's pa, had lived for a time as a boy, marked only by a few Ingalls family graves in a tiny fenced plot on someone's lawn. Or I could go to South Troy, Minnesota, since records indicate that Laura's infant brother died near there, and while the exact location of his gravesite or the house where he died is unknown, some Little House fans have been known to stop in South Troy just to visit a marker displaying a copy of his death certificate.

And sometimes I want to see the piney woods near Westville, Florida, where Laura and Almanzo had spent their doomed interlude in 1891. I understand there's even a historical marker there now, so that you can see exactly where they'd been miserable. I guess if I wanted to, I could consider all these places as entry points into my Laura World. I could keep changing the boundaries and make it bigger and bigger, a weird kind of manifest destiny.

There are also places I can't visit, of course. Given the chance I'd probably wander around the farmland surrounding Plum Creek looking for any sign of the Wonderful House, because *someone* somewhere has an idea of where it might have been. I wished I could see all the little houses now disappeared, even the burned-down house where the Ingallses had camped for the night at the end of *Little House on the Prairie,* even though I know that may well have been fiction, and even though this whole yearlong tour had taken me past so many other vanished places where a luckless family had once lived.

It was enough that these places had once been real, that they were still a *little* real.

My friend Kara agreed to see *Little House on the Prairie: The Musical* with me, an undertaking that required a drive to St. Paul, Minnesota, in October. It seemed to be getting as much publicity as a Broadway show, especially since it starred Melissa Gilbert as Ma, but just like the real-life Ingalls family, it was a road production, playing in small cities like Madison, Wisconsin, and Des Moines, Iowa, and Oklahoma City. It hadn't opened in New York and it didn't appear it would be coming to Chicago anytime soon. Kara said we could stay with a friend of hers in Minneapolis for the weekend, so off we went.

I didn't know quite what to expect from *Little House on the Prairie: The Musical.* I don't usually go for anything with a Colon, The Musical tacked on the end of it. But maybe the show was a good idea—after all, the books were full of music in their own way, all those lines of lyrics marching down the page whenever Pa played his fiddle. As a kid, I'd always tried to hear the songs in my head, even when I didn't know them at all, so I was curious to experience the show in musical form. Besides, I had seen so many different Lauras by now—all these pigtailed pageant players and look-alike contestants, book cover models and actresses and even a wide-eyed anime character—why not see one more Laura, a singing and dancing one to boot?

Kara had volunteered to be my Indian guide, and she wasn't kidding. My familiarity with the Twin Cities was limited to what I'd seen in the movie *Purple Rain.* I knew that there were lots of expressways, because Prince always drove his motorcycle around under them, but I wasn't prepared for how complicated they were. From a map they looked fine, but all the Internet driving directions read like tax forms. Luckily Kara could navigate.

"Do I go on 394 or do I stay on 94?" I asked her on the way to the theater when yet another boggling array of ramp signs appeared. "Or does it become all the same thing, or what?"

She peered down at the screen of her BlackBerry. "This says stay in this lane until we see the exit for 241B," she said.

"Are you sure?" I was panicking.

She held up the phone. "My spirit guide is not wrong," she said. And it wasn't.

We arrived at the Ordway Theater nearly an hour early and wandered around the vast, carpeted lobby with the rest of the growing crowd. What does one wear to the musical theater? Kara and I had no idea, so we'd worn nice dresses, just to be safe.

"Do you think we overdid it?" I asked Kara, as we walked by a woman whose sweatshirt was emblazoned with a moody trio of wolves. "I feel like Nellie Oleson on the first day of school."

"Oh, you mean the *snobby* one, right?" Kara said pointedly.

I had to laugh. "Well, yes."

But never mind, this was still the fanciest Laura-related excursion yet. We went up the grand brass-railed staircase to the mezzanine lobby where two bluegrass fiddlers played a duet. There were even little beverage carts that served glasses of wine, and, for six dollars, a drink called the Half-Pint, a concoction of vodka, açai berry liqueur, and Sprite. We each ordered one immediately.

"No matter what happens on that stage tonight," I told Kara. "Just being able to have a Laura Ingalls Wilder–themed cocktail makes it all worthwhile."

"Hear! Hear!" Kara said. We clinked our plastic glasses together. The Half-Pint tasted like a prairie breeze, we decided, only fizzier.

An Act to secure Homesteads to actual Settlers on the Public Domain, read the first line of the words on the screen. The Homestead Act of 1862 was projected onto a scrim that covered the stage, so that we could all sit in our seats and contemplate history while we waited for the lights to go down. The text was much abridged, of course: just the basics (free land, not to exceed 160 acres, must be age twenty-one or head of family, five-year residency required, some exclusions may apply, etc.) in two brief paragraphs. *Be it enacted,* began the first one. *And be it further enacted,* said the second. Below them, Lincoln's signature gleamed forth. The words were in white, floating on the blue screen that was lit just like a sky so that it all looked like a divine decree, like an offer that nobody, least of all Pa Ingalls, could refuse.

Next to us were two girls in track pants and hoodies; they looked to be in their late teens, both of them extremely pretty, like blond, bored angels. I would find out from talking to them later that they were two friends from Michigan. ("Upper Peninsula," one of them said. "Our town is really small.") They'd come here in a chartered bus to shop at the Mall of America, and while they'd hadn't read the books or seen the TV show ("My mom has," the other one said), they were here mostly because they'd always wanted to see a stage musical.

One of them got up and went off somewhere; the other, the one sitting closest to me, snapped pictures of the auditorium until an usher came over and asked to see her camera. The girl stepped out into the aisle so I couldn't quite hear their conversation, but after the usher left, she plunked back down in her seat and sighed loudly.

"He told me I have to delete my pictures," she said. "Can you believe it?"

I shook my head. "The show hasn't even started."

"He said everything here in the theater is copyrighted," she said. "Like what does that even mean?"

I had no idea, I told her. It did sound kind of confusing.

"It's just a *place*," the girl said.

Little House on the Prairie: The Musical didn't set out to dazzle the way *Phantom of the Opera* or a Bob Fosse production might. There wasn't much to the set besides a bit of split-rail fence, a section or two of boarded wall for the shanty scenes, and behind it all the backlit sky. "Sweet and simple" might have been the operative term for the set design, as if Laura Ingalls Wilder had written the memo herself. Nevertheless, compared to the wobbly community-theater charm of the summer pageants I'd seen, the show was still stunning: in fact it seemed to *pop*. The opening number portrayed dozens of chorus members Going West in pantomimed wagons headed stage right. Even from where we were sitting in the mezzanine, everyone looked clear, crisp, and in high resolution, though of course we were there in person.

The musical wasn't based on the namesake book or the TV show. Rather, it was a composite of the later Little House books, from *On the Banks of Plum Creek* onward, with events compressed and rearranged into a two-hourish-long epic set in Dakota Territory. In this version, Mary goes blind during the Long Winter, and the prairie fires that always threatened throughout the book series claim the wheat fields of the De Smet settlers (Little House convention dictates that *something* always has to happen to the wheat).

The story starts late enough in the Little House chronicle to have skipped all the problematic Indian stuff in Kansas, though Dr. Tan, the black doctor, is borrowed from one of the earlier books in order to make the cast more multicultural. At one point Laura yells something to Pa like, "We shouldn't have taken the land from the Indians back in Kansas!" and Pa bows his head.

I glanced over at Kara, who was smirking a little. "Ahem," she said.

Melissa Gilbert made Ma seem a great deal more fun than she probably was in real life, portraying a woman who still liked to dance a jig once in a while. (Of course, it helped that she didn't have a tiny fourth kid around, since Baby Grace had been written out of the story.)

As for Laura, she was definitely of the "spunky" school of Laura Ingalls Wilder impersonation, stomping around tomboyishly in a patchy dress like some Pippi Longstocking of the Dakotas. The actress who played her was a petite young woman who had that boundless, almost improbable-seeming musical-theater energy: she leapt and twirled and careened and even somersaulted across the stage prairie, sort of like Peter Pan in a petticoat. As impressive a performance as it was, it suddenly reminded me that I identify with Laura mostly from the inside, that usually I want to *feel* like her more than I want to see her.

The story was easy to follow but somehow hard to recognize. People went west, including this one family, with this one girl and her two sisters. There was a house, and then a town, and everyone was proud and happy. Then came the blizzards and sickness and fires and lost crops. Mary went blind and Laura vowed to "be her eyes." By the second act it began to feel more familiar: I heard lines I knew from the books and started to feel like I was there. A few things, of course, hadn't changed a bit: Nellie Oleson was still the scene-stealer, overdressed and awesome.

Over the course of the show, Laura's dresses become longer and tidier as she teaches school and is courted by Almanzo, and the story becomes less about Going West and more about growing up. Near the end, Melissa Gilbert as Ma sings a ballad called "Where Did My Wild Child Go?" in which she entreats Laura to stay true to herself. It's not a sentiment that's ever articulated in the books, but something that a lot of people who read them, myself included, tend to feel about Laura. Of course, it might also be something that fans of the TV *Little House on the Prairie* feel about Melissa Gilbert (where did our little Half-Pint go?), but it was moving all the same, possibly because Melissa Gilbert's voice wasn't naturally as strong as her costars', and you could hear that she was trying her very best under the bright lights.

The curtain call included a standing ovation.

"I liked that," said the blond girl next to me when the lights went up. Her friend had vanished again. "It makes me want to see more musicals."

Kara thought it was fine, but she still wanted her land back.

As for me, I enjoyed it, but it left me feeling a little empty. I knew the show was supposed to give you That Laura Ingalls Wilder Feeling, the spirit of a girl and a country as together they struggled to be both settled and free. Certain ideologies aside, it was not terribly different from my Laura World, but I felt like the music and the lights and the voices and Abraham Lincoln's autograph had somehow inflated everything beyond recognition, turned it all into a billowing dream from which I'd had to shake myself awake.

"But it's a musical, right?" I was saying to Kara on the drive back. "And I'm not really a musical person."

"And you know, you have to be true to yourself," Kara said.

I was glad we were going through Pepin on the way home. Since we had to go through Wisconsin on the drive back to Chicago, the route allowed an opportunity to revisit my first Laura Ingalls Wilder destination. The museum had been closed for the winter when Chris and I were there in March; now, in late October, it would be open only another week before the season ended.

"We'll just pop in and check it out really quick," I told Kara.

It was nice to see the little town again, this time in the fall afternoon sunlight that made the lake glint intensely enough that we had to shade our eyes as we drove down the hill to the marina. The town had been so subdued back in the late winter that already my memory had been conflating it with its nineteenth-century incarnation, morphing it in my mind into a sort of literary ghost town traversed only by curious visitors and phantom covered wagons. Of course I had been wrong: people in Pepin ran Sunday-afternoon errands and had motorcycle clubs and got burritos at the gas station. Somehow last winter I hadn't grasped this, but today it heartened me in a way I hadn't expected. Pepin lives!

The Laura Ingalls Wilder museum here was one of the more eccentric homesite museums, with a mix of TV show memorabilia and random donated antiques on display. Next to an *LHOP* lunchbox was a pig's-bladder balloon, which looked papery with age and slightly crumpled and not nearly as horrifying as I'd imagined.

Kara found a binder with biographical information on each member of the Ingalls family. A well-meaning history buff had written the biographies in accordance with a strict and curious template (which I shall paraphrase):

> When Laura Ingalls Wilder was born in Pepin, Wisconsin, on February 7, 1867, nobody had any idea that she would one day be known as the world-famous author of the Little House books. All her mother and father knew is that they loved her very much [etc.]. . . . When Carrie Celestia Ingalls Swanzey was born in Montgomery County, Kansas, on August 3, 1870, nobody had any idea that she would one day be known as the sister to Laura Ingalls Wilder, world-famous author of the Little House books. All her mother and father knew is that they loved her very much [etc.]. . . . When Caroline Lake Quiner was born in Brookfield, Wisconsin, on December 12, 1839, nobody had any idea that she would one day be known as the mother to Laura Ingalls Wilder . . . [etc.]

"Why write six different passages about each member of the Ingalls family when you can write one and just fill in the blanks?" Kara pointed out.

I bought a sunbonnet at the museum store, my sixth one.

"I had a feeling you would buy one on this trip," Kara said, as we walked back out to the car. "I bought something, too." She went through her bag in the backseat and pulled out a feathered headband, the kind they used to sell in dime stores for playing cowboys and Indians. "Picture time!" she said.

I started laughing. "Oh my God," I said. "Yes!" We put on

our mythical headgear and took pictures of ourselves standing together in the parking lot. It seemed a fitting way to end the trip.

"Didn't you say there was a log cabin somewhere around here, too?" Kara asked, when we were back in the car.

I'd forgotten about that: the Wayside cabin a few miles away to mark where *Little House in the Big Woods* had taken place. "Oh yeah, do you want to see it?"

She shrugged. She hadn't read the books. "I figured you'd want to see it again."

I'd thought so, too. All I had to do was drive a little ways down the highway—I still remembered where to turn—and then go the seven or eight miles up the county road to where the cabin stood. I considered it for only a moment.

"No," I said. "Let's not bother." There didn't seem to be any point. Somewhere along the way I'd stopped believing that the story was there. Anyway, it was time to head home. We drove out through the fall foliage that was so picture-postcard vivid that— I told Kara—I didn't even care that they weren't the Big Woods. I told her a little bit about how I'd spent all last winter dreaming about a place that looked like the Garth Williams illustration.

"And you knew it wasn't true, right?" she asked.

"Sure," I said. "But part of me kept sort of believing it. I don't know why."

It felt strange to admit that. All this time I'd been letting friends think that my Laura Ingalls Wilder thing was just a kooky kick of mine, the way people in the '90s got into swing dancing and saying "ring a ding ding." Why not make sunbonnets my own retro schtick? But I'd gotten teary at pageants and had something of an identity crisis in De Smet. I had a bundle of slough hay that I kept in a supermarket bag in the spare bedroom closet, the hay that had once been the haystick from Ingalls Homestead, and sometimes I liked to pick it up and smell its clean, dry scent. I was serious about this. Serious in a way that could make people wonder.

She didn't say anything for a moment. "Do you think that there's something you're trying to figure out with all this?" she asked.

I kept my eyes on the road. "Yes," I said.

12.

Unremembered

SOME OF OUR FAMILY VACATIONS, I remember, had included side trips in which my mother visited one of the places where she'd lived as a girl. Because of my grandfather's army career, my mother and her family had lived in California and Maryland and Kansas and Colorado and Germany, wherever he'd been stationed—sometimes in base housing, sometimes off base, dozens of places. She used to joke that she didn't know how to spring-clean because she never lived anywhere long enough. It was true. She lived in the first house she and my dad bought in Oak Park for two years, and it was the longest she'd ever been in one place.

The next house after that was the house where I grew up, and we lived there for eighteen years. It was the only house I knew, so my mom's old life was unimaginable, even with the glimpses I'd gotten on our family trips—these odd detours down side streets of Silver Spring, Maryland, and Leavenworth, Kansas, where my dad drove the car slowly while my mother scrutinized the houses and checked the numbers against the addresses she'd typed up. "I think it's here on the right," she'd say.

I only vaguely remember the houses. A few were bungalows, or boxy military-base houses. Once, in Leavenworth, we stopped in front of a stately brick officers' house, but for the most part the places were unremarkable. Sometimes there wasn't even a whole house to look at, but a set of wooden steps leading up to an apartment. My mom pointed out one such place to me and my brother. "That's where your aunt JoLee had to sleep in a closet," she told me. Sometimes the place was gone and we looked at a parking lot. "Oh, well," my mom would say. I don't remember ever getting out of the car.

It was not a long time ago that I lost my mother. Or when I'd first found that copy of *Little House in the Big Woods* at my parents' garage sale, or when my parents moved to the house they'd bought in Albuquerque, where a short time later, my mother succumbed to her cancer. It was in January of 2007 and it was not unexpected. We'd known at Christmas that it would be her last one. She said then that she was glad she'd made it out to New Mexico—which she'd considered a paradise, the Sandia Mountains visible from the high bluff where my parents lived—but she wished she'd had more time. She knew she wouldn't be living there, in their wonderful house, for much longer; she wouldn't have lived there even a year.

"Goddamn it," she said at Christmas dinner.

Then she was gone.

A year after that, I picked up a book from my childhood and found a trail I wanted to follow.

There was no explicit association between the Little House books and my mother, though. As far as I know, she'd never read them as a child; I remember hearing her speak only about how much I adored them, whereas, she said, she'd loved *Rebecca of Sunnybrook Farm*. There's no shared experience or specific memory; she never said, "all's well that ends well," the way Ma did; there was nothing to indicate that my pursuit of all things Laura Ingalls Wilder would lead to my mother. And yet all along I wondered if there was some deeper reason I was doing all this, and for a while I suspected it might be, at least in part, because of Mom.

That's all it ever seemed to be: a suspicion. On those trips where I saw the places where my mother lived, I must have thought of Laura, too, of one little house after another forming the story of a life. I lived my whole childhood in one place, a sense of security I can't begrudge, but maybe I wanted nothing more than to always be leaving a place behind. Maybe I'd thought life was more visible if you could see all the spaces where you'd been. Maybe I still thought that.

And then there'd been a moment at the museum in Burr Oak. In the parlor, Monica had showed us an old photograph of a woman named Mrs. Starr. I knew who she was from reading *Pioneer Girl*. She was a well-off doctor's wife in Burr Oak who had once proposed to Ma that she adopt Laura, saying she wanted a little girl to help her around the house and keep her company, and perhaps also thinking that the Ingallses had more children than they could feed. Ma had politely declined, saying that she couldn't spare Laura.

I stared at the photo (Mrs. Starr was a stately-looking older woman, her face hard to read) and recalled reading in *Pioneer Girl* that the conversation between Ma and Mrs. Starr had happened in Laura's presence. She wrote that it had made her feel strange and frightened. "It seemed to be possible that I could go on being me—Laura Ingalls—even without Pa and Ma and Mary and Carrie and Grace," she'd said. It was a strange way to think about being alone, but it made perfect sense, and I'd suddenly remembered it, and remembered that my mother was gone, and how was it possible that I could go on being me?

Maybe the Little House books have always been a way to *unremember*—a word that I kept coming back to ever since I'd read it in *Laura*, Donald Zochert's book. *This little unremembered house*, he'd written. I know technically it means *forget* but somehow, in my mind, the definition changed. To me unremembering is knowing that something once happened or existed by remembering the things around it or by putting something else in its place. Laura Ingalls Wilder unremembered being hungry by writing *Farmer Boy*, and Rose Wilder Lane unremembered her terrible childhood by helping her mother write about hers. I unremembered my mom's cancer and death in the Burr Oak cemetery. You don't deny something when you unremember it, you just give it a place to live.

It was dark by the time Kara and I got back to Chicago on our return trip from Minneapolis. I dropped Kara off and then headed back to the apartment and Chris. We had dinner and I told him about the musical (unremembered history, perhaps?), and how I saw Pepin again, and how much I'd missed him in every single last place.

"So where are we going next?" he asked. "Are we going to have to go off in a log cabin in the middle of nowhere?"

I could tell he was willing to go. He'd read the whole official Little House series and the three unofficial books, too. He'd gone to De Smet and Walnut Grove and Burr Oak and even the ill-fated Homesteading Weekend chock-full of End Timers for me. I looked at him, with his beautiful big head and wearing one of his obscure band T-shirts that he always has to explain to me, and thought about how I really *would* be in the middle of nowhere without him, which was the last thing I wanted.

"We're done with the Laura trips," I told him. "I'm home."

This year we got to be home for Christmas, which is to say that my dad flew in from Albuquerque and my brother came down from Wisconsin to stay with us in our apartment, and for the first time in my life I would cook them all a Christmas dinner. For the past two Christmases since Mom died, none of us had really figured out how to do the holidays; we were still trying to learn how to work as a family, figure out who we were. Well, we knew this much: we loved prime rib. I'd gotten a roast at Costco that would have cost Laura three full months of her teaching salary at the Brewster school and it was waiting in the fridge.

It did not seem strange, though, to see my father on his own. My dad had the same kind of singular presence Pa had, and growing up I'd loved how much time I'd spent with just him, over dinners when my mother worked late. His most wonderfully Charles Ingalls–like endeavor had been buying an old VW Beetle as our family's second car and continuing to pour money and love into fixing it up even after it had proved unreliable, so much so that it had burst into flames in our driveway. He'd gotten the engine rebuilt and when he'd said, in classic Pa fashion, "That fire was the best thing to happen to that car!" we'd all felt more proud than unlucky.

I'd asked him for only one thing for Christmas, which was to transfer the dozens of family home movies to video. We hadn't seen them in twenty years. I barely knew what was in the movies anymore, but I'd hated to think of them all rotting away in a box in my dad's garage. Now my dad had given my brother and me both a set of gift-wrapped DVDs with the first batch of old films, and on Christmas Eve we watched them.

There was the house I didn't remember and then the house I knew. I saw our backyard and a party and my grandparents and Christmas. At the first sight of my mom my eyes filled up, but I held on because it was about time I remembered. I'd thought I couldn't see her anywhere, but I could remember and I could see her here.

I sat in the dark next to Chris and my family while the video remembered the film. The old Super 8 stock flared and flashed sometimes, and while the video was silent, something about the motion around the edges reminded me of the old ticking of the projector. I could see all the camping trips we'd gone on, back when we'd had a borrowed tent and then, later, our own. The names of all the places we'd been came back to me in the right order, like a story I'd learned: Trout Valley, Fish Lake Beach, Landuits Lake, and Lake Louise. It was like my own Laura saga. I loved this part best.

I saw footage of myself, maybe seven years old, with my brother running through rows of tall pines. The light was so dim the film grew grainy. I didn't know whether I was remembering or unremembering anymore, but as I watched myself run, I was sure

I knew everything I'd thought that day: We would live here now. We were in a new country. If we stayed here long enough we could know all of the world, the woods and the creeks and the fields and the lakes. And we would know all the little houses, a bright *now* in every one.

ACKNOWLEDGMENTS

❀

I am thankful for the encouragement of Megan Lynch, my editor, and Erin Hosier, my agent. Their early support for this project helped me greatly in those anxious first months of writing. Michael Taeckens heard me talk about "this Laura Ingalls Wilder book that I'll write someday," and suggested that I write it sooner than later, and I am forever grateful for his advice and friendship.

Many people helped and inspired me with their deep knowledge of Laura Ingalls Wilder's life and work: Sarah Uthoff, Amy Mattson Lauters, Rebecca Brammer, Nancy Cleaveland, Pamela Smith Hill, John Miller, and Bill Anderson. Thank you all for answering my questions; meeting you has been an honor. Much appreciation as well to Barbara Walker, Donald Zochert, William Holtz, Anita Clair Fellman, Kathryn Lasky, Stephen Hines, and Ann Romines for their Wilder-related works and research.

Sandra Hume was my first "Laura friend," and I'm glad for her humor and generosity. I feel fortunate to have met Catherine Seiberling Pond and Erin Blakemore during this book's journey. I am very grateful to

Meribah Knight, Mike McComb, Amy Finney, and Virginia McCone for their contributions. Many thanks to Dean Butler, who helped me at a crucial juncture.

Several friends served as writing buddies, travel partners, fellow butter churners, or just as moral support: Kara Luger, Jami Attenberg, Jen Larsen, Monique Van Den Berg, Wendy Wimmer Schuchart, Cinnamon Cooper, Anne Holub, Rose Lannin, MacKerrow Talcott, Claire Zulkey, Kate Harding, and Laura Pearson. Thanks also to Jody Michael, Emily Rems, and Ellen Willett.

I owe a debt of gratitude to Kathleen Tucker, Abby Levine, Josalyn Moran, Michelle Bayuk, Margaret Coffee, Nick Tiemersma, John Quattrocchi, Pat McPartland, and everyone else at Albert Whitman & Company for getting behind *The Wilder Life* with as much enthusiasm as for one of their own books.

I'm very happy to have Sarah Bowlin, Geoff Kloske, Mih-Ho Cha, Claire McGinnis, and Liz Hohenadel on my team at Riverhead.

While a few of my research pursuits did not make it into the final version of this book, I appreciate that Deirdre Churchill, Eve Richards, Betty Charbol, Emily McConnell, Eve Dutton, Cathie Maitland, Laura Bogue, Jess Hutchison, and Marilyn Ringland could take the time to talk to me.

Many thanks to the staff, volunteers, and supporters at all the Little House museums and homesites: the Laura Ingalls Wilder museums in Pepin, Wisconsin, Burr Oak, Iowa, and Walnut Grove, Minnesota; the Spring Valley Methodist Church Museum in Spring Valley, Minnesota; the Little House on the Prairie Museum in Independence, Kansas; the Historic Home and Museum in Mansfield, Missouri; the Laura Ingalls Wilder Memorial Society in De Smet, South Dakota; the Ingalls Homestead, also in De Smet, and the Wilder Homestead in Malone, New York. Special thanks to the Herbert Hoover Presidential Library in West Branch, Iowa, and to the Little House Heritage Trust.

Thank you, Laura Ingalls Wilder and Rose Wilder Lane, for the books that shaped my inner life and helped me find my way in the world.

Thank you to my family. Thank you, Mom. I miss you.

Thank you Christopher, for being at my side—for reading the books, reading my chapters, and for driving the car through Wisconsin, Minnesota, South Dakota, and Iowa. I couldn't have done it without you.

SELECTED BIBLIOGRAPHY

❀

Works by Laura Ingalls Wilder

(Published in New York by Harper & Brothers, later Harper & Row, unless otherwise noted)

THE LITTLE HOUSE SERIES

(The page numbers in *The Wilder Life* refer to the revised editions published in 1953.)

Little House in the Big Woods, 1932.
Farmer Boy, 1933.
Little House on the Prairie, 1935.
On the Banks of Plum Creek, 1937.
By the Shores of Silver Lake, 1939.
The Long Winter, 1940.

Little Town on the Prairie, 1941.
These Happy Golden Years, 1943.

POSTHUMOUS PUBLICATIONS

On the Way Home: The Diary of a Trip from South Dakota to Mansfield, Missouri, in 1894, with a setting by Rose Wilder Lane, 1962.

The First Four Years, 1971.

West from Home: Letters of Laura Ingalls Wilder, San Francisco, 1915, edited by Roger Lea MacBride, 1974.

A Little House Sampler: A Collection of Early Stories and Reminiscences, by Laura Ingalls Wilder and Rose Wilder Lane; edited by William Anderson. Lincoln: University of Nebraska Press, 1988.

A Little House Traveler: Writings from Laura Ingalls Wilder's Journeys Across America. New York: HarperCollins, 2006.

Laura Ingalls Wilder, Farm Journalist: Writings from the Ozarks, edited by Stephen W. Hines. Columbia: University of Missouri Press, 2007.

LAURA INGALLS WILDER BIOGRAPHIES

Anderson, William. *Laura Ingalls Wilder: A Biography*. New York: Harper-Collins, 1992.

Hill, Pamela Smith. *Laura Ingalls Wilder: A Writer's Life*. Pierre: South Dakota State Historical Society Press, 2007.

Miller, John E. *Becoming Laura Ingalls Wilder: The Woman Behind the Legend*. Missouri Biography Series. Columbia: University of Missouri Press, 1998.

Zochert, Donald. *Laura: The Life of Laura Ingalls Wilder*. New York: Avon Books, 1976.

LITERARY AND CULTURAL CRITICISM

Fellman, Anita Clair. *Little House, Long Shadow: Laura Ingalls Wilder's Impact on American Culture.* Columbia: University of Missouri Press, 2008.

Miller, John E. *Laura Ingalls Wilder and Rose Wilder Lane: Authorship, Place, Time, and Culture.* Columbia: University of Missouri Press, 2008.

Romines, Ann. *Constructing the Little House: Gender, Culture and Laura Ingalls Wilder.* Amherst: University of Massachusetts Press, 1997.

ROSE WILDER LANE

WRITINGS

Free Land, 1938. Reprint edition. Lincoln: University of Nebraska Press, 1984.

Lauters, Amy Mattson, ed. *The Rediscovered Writings of Rose Wilder Lane, Literary Journalist.* Columbia: University of Missouri Press, 2007.

Old Home Town, 1935. Reprint edition. Lincoln: University of Nebraska Press, 1985.

Young Pioneers. New York: McGraw-Hill, 1961. (Previously published as *Let the Hurricane Roar.* New York: Longmans, Green, 1933.)

BIOGRAPHIES

Anderson, William. *Laura's Rose: The Story of Rose Wilder Lane.* De Smet, SD: Laura Ingalls Wilder Memorial Society, 1986.

Holtz, William. *The Ghost in the Little House: A Life of Rose Wilder Lane.* Missouri Biography Series. Columbia: University of Missouri Press, 1993.

OTHER WILDER-RELATED BOOKS

Anderson, William. *The Little House Guidebook*. Photographs by Leslie A. Kelly. New York: HarperCollins, 1996.

The Laura Ingalls Wilder Country Cookbook. Compiled by Laura Ingalls Wilder; commentary by William Anderson; photographs by Leslie A. Kelly. New York: HarperCollins, 1995.

Walker, Barbara M. *The Little House Cookbook: Frontier Foods from Laura Ingalls Wilder's Classic Stories*. New York: HarperCollins, 1979.